HOWARD F. BAER

SAINT LOUIS TO ME

HAWTHORN PUBLISHING COMPANY INC.
10617 Liberty, St. Louis Mo. 63132   314·428·4460

For Isabel,
With a fond hope that her patience with me
will include this effort

ACKNOWLEDGMENT

Notes of this sort, most of which are about things, places, people and events remembered, have not been possible without consultations and refreshments of memory. I am, therefore, grateful to many, among whom are: William Cohn of the Jewish Community Centers Association; Judge Thomas F. McGuire and Richard D. Schultz of the Zoo; Oscar O. McCracken of the Civic Center Redevelopment Corporation; Dr. Peter Raven of the Missouri Botanical Garden; Alan Brimble and James Wood of the Art Museum; Robert Shelton of Blue Cross, and William Zalken, ex-manager of both the Symphony and the Municipal Opera.

A special debt is owed to that ebullient friend and source of information, Alfred Fleishman, to whom, in my view, our St. Louis is as deeply indebted as am I for his constant and energetic expressions of love and respect for his city and his fellow man; and Harry Wilson, chairman of Fleishman-Hillard, has criticized helpfully.

But Sue Ann Wood Poor has taken time, trouble and special interest in advising me, and Martin Quigley, editor of *The Midwest Motorist*, has made the volume possible, as has Arielle North, the editor.

I am grateful to all of them.

CONTENTS

FOREWORD

"Who knows whether in retirement I shall be tempted to the last infirmity of mundane minds, which is to write a book?"

Geoffrey Fisher

This book is not an objective look at the present St. Louis scene. Rather it is a subjective attempt to record some of the experiences of one man who, during his half-century of living here, has learned much, has been deeply enamored of his adopted home and has seen some of its wheels go round. And he has been bold enough to express some opinions concerning what he has seen.

Having reread Kirchsten's *Catfish and Crystal* lately, a book published some 17 years ago, it is apparent that events move all too swiftly. Already his descriptions of the Tucker administration, the position of the black in St. Louis, and the general political atmosphere are sadly dated.

This writer yields to none in his degree of affection for this city on the Mississippi where once the West began, a place of charm, dignity and poise. So it is that while he points with joy or alarm, praises or decries, he has tried not to prophesy--well, anyway not much--realizing that game has had notably few winners.

He knows he is often cantankerous and faultfinding, has often failed, and is now in fact an old curmudgeon. Nevertheless he has had great joy in running the course!

HOWARD F. BAER

SAINT LOUIS TO ME

FOOTNOTES ON FIFTY YEARS

Any resemblance between the individuals described or named in this book, and persons living or dead is neither coincidental nor unintended. On the contrary, none of the persons have been imagined--all are very real indeed to this writer.

CHAPTER I

"and tell old tales, and laugh at gilded butterflies, and hear poor rogues talk of court news; and we'll talk with them, too, who loses and who wins; who's in, who's out."

King Lear

Somerset Maugham, a writer whose works, whose easy style, whose plot ingenuity I have always admired, once wrote a short story in which the youthful hero did everything his cautious father advised him not to do. The boy was selected to replace a member of a tennis team who had fallen ill, and was asked to go to the Riviera to compete. His father was reluctant, thinking the 18-year-old lad too young, but finally gave his consent, cautioning him not to gamble, not to lend money, not, above all, to be taken in by any predatory loose women. If you have read the story you know that not only did he do well in his matches, he gambled at the casino and won heavily, he lent money which was returned, and he was pleasantly seduced by a toothsome hooker who fully intended to rob him but, by fortune's whim, ended by being the sucker. Thereby he made his father extremely unhappy both because of the humiliation the old boy had suffered at seeing his advice so successfully flouted, and because of his concern that the lad's character would be ruined by such an early and delightful introduction to the primrose path. Whether, in fact, the youngster's adult life was an anticlimax or whether, as one of his father's associates suggested, he was born to be lucky, we can only surmise, for Maugham never followed his career.

When I left West Virginia for St. Louis in 1927, I also was carefully counseled, by my Uncle Joe, the uncle for whom I had the most respect, to stick to business, not to be beguiled by outside civic or social affairs, in short, to mind the store. For Uncle Joe, and for that matter all the adult members of my family, had great contempt for some of their contemporaries in the West Virginia community who were prominent in community affairs and shaky financially.

I had the best of intentions, and almost certainly would have been better at the Aloe Company had I not been constantly engaged in so many diversions--but then I have never been able to say no very firmly.

Certainly I have no claim to the unmitigated success of Maugham's young hero--but then who knows what failures would have been his had his creator let him grow old?

It does not take long to swamp oneself in these things. Workers are always wanted, and once it is known that a man or a woman is someone who will work, job offers are plentiful. Quickly then a young man begins to feel himself a part of the town in which he lives, to believe that he is making a contribution and to see how the wheels go round. This sort of thing is not for everyone, but if you are one to whom it does appeal, the fascination can be great.

*****

One small but satisfying success involved the stadium. As I look out of the window, I admire its handsome series of 96 arches, each repeating the curve of the superb Jefferson Memorial Arch. Nearby stands the new Breckenridge Tower which has rescued (and enhanced) Cervantes' monumental error, the Spanish Pavilion--proving that architectural mistakes occasionally can be rectified.

The story of the stadium goes back to a beautiful autumn

day in 1961. I was sitting with Jim Hickok on the stern of a fishing boat cruising the Gulf Stream just off the Island of Bimini. As usual the fish were not bothering us nor we them, and the conversation was desultory. I said:

"Hickok, you dumb so and so, you are one of the greatest heroes St. Louis has ever had after collecting an unbelievable $20 million toward a stadium, and now you are about to make a colossal bonehead play."

"How come? Why do you say that?"

"Look, you are going to spend $53 million on it, more than has ever been spent on one thing in St. Louis; and you are going to do it without an architect. How stupid can you be?

"That's not so--we've got Sverdrup."

"Sure, you have, and he's an engineer, not an architect. He's really got you bamboozled--and by the short hair."

"Well, who do you think we should have?"

"Oh, that's easy. The greatest modern architect on sports structures is an Italian named Nervi. His stuff is marvelous, uses thin concrete. But you won't get him, and if you could you couldn't afford him politically. But for God's sake, get some good architect; America has plenty."

"Are you going to Italy?"

"It happens I am next month."

"OK, go see that guy."

"Are you serious?"

"Sure."

Charles Ferris of the Federal Land Clearance authority and his associate, O. O. McCracken, had dreamed up the stadium idea in 1958 when St. Louis was at a low ebb. There had been no new construction for a decade and everywhere there was talk of doom for the area. Saarinen, the architectural genius, designer of the Arch which was about ready to be built, had expressed concern for the miserable setting surrounding his design--this also influenced Ferris in his concept.

11

Hickok, president of the First National Bank, had caught fire, and he and Preston Estep of General Bancshares had tramped the streets and raised the equity money. It was an effort, something akin to a miracle--a miracle headed by Gussie Busch's commitment of $5 million from the brewery. His ball club would play there and it was to be called Busch Memorial Stadium, and his contribution was seconded by Buster May's $2.5 million from the May Department Stores, for which he received exactly zero--not even an honorable mention.

Jack Sverdrup, the war hero, the great engineer of Sverdrup and Parcel, had gambled some design money and had the inside track. He was powerful, dominating and demanding. There was no question that he would build it, and he had graduate architects in his firm. He neither needed nor would brook any interference.

Somehow, however, I was stuck with a feeling that would not go away, that maybe something could be done, and, as I was in Rome but a few weeks after the argument with Hickok, I called on Professor Nervi. It happened that Edward Greensfelder, who has done so much for St. Louis institutions through his stewardship of the A. P. Greensfelder Trusts, was with me and expressed an interest in meeting the great man.

Before going to his office we went to see two of his great sports center structures and they were beautiful. The concrete shells soared and curved into magnificent shapes--it was pioneer 20th-century design at its best: Nervi was then 73 but was obviously vigorous and had with him two tall strong sons, both architects, his trained assistants. He spoke no English and we used an interpreter. As I had expected, there was no interest on his part. He was swamped with proposals, was already too busy and showed us designs for the Hague, South Africa, Scandinavia and much more that has escaped me.

I could see that this was a dead end, but I asked him whether he thought his lack of any familiarity with American football

12

and baseball would handicap him. He said absolutely, that he was used to soccer, boxing, tennis and track events, that he would have no feeling at all for an American stadium. It was an interesting visit, but it came to nothing. His influence, however, exists in what I consider the most beautiful building in St. Louis--the Priory School Chapel on Mason Road. This small exquisite gem, built in 1960, is an early work of Gyo Obata, designed when he was only 37, but it is my understanding that Nervi went over the plans with him, and greatly influenced them.

Then Buster May, who knew what I was trying to do, caused an exhibition of Nervi's designs at the Art Museum. Well, that was fine, but those who would make the decision do not make a habit of spending time in the Museum and I had a dim view of that doing much good. I have the same affection for Buster May that all St. Louis has, for how could anyone not like this man who has been so courageous about his physical problems, so generous with his money to so many causes, so warm in his feeling for people that I have never heard him say an unkind word about anyone? But while he is persistent, he is not an abrasive fighter. He would not oppose Sverdrup even though he could have wielded a $2.5 million stick,.the May Company's contribution. As for me, I kept talking whenever I could get anyone to listen.

About then the General decided he had had enough; it was time to get rid of me. He called me and asked me to stop by his office. I did. Everything about Jack Sverdrup was a little larger than life, and to say that he was an imposing figure does not begin to describe him. He was huge, a true Viking, his face was craggy and handsome, his coffee cup held a pint, the case of mounted .44 automatics, souvenirs of his war experiences, was formidable, his language was forceful. The word for Jack was intimidating--for this was the legendary general who had built airfields in the South Pacific where the Japanese could not, the man whom MacArthur called the perfect engineering officer, the builder of roads in the Burmese jungles against all known odds. He said:

"There are two kinds of people, doers and lookers-on; you are a doer--so am I. This stadium is my project. I am an engineer and I build roads in the Asian jungles, bridges all over the world, but I have no real project here and am not known in St. Louis. This is to be my memorial."

"And, General, you want me to get out of your way?"

"Yes, that's it."

At that moment I felt pretty small--even humiliated. Behind that blue-eyed steely gaze I thought I could sense his thought that no little Jew-boy was going to upset his applecart. I wilted.

"OK, Jack, I guess that's it." And I left him. But when I got back to my office I said to myself, "No, by God, that's not it." I wrote him a letter. I can't find a copy now, some 15 years later, but I remember quite well that I said I had been wrong in agreeing with him, that my opposition could not amount to much, but that such as it was I had to continue. Nor did I have any doubt that he would do as he wished, but I had in mind one last effort.

Within a week or so there was the usual monthly meeting of Civic Progress at the Racquet Club. The members, the heads of the 21 largest corporations, had been responsible for Hickok's success in raising the $20 million of seed money. I made a talk, a plea for an architect, saying that I had told this tale too often, that never again would I bring it up, but I could not let the occasion pass without one last plea for a good architectural design for something so important to the city. And I sat down. Silence. Then miracle of miracles. Gussie Busch rose to his feet.

"Howard is right. I've got $5 million of Busch money in this thing. When my grandchildren walk around this town they

14

ought to be proud of it. Get an architect!"

I say it was a miracle because great citizen that he was, no one would expect an appreciation of the visual arts from him; it simply was not his cup of tea, but he understood what I was saying and he was the cause of what stands there today.

A week later Hickok called me.

"About this stadium thing. Would you settle for a man named Stone?"

"You mean Edward Durrell Stone?"

"I guess so, let me look; yeah, that's him."

"Well, Jimmy, I'll tell you, a lot of the moderns don't like him, think his embassy building in India is too fancy. But he's an architect, a good one, yes, yes, yes! Terrific!"

It never occurred to me to wonder who had wanted Stone. I knew it wouldn't have been Sverdrup, and Hickok had never heard of him. Only recently I learned that O. O. McCracken, who had left government service to manage the Stadium project, had wanted Stone all along. It was rare judgment on his part, an evidence of the excellent service he has given and continues to give to the city.

It was about two years later before Jack Sverdrup could bring himself to speak to me. He was furious. But gradually he began to see that we had done him a favor. His name, not Stone's, is on the building and the design is widely admired.

*****

That was a winner, but the business of the Spanish Pavilion was not. I suppose it might be said that the Cervantes failure in moving the World's Fair building here was not really so great, the end result stands there in the form of the hotel, imposing, handsome and unquestionably enhancing the area.

The Spanish Pavilion had been, perhaps, the outstanding building at the New York World's Fair in the 1960's, and with its superb restaurant, paintings loaned from the great Prado Museum and flamenco dancers, it had been a winner. Harold Koplar, of the Chase Hotel, a close friend of the Mayor, had suggested it would be a spectacular ten-strike to purchase and move the building here instead of seeing it demolished, the usual fate of fair buildings. Cervantes was then newly elected and he was a charger; no idea was too far out for him and he was never in doubt. He determined to get it and twisted every arm he could grab to get the $2 million he thought he'd need. Oddly enough the business community went along with him in spite of their almost unanimous feeling that the project was ridiculous. Actually they were a little afraid of him and decided to play along.

At one point he took a plane load of people to New York to look at the building which was still standing, but was now dark and deserted, the fair having ended several months earlier. I was one of them. What interested me most was the stage which had been built for the dancers, an attraction which had been enormously successful, because both the Mayor and I visualized a working theatre.

For a long time, beginning in college, I had been intensely interested in the little theatre at Princeton known as the "Intime," and I had briefly dreamed of being a playwright. I had written, acted and directed and after graduation was the amateur director of the Kanawha Players, an amateur company in Charleston, West Virginia. It was for that reason that I was so happy to be elected a director of the Municipal Opera--and I still love it. Well, who does not? As all baseball fans think themselves potential managers, so do theatre buffs regard the theatre--they are, or could be, producers. Bill Zalken puts it better: He quotes Oscar Hammerstein who said: "Everybody knows his own business--and show business."

Anyhow, I, with many others, had thought for some time that Broadway was dying. A one-scene dramatic show in 1925

16

could be brought in for some $15,000 or $20,000, a big musical for perhaps $100,000. Now the costs have increased tenfold, and the chances of success are no greater. The finance question and the domination of television both have stifled the prolific creation of the theatre which seems to exist now only in England, and that too is sinking. In the 50's there began to be a widespread belief that the future of the theatre arts in America would have to be in the repertory theatre--that it would of necessity be outside New York; and about this time in Minneapolis there appeared the magnificent Guthrie Theatre which many thought would be the forerunner, the spearhead of the movement.*

With all this in mind I for one looked forward eagerly to the visit to the Spanish Pavilion. There was no question that the building was beautiful, but the theatre was quickly a disappointment. It looked more like a high-school stage than a legitimate theatre; a platform is what it was, with no backstage space, no fly space, no dressing rooms. The depth was too shallow for scenery, the height was inadequate--in a word it was not a theatre, but was a shallow stage designed only for the dance act at the fair. But the auditorium and its seating were superb; the lobby had a beautiful bar and the restaurant spaces were gorgeous--the possibilities were there.

About this building I began to develop a wild idea, one which I thought would have little chance of realization but which, the more I thought about it, seemed eminently sound. It went like this:

The Muny Opera was a summertime activity, its actual season ran for not more than 85 or 90 nights during June, July

---

*As was the case of Mark Twain's death, however, the opinion as to the theatre's demise, has been exaggerated--and some on- and off-Broadway houses are currently lighted each night.

and August, to which had to be added the heavy preparation time of March through May. But it had a fine house and business staff headed by William Zalken, a seasoned professional, and a subscription list of great size and substantial strength. The staff had little or nothing to do from September through March and, best of all, the Opera had money--reserves built up through decades of profitable operations.

Suppose, just suppose, the Muny were to undertake in the Spanish Pavilion the creation and operation of a great, really great, theatre, a regional repertory playhouse! It would lose a little money, surely, but the Muny could stand that if the loss were not too great. But think of the pluses--the location in a building with great food facilities, the downtown's popular stadium area, and with access to the great subscription list which the Muny owned. How could it fail?

Tentatively then, I approached the mayor. He jumped at it like a trout to the fly, as of course he would, because he already could see that he had a white elephant on his hands. Then I talked to some of the Muny's more conservative board members and their reactions varied. Dick Amberg's was amusing: he looked at me and growled, "It's a hell of an idea, really great; but I hate to see you pull Cervantes' chestnut out of the fire."

Some, as was to be expected, felt that it would be folly to tamper with the time-tested formula which had served the Opera so well, and they opposed it.

The younger members (and the young at heart) thought it worth looking at and agreed to investigate the scheme when I suggested we get the services of the best theatre man we could find to give us an opinion. We had heard of one Norris Houghton who had created the theatre at Lincoln Center in New York, and had been a director, producer, all-around authority, and had retired to teaching at the State University

18

of New York. A call to Richard Rodgers confirmed that Mr. Houghton was the best man possible for the job. Happily he was agreeable to making a study for us, and the Opera appropriated $5,000 for his effort.

We asked him to tell us three things:

1. What could we do to make the stage a true theatre?
2. Is it possible to build a really first-rate repertory company in St. Louis?
3. How much money would the theatre lose? That is, what should its budget be and how much income would it expect?

In three months he was back with answers, fine satisfactory answers to all three questions. Yes, the stage could be modified, in support of which he had three architectural designs to show us. Yes, a repertory theatre could be assembled; and yes, within three years it might be self-supporting, and even the first two or three seasons would not lose more than $100,000, an amount easily absorbable by the Muny's earnings. We were excited by the study; it exceeded our fondest hopes, but the excitement was brief.

The catch was the modification of the stage. Cervantes and his group--again Hickok was deeply involved--had collected $2 million with great difficulty and a building and loan had agreed to lend some $3.5 million on a mortgage. They were ready to start construction. The estimate of added cost for the stage was $275,000, and although this would have added only about 5 per cent to the building's cost, the Pavilion group would have no part of it, nor would the Opera. We were dead: either it was an idea whose time had not yet come; or, and quite likely, it was simply no good. It was definitely a loser, but I still think it would have worked. Nor should it be revived now as the Webster College Loretto-Hilton Theatre has, at least for this era, filled the need surprisingly and even superbly well.

*****

19

My first involvement in St. Louis civic affairs was with the old Community Chest (now the United Way) when Gale Johnston got me to be a team captain in the north 12th Street area, a perfectly rotten section for collecting money. But by 1938 I had worked up in the ranks and was asked, along with Henry Hitchcock and Sam Conant, to be vice-chairman of the campaign, the chairman to be James L. Ford, a vice-president of the First National Bank. It was a significant campaign, not, the good Lord knows, because I was in it, but because of Ford and what came afterwards. The town was at low ebb, the Depression was still on; the smoke evil in St. Louis was at its worst; business was bad and the Chest campaign had not been successful in years.

Jim Ford had been president of the Franklin American Bank, an institution which in the early 30's had been saved from going bust only because Walter Smith of the First National Bank had taken it over at the zero hour. Ford had been given a vice-presidency, but he was discredited and had nothing to do. He sat there, a nearly broken man. In those times, with money so scarce and civic pride so low, no one wanted to chair the annual drive, least of all Jim Ford. But he had little choice, the campaign organization had convinced the First National that it was their turn, so they, having nothing else to do with Ford, tagged him for the job.

With all our gloom and pessimism the campaign was fun. Hitchcock, Conant and I became fast friends (Henry and I still are, but Sam is gone now) and we bolstered Ford, holding up, as it were, both his arms. Jim was timid, modest and nervous almost to a fault. I suppose most of the starch had been taken out of him by his bank failure and he spoke haltingly at the first report meetings. But part of the chairman's job always is to make speeches and he had to do it so we developed a technique to assist him--namely to get three quick drinks into him at the old Statler before the big weekly meetings. With

20

that time-tested aid he performed nobly. The campaign, however, lagged badly, bogged down; it seemed we would do no better than the others who had gone before us.

Then one day a miracle, in the shape of a metamorphosis, came to Jim Ford. He caught fire and righteous indignation burst from his every pore. He preached to everyone he saw, to all the inadequate givers he was soliciting:

"This town stinks. We can't do anything; we can't raise our Community Chest quotas; our smoke and smog smother our progress; what kind of city are we anyhow?"

And more--much more. Sam, Henry and I were at first amused, then amazed and finally awed. So were others including his bank. He put that over and then--the bit of success now in his teeth--he was the logical man to tackle the smoke problem.

He borrowed Ray Tucker from Washington University's engineering department and within two years the town was one of the nation's cleanest instead of its dirtiest. He stands high and clear in my memory, as a fine man who made a great comeback. He was good for St. Louis.

*****

In 1952 I was asked to be chairman of the Chamber of Commerce, a position for which I thought myself singularly unqualified, and in which I could not see much cause for interest. I said as much to Dave Calhoun, who was not only my mentor but who had a finger in every civic pie. Dave's argument for my taking it was a double one: first, that I had to eat lunch somewhere and the monthly board meeting would at least provide one day's lunch out of 30; and second, that the post had never before been occupied by a Jew and didn't I think that was a worthwhile precedent? Al Fleishman agreed, so I accepted.

21

The Chamber, at that.time, sparkled about as much as a wet towel and, so far as I could see, accomplished little or nothing. Its support among the business community amazed me: the dues income was substantial, but what the companies received in return was miniscule. There was action in St. Louis but it was all in the then-new Civic Progress organization, and of this the Chamber staff was jealous. It would be decidedly nice if I were able to record that I changed all this for the better; but there wouldn't be a glimmer of truth in it. Neither I nor my company, a relatively small one, had the clout, the energy, nor the imagination. But I did have a couple of interesting failures.

The one-time Republican Mayor Aloys Kaufman had succeeded George Smith as the Chamber director and suggested that perhaps we could get a pro-football team here, that the Chicago Cardinals were not doing well under the shadow of the more successful Bears, and that I should call on the owner, Walter Wolfner. As we were due in Chicago for a social weekend about then, the effort would certainly not be great and I called for an appointment. Wolfner was the stepfather of the Bidwill boys, having married their widowed mother, and while he was divested of his supposed ownership later on, he was very much in control at that time in 1953.

St. Louis knew something about him, he was a brother of the distinguished eye physician Henry L. Wolfner, who had long practiced here and was responsible for the Wolfner library for the blind. But unlike his brother, Walter was generally thought to be a tough cookie--and, in fact, unpleasant. When I called on him at his office under the grimy White Sox Stadium, he was anything but receptive. I told him that I represented the Chamber, that I thought we were ready for a big-league team, that we had heard he was not too happy in Chicagoland, and we'd like to invite him. He asked whether we would guarantee the sale of X thousands of season tickets, and I said that we could not, that such was not our practice, but that if

22

financing was needed there were good sportsmen in St. Louis who were always interested in investment. I mentioned, as examples, Sidney Salomon, Jr., and Bill Veeck. He grunted, said that was not a consideration and that there was no interest. That ended it, but not quite--there was a sequel.

About two years later, several years before the Cardinals did move to St. Louis, I got a call from Salomon to this effect:

"Do you know that both sports editors, Bob Burns and Roy Stockton, have been spreading a rumor that Walter Wolfner has said he would have moved the Cardinals down here had you not demanded a piece of the club for me and for yourself?"

"Ridiculous, Sidney, of course I never did any such thing."

"I know you didn't--but they are saying it."

I laughed, "So what difference does that make? I couldn't care less."

"No, Howard, it does make a difference. They can't do that to me or you. Will you be in your office tomorrow morning?"

"Sure."

"OK, I'll have them there."

And duly there appeared Sidney and both the sports writers to whom he laid down the law in no uncertain terms. I will say that both of them were a little sheepish, admitted by inference their having said more than they should have and that was the end of it. But I was impressed by Salomon's desire to clear himself and by his concern for me. He has been a controversial figure in St. Louis all his adult life, tainted by his association politically with suspect figures, but I never heard an authentic bad word about his personal or financial morals. From that day on I was a defender.

I regret only that disillusionment has come to me recently.

The other failure, involving a quite substantial effort, was in connection with the about-to-be-created Air Force Academy. It was the joint idea of Kaufman of the Chamber, Calhoun, and Charles Thomas of Monsanto that St. Louis had a very good chance to attract the Academy here. They thought they were not without influence since Eisenhower had appointed Harold Talbott, the brother-in-law of Thomas, as Secretary of Air, and the Secretary himself encouraged us to throw the St. Louis hat in the ring. The site we envisaged was on the bluffs above Alton, a location with a magnificent view up the Mississippi with flat farm land behind it, ideal for aviation, with ready access to the universities, hospitals, etc. of St. Louis, with superb waterfowl shooting for the officers. Within a short time we had dreamed up a package of pluses which seemed to us to offer perfection itself.

And indeed we did stay in the running until we were one of the last three sites under consideration; Colorado Springs, someplace near Chicago, and Alton, The Colorado site looked impossible to me. There was no water, so it would have to be brought through the mountains at an astronomical cost; and the altitude was 7,200 feet. I checked with a cardiologist, who said the critical altitude was 7,000--anything over that would be a definite handicap to visiting athletes, and, therefore, we argued that visiting teams simply would refuse to come. We were excited and we were naive.

At that point Principia, the Christian Science college also at Alton, balked. Afraid that their serene atmosphere would be shaken up, their privacy disturbed, they protested to Washington. That hurt, and the Secretary was definite in his statement that they did not want to antagonize local elements; a fine excuse for him but not the real reason. For we had been spinning our wheels. Ike had all along promised it to his old and good friend, Dan Thornton, the Colorado governor.

*****

It may be fairly said that if there is one villain concerning whose perfidy all would now agree it is the bureaucracy. The average citizen may not quite know of whom it is composed, but he does know that his representatives at federal and state levels continue to increase its size and functions. He has been told to hate it, and I think quite properly. Of late it seems to feed on its own ineptness and to grow apace. Each and every presidential, gubernatorial and senatorial candidate rails at the numbers of such bureaucratic employees, feeders at the public troughs, but invariably they find that during their own tenures the monster has not been reduced in numbers; it has been increased.

Partly it is due to the congress and the state legislative bodies who will not cease from creating more and more regulations, partly to the wishes of the body politic for public assistance in welfare, education, health, environmental protection and so on, and partly--and not to be over-looked--because of the political influence the vast numbers of bureaucrats now have with the law makers. The new kingdom within the democracy has acquired its own considerable power. My own recent experience has been slight but quite definite. Example:

In the spring of 1973 there was a call from the Attorney General, Jack Danforth, a young man who had achieved a fine record, first in having been elected Attorney General against overwhelming Democratic party odds; and, in 1970, losing his bid for the Senate to the veteran Stewart Symington by only 30,000 votes. I scarcely knew him, as I was a contemporary of his father, Donald, which is to say I was some 35 years his senior. Would I come to Jefferson City to lunch with him? Well, why not? The weather was pleasant, the drive but a couple of hours, and I admired the Danforths, especially Jack's older brother, Bill, the brilliant chancellor of Washington University. What he wanted of me was, however, dismaying, outside of my ken completely, and I did not see how I could do it.

He explained that in December of 1968 the Congress, alarmed at the growing crime rate in America, had passed the so-called Safe Streets Act which was designed to pour large amounts of money into law enforcement assistance--the object being to control and reduce crime. Fine, I was for that just as I was for motherhood and against sin. There was, of course, an agency in Washington to oversee, make the rules, and disperse these millions, but the actual spending of it was within the 50 states. In accordance with the regulations, the Missouri Law Enforcement Assistance Council--MLEAC--was established here. Its job, then, was to spend the $14 million a year which was Missouri's allotment and to oversee special emergency federal grants of several million more which came to St. Louis and Kansas City. The Council had been appointed by the newly elected Governor Bond and consisted of prison and police professionals, members of the legislature, parole and rehabilitation experts, and prominent citizens who were presumably interested. Danforth was the new chairman.

But the organizational setup did not stop there. The state had been divided into 19 regions in each of which there was a staff and a local council of volunteers. Region V, St. Louis, was the largest, had about 40 employees, none of whom had anything to do directly with catching, convicting, disciplining, incarcerating or rehabilitating criminals, and received the most money. Kansas City, a smaller city, received less money and had a smaller staff, perhaps 15 or 20. Poplar Bluff and Hannibal had staffs of but two or three, some part-time, but around the state there were altogether more than 100 staff employees.

Their job, then, was to see that these millions were intelligently and properly apportioned to police, courts, prisons and any other law enforcement agencies in order that the Missouri criminal justice system might be improved. It might be (and was) spent for flashing lights on a sheriff's car,

26

for computerized communication systems, for flags to grace a judge's office, for a medium-security prison, for parole officers--for anything, in fact, having relevance to the problem. The law seemed clear in that the final authority lay with the central council at the state capital, although the act specified a certain and rather indefinite amount of local control, and was accompanied by varied and multifarious regulations.

Danforth felt that he had inherited a nest of confusion. What he wanted was someone to look at the process, the system, to come up with a plan which would recommend any needed changes in the structure, and which would give particular attention to the proportion of spending to be authorized locally and the amount reserved for disposition by the State Council. Further, the director was about to leave, and he wanted a new man.

At once I protested my absolute and utter lack of the slightest qualifications for any such effort. I said that I knew nothing of and had no experience in law enforcement matters, had not even known of the existence of the organization, and did not see how I could be of any service. Danforth, however, argued that the task was that of a businessman, an administrator, that no legal knowledge was necessary and that I ought to try. And he capped this argument by saying triumphantly, "My father says if you will get interested and say you will do it, you can!" And, always a sucker, I said I'd try; whereupon he handed me a pile of literature, forms and regulations about a foot thick.

I remember thinking that I could scarcely look for answers if I had no idea of what the questions were, and I do not exaggerate in saying that it was a good two or three weeks before I did begin to see the questions and the problems. Nor was the task made any lighter by my inability to understand the new language which can best be labeled as bureaucratic, a medley or conglomeration of newly coined words and phrases apparently designed to pile confusion on bewilderment.

By then I knew that I could not do it alone in a vacuum, but that I might be able to make some contribution if I could get help from one of the large accounting firms, most of which now have systems analysis departments. Accordingly I spoke to J. K. Thompson of Arthur Andersen, a good friend of long standing, and he readily agreed to provide the service. Danforth had no objection to a small expenditure and Steve Stauffacher, a brilliant young man whom Thompson had assigned, and I went to work.

We visited the staff offices in nearly all the the 19 regions, we analyzed the forms, we heard the complaints, we listed the suggestions for improvement, we studied the procedures in other states--finally we understood what was going on, or thought we did, and we wrote a report.

What we said was that the State Council in Jefferson City had the authority but did not use it sufficiently, that it ought to reserve to its own judgment the spending of money for other-than-local purposes, i. e., a prison to serve several counties, a training school for police or payroll officers in a large area; that there was far too much paper work in connection with small projects; that the smaller regions ought to be combined and, finally, and of most importance, that there had never been an evaluation by a third party of any of the projects financed. We knew, but had never quite realized, that there never is any evaluation of public expenditure, at any level whether federal, state, county or city.

Well, yes, once in a while an article will appear emanating from the General Services Administration as to a lack of value received for the millions spent, but, in general, unless the stealing is so flagrant that it cannot be ignored by the press and the Department of Justice, nothing is said; and there would appear to be no protection for the citizens of this country except to vote the lawmakers, the appropriators and the executive branches out. But this does not often serve because the voters are misled and cannot be properly informed. But to return to this homemade Missouri example:

Steve and I knew the so-called "Baer" report would be highly unpopular. By implication it accused the staffs of the bureaucracy of needless complication, of wastefulness, of being excessive and, in some cases, incompetent. It suggested the elimination of some jobs; wanted to take some of the local candy away to be spent at the state level; it wanted an evaluation process to look at what was already being done to see whether money had been wasted, and expressed the thought that the employment of all regional directors ought to be approved by the State Council. And we were correct--they did not like it, particularly the idea that they might not control their own local, petty patronage.

But Danforth did, and so did others such as George Camp, the brilliant young director of prisons, Senator McNeal of St. Louis, and Charlie Mann, the devoted and expert head of the Bureau For Men. It was, however, anathema to the local staff directors and their assistants, and they ran crying to their home-town members of the State Council, some of whom were politicians. I suppose if you or I were a state senator from Hannibal or Joplin, and our acquaintance, for whom we had gotten a state job, came to us with a story that those long hairs in St. Louis and Jefferson City think they know more about crime in our neck of the woods than we do, and that those city boys have no business running our affairs, we'd believe them.

Whether Jack was as naive and idealistic as I was, I can't say; in any case he said we would fight, and we went to it, deciding to take one step at a time. The bureaucrats swarmed about us like hornets. When the Council met, the staff members assumed that they were to be present (and their expenses paid) so that we were forced to deliberate in a fish bowl. Nevertheless, at the start we were successful and we began to believe we could be constructive. It seemed to me from the beginning that the matter of evaluation of expenditures was the heart of the problem, and any solution to it eluded us. For one thing the court system simply would not cooperate and refused any information. Jealous of their complete authority and disciplined only by the State Supreme Court, the circuit judges and their staffs showed no interest in what we were doing; and the last people wanting any evaluation of their pet projects were the local regional staff members.

So far as I could see the single largest expenditure was going into a state-wide computerized communications system. That it could do wonders no one questioned--a police or highway patrol officer stopping a suspected criminal could get his state-wide record within minutes, even seconds, and his national FBI rundown in but a few moments more. Fine, but at what cost? The display of electronic hardware at the State Highway Police Headquarters, where the central brain was located, was overwhelming, but was all this necessary? One thing is sure, it was and is the perfect toy for bureaucracy. Its growth, like governmental employment itself, feeds on its own activity and on the inescapable fact that the lay public, the citizens, have little idea what it does and therefore do not know how to challenge it. It is not the fault of the machines, which keep on multiplying their own abilities to perform tricks which are seldom seen or used; the problem is that those in charge cannot escape empire building.

We thought we could bite that bullet too, and I came up with what I thought was a pretty bright idea--we would get McDonnell to assess the value of it. I did not see how we could miss, for the McDonnell Automation Center at the aircraft company was stupendous in size, did not do business with the state and thus would be in the clear as to conflict of interest, and was knee-deep in computer know-how. I told Danforth I had no influence with Old Mac but that he would have, and that he ought to ask him to contribute a study and report. He agreed and soon told me that the mission was accomplished, that he had lunched with the old fox and that while Mac would not do it, he recommended to us a newly retired executive who was an expert, Kendall Perkins. Here then, without spending the many thousands we would have had to pay a great business engineering firm like Battell, or Booz, Allen, we had a completely impartial, expert veteran.

About this time we had found a replacement for the top staff job, a man who had been head of the St. Louis County prison system, and we had more high hopes. He had already made an excellent record, was highly regarded by Charlie Mann, our prison expert, and believed in what we were trying to accomplish. His name was Robert Gruensfelder and now, two years later, the choice still looks good to me. But just as the Baer report was anathema to the bureaucracy, so he proved to be because he was committed to it.

The Perkins evaluation report on computers was cogent but again nothing happened; its recommendations for simplification and lesser expenditures were ignored. Volunteers in the local councils, of which there were 19 just as there were 19 regions, augmented the political power of the staff men. In all, then, there were 456 politicians and citizens of local importance, and their powers of complaint to the legislature were substantial. They were asked to explain to their favorite State House friends that Danforth was building an empire, that it might be best to threaten him with the very existence of the agency by cutting off the very small, state matching fund necessary for the federal appropriation, and, in general, to raise hell.

After two years Danforth felt that he did not want to be destroyed in such a cause. There had been no strong support from the Governor's office, and obviously it would have been impossible to win by force with an antagonistic Democratic majority in the Assembly. When he resigned so did I.

The MLEAC agency still operates exactly as it did before either Danforth or I were part of it. The bureaucrats have their own 19 little spoils systems (well, not so little at that). The money still comes from Washington and is, with the aid of tons of paper, cheerfully disbursed. There are, to be sure, occasional rumblings of complaint. I look now at the reprint from *Science* magazine which has recently appeared in the *Post-Dispatch*. Two reports from such reputable private agencies as the Twentieth Century Fund and the Center for National Security indicate the program has been a failure. Some *forty-six hundred million dollars* (count 'em!) has been spent to little purpose. Both reports come down heavily on the "layers of bureaucracy and red tape." And they decry the lack of evaluation--but we could have told them this two years before.

Withal, I know of no concern on the part of anyone in the State of Missouri, from the Governor on down through the ranks, as to the waste. But enough--like Pogo who has seen the enemy and it is us, I have seen the bureaucracy, and it is clear that like cancer it is both insidious and feeds upon its own wild growth. In a way this new third force in our country is worse than the criminal, for the wrongs it perpetrates, its rip-offs of the public pocketbook, are not illegal. At least the criminal can be prosecuted, while the bureaucrat cannot. But the latter's damage to us is just as real and it is endless.

*****

The little I had to do with the Arch was pretty much the extent of my relationship with Luther Ely Smith. This superb man, graduate and loyal son of Amherst, well-known and highly regarded in St. Louis, was the first man I had ever known who was effective in the public affairs. As a young man I had met many members of the business and civic power structure, but these were inclined to leave government alone. Smith had, however, been helpful in the Milles Fountain matter and was, after the end of the war in 1945, once more laboring hard at the climax of his life work--the Jefferson National Expansion Memorial--now known as the Arch.

His effort began in 1933 when, at his urging, a committee was formed by Barney Dickman, the then mayor, to work for the establishment of a federal memorial to commemorate the Louisiana Purchase of 1803 and to honor Jefferson and the exploration of the West. The country was then at the very nadir of the Depression; it did not seem to many of us that there would ever be any revival of building. But Smith's vision and hope were great. He was dogged, and almost single-handedly he slugged his way through the mire of indifference, lack of funds and plain antagonism. From time to time he had help--mostly, as I remember, from Buster May who could always be counted on to support anything good for St. Louis--but most men would have given up many times.

As with all great human accomplishments, there are secondary benefits; and, although the Arch stands splendid in its graceful glory, the lesson of persistence, the spirit of never giving up, seems to me even greater in its significance. Surely those sturdy souls who braved the impossible rigors of winter storms in the mountains, trudged endless miles in the prairie winds, and braved the perils of marauding Indians in order to build the West, were matched by Smith in his determination to honor them. Sadly enough, he lived to see neither his Arch shining in the morning sun, nor the museum which of late has been added to it; but this often is the fate of those who strive mightily. Even Moses did not see his land but from afar.

The Arch was dedicated in 1968, its superb educational museum in 1976. Millions have ridden its elevators, more millions visited the area, and henceforth, as far as anyone can see, the stream of visitors will be endless. Even without the museum, the Arch has for some time drawn more visitors than the Washington Monument. But Smith died in 1966.

These were some of his obstacles:

In 1935 he had to get the city to agree to a bond issue to match federal bonds. Again in the same year the city actually voted $7.5 million to match the federal $22.5 million, this itself a small miracle.

Promptly the validity of the bonds was attacked, and he had to shepherd the suit through the State Supreme Court. In December 1935 and in 1936 two irate citizens sued to block sale of the bonds. In 1936 a citizens' committee was formed to oppose the project. It planned to convince Congress that President Roosevelt had been "duped" into authorizing the Jefferson Memorial. Later in 1936 an injunction, granted to 38 firms and individuals, caused a year's delay.

In 1937 the dispute with the Terminal Railroad as to the removal of elevated tracks began and continued until 1949. In 1939 Smith, through Congressman Cochran, defeated a move by representatives from Kansas and Pennsylvania to block federal appropriations.

In 1945 Smith raised $225,000 for an architectural competition and employed the distinguished George Howe to conduct it.

Though Smith did not see the Arch, his satisfaction must have been great at the time of the judgment of design submissions and the selection of the winners. He could catch the scent of victory. I had been back from the Army for only a year when he designated me as chairman of the competition committee, but the title meant little for he alone did what was to be done, from the raising of the prize money to the selection of the speakers at the awards banquet.

The jury was a distinguished one, as was to be expected,

Howe having selected the members. Among them were Fiske Kimball, director of the Philadelphia Museum; William Wurster, dean of architecture at MIT; Richard Neutra, the internationally known modernist architect; Charles Nagel and Louis LaBeaume, both St. Louis architects and museum directors; Roland Wank of New York and Herbert Hare of Kansas City. The occasion was well attended and gay, with Bill McDonnell, the toastmaster, presiding and at his best--and his best was very good indeed. After the dinner the jury and others who had a part in the project assembled at our house for a very lively evening which, full of optimism, lasted late into the night.

Having met and been impressed with such talent, some years later I asked two of them, Neutra and Wurster, to design branch buildings for our company, and Neutra in his upper years became our friend.

I can add nothing to the reams that have been written about the monument, but recently I have seen what Saarinen himself said about the conception and birth of the idea. The following are excerpts from a letter he wrote to the *Post-Dispatch:*

"I argued the case for the pure monument as opposed to the utilitarian. I felt that monuments like the Lincoln and Washington served their real purpose of reminding us of the great past, which is so important in relation to looking toward the future. I can remember thinking how, in Washington, the memorials to our three greatest men, Washington, Lincoln and Jefferson, each has a distinct geometric shape. The Washington Monument a vertical line; the Lincoln Memorial a cube; and the Jefferson Memorial a globe. There is something simple and satisfying in that, and I wondered whether St. Louis should not have a shape along similar lines.....We thought of a huge concrete arch. Such a shape was in no way unfamiliar to us. There are the dirigible hangars in France by Freyssinet, the arched concrete bridges by the Swiss engineer

Maillart, the arch that LeCorbusier designed for the Palace of the Soviets. Then we thought maybe an arch is a good idea, but we began to wonder whether one leg should be placed on each shore of the river. No, there seemed to be enough bridges. Then we came back to the thought that placing it on the west bank was not bad at all. We tried it in many different ways. We tried it obtuse, close to a semicircle, and it looked too much like a rainbow. We tried it quite vertical and pointed, and it looked too ecclesiastical. Anyway, we chose an arch form which was neither flat and round nor too pointed.

"More and more it began to dawn on us that the arch was really a gateway and, gradually we named it the *Gateway to the West.*"

If Smith was the Moses of it, then surely Buster May was his Aaron, the aid who held up his arms so many times when he was near exhaustion. And there were stalwarts in the Congress like Leonore Sullivan, as indeed there needed to be, for all the original estimates again and again had to be revised upwards.

There it stands now--a 22-acre national park, the only one within a city, a beautiful monument, a spectacular architectural-engineering tour-de-force memorial to Jefferson and the western pioneers, and a graphic educational story for those who will but look. More than a national park, it is also a useful festival area for the city itself--an asset of which much is being made. Between it and the Old Court House lies a small open park of one block, and on it is Luther Smith's name. I can think of none in my time who deserved more of his city and his nation.

*****

I don't know how to define a great man. Is he different from a genius? Well, it doesn't matter too much for I have known

36

few of either. Point of fact, I guess the only one I've ever had much to do with is Jim McDonnell, and I think that by any standards he qualifies on both counts. Surely any man who starts with nothing but a briefcase and within 40 years employs 40,000, builds the western world's finest military machines, has sent his emissaries into limitless space without losing one man, has to be worthy of any label you can imagine.

As has been noted elsewhere in these records, I had some associations with him when he was president of St. Louis Country Day School. I was first his treasurer and then his vice-president. What I quickly learned about him was that failure was not in his vocabulary, and his persistance was such that, once he determined on a course of action, he simply would not recognize an obstacle.

The following example has nothing to do with electronics, aviation, space technology or ballistics, but it does offer a small footnote to his ability.

In the early 50's Country Day School was located on Brown Road in north St. Louis County, almost adjacent to the airport. It was clearly in the wrong place. Its clientele lived far to the east and south of it, and would increasingly come from central west county some 10 to 15 miles distant. Besides being inconvenient, the school's surrounding neighborhood was becoming commercial in such a manner that it did not provide the best environment for a school of teenagers. Jim determined to move the school.

Quietly he had a real estate firm obtain options on a number of parcels near Mary Institute on Warson Road, the school's present property. The price was but a trifle more than $200,000, a sum which he decided to get the easy way, i.e., from four $50,000 donors, one of which would, of course, be himself.

I was to meet him at lunch to discuss some small school affairs one day, and about 10 that morning the phone rang.

It was Donald Danforth, the chairman of Ralston Purina.

"Say, Howard, Jim McDonnell is outside my office. Do you know what he wants?"

"Well, Don, I guess it's $50,000. You know he wants to assemble this land, and I think he plans to get three guys to go along with him."

"Now look, I am not going to do it! I have been president of the school; I've done my share, given them quite a lot already. I won't do it."

"OK, Donald. You are, as they say, free, white and 21, and can make up your own mind. But you asked me and I'm pretty sure that's what he's after."

"Thanks anyway." And that was that.

Our date for lunch was at 12, the standard hour for St. Louis businessmen, but he was late. I read the paper, fidgeted, and he finally showed up at 12:45 p.m. And he had--you guessed it--Danforth's check for the $50,000 in his pocket; and by the time lunch was over he had my check for $5,000, which I did not have. I borrowed it at the bank without much enthusiasm, but there was no resisting him. He is not long on his sense of humor; life is serious with him; but he is the most ingenious doer I have ever known.

*****

G. B. Shaw said somewhere in his *Man and Superman* that "The reasonable man adapts himself to the world; the unreasonable one persists in trying to adapt the world to himself. Therefore all progress depends on the unreasonable man." You may not always believe in Mr. Shaw, but you must admit his provocativeness, which brings us to David R. Calhoun--in his day, Mr. St. Louis.

Dave was eminently a reasonable man. He looked upon the world, his world, his St. Louis, and it was good. He loved his

38

peers, what he was doing; and he wanted to sail calm seas; if he could avoid it, feathers would not be ruffled. And he had everything--the world his oyster.

Darkly handsome, the product of attractive, socially prominent parents, self-confident, he nevertheless never appeared arrogant, cocky or overbearing. He could easily have been the wasp among all the wasps, but while he was one when he wanted to be, he had the common touch. Somewhere he acquired the gift of thoughtfulness to a degree given to few, and he would go far to avoid hurting anyone for whom he had the slightest respect. But, of course, like Shaw's reasonable man, he wanted to adapt himself to his world and there was no touch, not the merest suggestion of radicalism about him. He was, therefore, the perfect trust officer.

Whether he would have been more valuable to himself and to St. Louis with a college degree is unknowable. That he did not get one is odd, for the contemporaries of his circle in the early 1920's were generally traveling the college route, but Dave passed but briefly through the University of Virginia campus and came home to work for the legendary, hard-boiled, shrewd Ed Cave at the old Ely-Walker Wholesale Dry Goods firm, which Dave's father had previously headed. At this endeavor he quickly proved himself the superb salesman, which he was all his life; but it was obvious that he could not be comfortable with Cave who, brilliant businessman that he was, sat in his office with his hat on, coatless but with open vest, and exuded toughness. So they parted company and Dave went to work for the St. Louis Union Trust Company.

All along he had been a close friend of Ben Loeb but, though I had met him several times, our paths began to cross only after 1945, when the war was over. We had both returned to St. Louis--I from the military and he from his war effort, which was running the Trailmobile Company in Cincinnati. Whether he knew he would go back to St. Louis Union Trust before his return to town I don't know, but the aging but astute Jim Grover picked him--and neither he nor his directors were ever sorry.

Now the trust business is a complicated, even tricky endeavor. It requires vast banking, investment and legal knowledge, discretion to the nth degree, and integrity to the extent needed in perhaps no other business. The chief executive, in common with all other corporate heads, should naturally be a capable administrator, and he ought also to be able to inspire confidence, for the essence of the trust business is the handling of other people's money, and about this people are apt to be pretty touchy.

Dave was neither a lawyer nor a banker, but his discretion was absolute, his integrity unquestioned, his salesmanship the best, and he inspired confidence. Moreover, his diplomacy both in social and business affairs quickly became almost legendary. He managed to keep the closest of ties with Gussie Busch, in spite of the longstanding schism between the Busch family and St. Louis Country Club. Were he still living, I think he would not resent my saying that he never knew the intricacies of the trust business, or the banking laws--knowledge that ordinarily would have been expected of a man in his position. The Trust Company owned one-third of the stock in the First National Bank and exercised control, so it would seem that the chief officer of the largest trust operation between Chicago and the West, and the *de facto* head of Missouri's second largest bank, ought to be technically qualified. But, of course, technicians can be hired and his lack of these skills was far overbalanced by his assets.

For some time Ben Loeb had been on the board of the Mississippi Valley Trust Company and later, after the merger, the Mercantile. He strongly influenced Jewish business toward that bank. In 1945 there were no Jewish directors of the First National or the St. Louis Union Trust Company except Sidney Shoenberg who served on both. He, however, was aging and, in any case, in spite of his great wealth, had never headed a business enterprise. It was never spelled out to me in so many words, but I knew full well that Ben suggested me to Dave and I joined the Trust Company board; a year later, at the invitation of Bill McDonnell, I joined that of the First National.

The myth of the hero has been popular with mankind since the early mists of history. Even Ecclesiastes sang "Let us now praise famous men," and do we not sigh sadly that we have no heroic leaders now that Churchill and Roosevelt are gone, and look back at the founding fathers in wonder that so small a set of colonies could have produced their breed?

As for me, I have always been a hero worshipper. When I was at school there was St. John, at college Lloyd-Smith, and when first in St. Louis (and always) Loeb, Shepley, *et al.*, during military service Marshall, Ike and Bradley. And quickly then my affection for and awe of Calhoun was fixed.

Well, why not? For his list of credits is long. I do not here take account of his many directorships in important companies, his leading of civic projects such as bond issue campaigns, and the like, but only the things that concerned me. Without him I should not have had the interest in banks, the Zoo, the Chamber's chairmanship, the presidency of the Muny, the membership in Civic Progress and the breaking of some important barriers in which I think some of us have been helpful. Yes, he was a hero to me, as he was to many others. I saw him frustrated only once, and that disappointment was to him a deep one.

The year was 1952 and Ike was about to run for President, but first he had to get the Republican nomination. Now Ike, a great, old-time social friend of St. Louisan Willard Cox, had come to St. Louis several times after the war, had met Dave, and had been with him elsewhere. Ike liked him, was impressed with his charm, ability and connections, and asked him to be his finance chairman. Dave's excitement was great; he was but 50, and if perchance the lightning struck, his position in the Eisenhower administration would be a firm one. The political aide furnished during the early stages counts for the most with any politician, and Dave not only believed deeply in Eisenhower, he saw this invitation as an opportunity both for him and his bank.

Moreover, the task had its own time limitations, for he was to be finance chairman only until the primary election. After that, either Ike would be nominated and the Republican Party would take over, or else Ike would lose in the primary and the campaign would end. Dave consulted with his chairman, James Grover, who had no objections and was even enthusiastic, and accordingly went before his board asking for a six-month leave of absence to undertake the job. He was careful to say that he knew the request was unusual, that if even a minority of his directors were opposed he would not undertake it--but he thought the matter would be routine, could not imagine any opposition. Whereupon he was stopped dead in his tracks.

The opinions voiced were to the effect that Democratic money was as valuable to St. Louis Union as Republican, that we ought not to take any political side, that it would be bad for one of our officers to be in the limelight. In vain did the "younger" board members, Henry Pflager, James Lee, Johnson and I argue for Dave. The majority in that year of 1952 could have been trustees in 1840 when the railroads were turned down and went to Chicago.

And Dave quickly wilted. He had been the Trust Company's president but a short time, had already said he would accept a negative decision from even a small minority, and so the effort failed. Ah well, the saddest words of tongue and pen are "It might have been." Perhaps he would have been at the Court of St. James, Paris or Rome representing his country, and certainly St. Louis might have had the Air Force Academy. No one, however, need feel sympathy for Dave, whose career was, I am sure, just as he wanted it--crowded to the full with the success of his own company; board memberships on a dozen of the bluest of blue chip companies such as American Express, Monsanto, Equitable Life, Emerson Electric and Anheuser Busch; trustee of anything in St. Louis he wanted, from Washington University to the Zoo, and top of the social heap. His golf was good and his friends legion.

Just as perfection eludes all mortals, so Dave was neither genius nor saint. He was, as I have said, a conservative, a compromiser, a resister to change and, if Shaw was right, not a creator of great new vistas. But then mankind is generally uncomfortable with the radicals, even the greatest of them: witness the poor reception given Socrates, Jesus of Nazareth, Galileo and Darwin. And if you are comfortable and happy in the warmth and cheerful air of St. Louis, as so many of us are, then I submit you owe a debt of gratitude to Dave, who did so much to keep and enhance the charm, the strengths, the values which mean so much to the average man.

CHAPTER II

Lord, I ascribe to thy Grace,
and not to chance as others do,
That I was born of Christian race,
and not a heathen or a Jew.

Isaac Watts

If you are Jewish, one of your ever-present considerations is the relationship of the Jew to the community in which you live. It follows then that if you are not Jewish or Italian or Oriental or black, but simply a run-of-the-mill Gentile--which is to say white, Protestant, not especially intellectual but prosaically middle-class American--you don't worry too much about your place in the community. (If, however, you are a socially ambitious, upper-class Gentile and want to graduate from Normandy to Bellerive or--wonder of wonders!--to St. Louis Country Club, why then, you are *very* conscious of your place and think about it constantly.)

But the Jew, whether in St. Louis or New Orleans, Des Moines, Joplin or Belleville, always is aware of his relationship with his coreligionists as well as with the outside community. To begin with, he tends to be wary because he has been raised on a diet of anti-Semitism. This diet has varied enormously, has taken many forms, some of the most violent of which were the poisonous periods of the Spanish Inquisition, the long history of being an outcast from nearly all Medieval European

44

society,*the Russian and Polish pogroms, and the climax of the Hitlerian holocaust of the 1940's.

The Jewish neighbor of yours, the Country Day and Harvard graduate, the member of Westwood or Meadowbrook and perhaps the Noonday or Missouri Athletic Clubs, has also experienced it in its ever-present if much milder forms, and has heard it talked about in his home, his schools and among his contemporaries since early childhood. The chances are good that at public school he has been called Sheeny or Yid. If he is middle-aged or older, he feels that he knows the truth of what Henry Miller wrote about the Jew in a Gentile world, when he compared him to a man in a cage with a lion. So long as the lion is content and well fed, he tolerates the man and the man is safe. But let the lion get hungry, sick, irritable, and the man has no defense, is in grave danger. So it is that generally the Jew has maintained a low profile, made no moves, hoped that with each recurring public scandal the perpetrator would not be Jewish and thus tarnish his image. Even if he has not read nor even heard of Henry Miller, he is likely nevertheless to subscribe to the lion-cage theory. This attitude was markedly noticeable in the late 30's, when Hitler and his American followers such as Gerald K. Smith and the Klan were on the move.

The Jew has been ultracharitable, often because he was truly motivated, but just as often because he thought his giving would improve the image of his people. He has realized that because there were strikes against him, he must top his competition, be a better student, work harder, be smarter, earn more in order to attain eminence or even just stay on the same plane with contemporaries who make small effort.

There are, however, two differences between the situation

*cf. Shakespeare's *Merchant of Venice* and Marlowe's *The Jew of Malta.*

45

in 1977 as I set this down and in 1926, when I first came to St. Louis. The first of these is that nationally the Jew has more confidence in himself.

Whether or not he is a Zionist, he has nevertheless observed the Six-Day War, seen his people not as sickly wraiths led to the slaughter as in Germany, nor as pale, nonmuscular intellectuals to be laughed and sneered at by the world, but as tough, battle-hardened sons of bitches. This sense of pride in the raw strength of battle evidenced in Israel has affected even the anti-Zionist Jews everywhere. Not since the days of the fabled Judas Maccabaeus about 2,100 years ago have his people been warriors; and the wealthy Jew of German descent who deplored the idea of a Jewish "homeland" as anti-American still gloried, if secretly, in the victory.

Most of us would agree that he is to be pardoned for some pride, if after 2,000 years of sniveling at the heels of the barons, he stands taller in his own estimation.

But, of course, this hardly helps him socially, and what we are talking about is the Jew (and especially *this* Jew) in the city of St. Louis.

While I had been here several times during the process of courtship during 1925 and '26, it was not until 1927 that we moved here, became once and for all time residents, and began life in the metropolis on the Mississippi, which politically was partly German and partly Irish-Catholic controlled, socially was Waspish to its core, and in the Jewish social structure was dominated by those of German ancestry--socially, philan-thropically and in business.

A half-century ago the Jewish social scheme of things was definite and centered around two clubs--the city Columbian Club, on Lindell at Vandeventer (in a building later occupied by the Automobile Club), and Westwood Country Club, which in those days was in Kirkwood.

There were about 400 families in both clubs and few of any

Russian descent. The German-Jew was to Jewish society what the original British society was to 18th-century New England, only in St. Louis they bore such names as May, Schoenberg, Rice, Stix, Baer, Goldman, Waldheim, Aloe, Rauh, Bettman, Rothchild, Glaser and Eiseman, instead of Cabot, Adams, Lodge, etc. Few of those named had college educations but there was (as always with the Jews) a large cadre of college-trained professional lawyers and physicians, including the distinguished Dr. Max Goldstein who established the Central Institute for the Deaf, Hanau Loeb who was Dean of the Saint Louis University Medical School, and many other members of the professions.

I was but 25 and duly impressed with the hierarchy. Now, from the great distance of a half-century, I see that I should have been--for those of the Jewish social set were mightily impressed with themselves. Except for the professionals like those listed above, the general tone was anti-intellectual and antieducational. If this seems strange in view of the age-old respect for education, teaching and scholarship which lies deep in Judaism, nevertheless, it was there. Indeed, when some of the boys of wealthy families did not go to college, in spite of their parents' great wealth, it was a point of conversation, but the answer always was: "You should have the education-- they've got the money." The idea was, of course, that if you were smart enough to get rich without college then what the hell!

The Jewish tradition of learning for its own sake, for its character-building aids, for its interpretation of the Talmud, and for its fostering of theological scholasticism, existed then and still does. But that tradition was prettly largely in the Orthodox circles, and these were and are socially beyond the pale, for the German Jews, after casting off the European yoke, were rushing pell-mell to become Americanized. In this, I cannot see that they were very different from the Irish, the

47

Italians or the Poles. America was the mecca for the poor and persecuted of Europe in late 19th and early 20th centuries. Since it held out freedom, hope and opportunity, was it not inevitable that the young immigrant would want to be as American as possible and as quickly as he could? But the United States after the Civil War was almost at once vulgar, materialistic, bursting with economic energy as it grew in wealth, and the German-Jew followed the pattern of its vulgarisms as well as its love of freedom and democracy.

He had his own pecking order; his contempt for the Polish and Russians who came a generation or two after him was drastic, and that prejudice did not retreat until after the second World War. Before the Germans there had been the Portugese, with family names like Baruch, Cordozza, Brandeis, and they were revered; but they were few, and, so far as I know, only Brandeis of Supreme Court fame had any St. Louis background.

The situation then, about 1927, was this: The Jewish community--I should think about 35,000 in the metro area--was reasonably prosperous; it had its own hospital and charity federation, but still supported the Community Chest more than in proportion to its numbers and wealth, and had an upper-crust society of some 400 or 500 familes which were happy, contented and snug in their memberships in the Columbian and Westwood Clubs. There were a few, perhaps five or six, with memberships in the Missouri Athletic Club, none in the Noonday, none in the Racquet Club and, of course, none in any of the country clubs other than their own Westwood.

There were a few bank directors, but almost no bank officers in any executive positions. The real V.I.P. executives in the business community were pretty much confined to the two larger department stores, Famous-Barr (May Company) and Stix, Baer & Fuller. In addition there were the old and respected wholesale dry goods houses, Rice-Stix and Ely-Walker--the two fading embers of what had been the St. Louis distributional industry to Arkansas, Texas and Oklahoma. But neither of these was to last very long as mercantile patterns were changing and Texas quickly bypassed St. Louis as the dominant factor in the Southwest.

The breweries, the chemical companies, the steel mills, the giant shoe manufacturers--in none of these were Jews prominent during the first decades of the century.

Social institutions were not all there was to organized Jewish community life. Important also were the temples or synagogues, the two most prestigious being the old Temple Israel, then headed by Rabbi Leon Harrison, later succeeded by Ferdinand Isserman, and Temple Shaare Emeth, whose Rabbi was Julius Gordon. These were "reform" congregations. While there were two others, United Hebrew and B'nai El, led by the fine Rabbis Thurman and Miller, their social standing was not to be compared. Jewish formal religion is divided into three sects--I use the word for lack of a better--Reform, Conservative and Orthodox, each represented by differences in ritual, and of each there were several congregations. I have no idea as to the number then, but today there are a total of 16 divided as follows: seven Reform, three Conservative and six Orthodox. For those to whom the various sorts of Judaism are mysteries, it may be useful to note that the Orthodox practice the old-time fundamental religion and are responsible for the peculiar hats, Kosher foods and the like. Reform Judaism is American (but based on a similar, earlier German movement) having been founded by Rabbi Isaac M. Wise of Cincinnati in 1876 and designed to bring Judaism into the modern age, to adopt it to Western society--in effect, to Americanize it. Conservative congregations lie somewhere in-between.

There have been too many scholarly analyses of religious prejudices and discriminations for me to pontificate on

49

something of which I have only a layman's experience, but I would like to express a thin hope that perhaps Henry Miller was wrong.

It is just barely possible that a more liberal attitude genuinely exists. In some curious way I believe this could be the universal (in the western world) decline in the belief in immortality and even of a supreme deity. I suppose what I am saying is that along with organized religion goes bigotry, suspicion and hatred, and, with the great 19th and 20th century advances in science, especially since Darwin, there has been more lip service to the tenets of Christianity than unquestioning belief. Whether communism has also contributed to this I've no idea, but it is clear that the great monolithic Roman structure is badly shaken.

It would seem the safety and security of an all-embracing creed--one which undertakes to provide snug comfort and sweet solace from the cradle to the grave and everlasting paradise thereafter--has a greater hold on the people where the general level of ignorance is high and public education is low. Then, too, the adherents, fearful of any cracks in this security, are suspicious of those outside the fold. It is hardly necessary to mention civilization's many brutal and genocidal religious wars, its inquisitions and, finally, the charnel houses of Europe in World War II. Nor is the end in sight; Catholic and Protestant kill each other in Northern Ireland; Moslem shoots Hindu in India; Arab, Moslem and Christian turn on the Jew in Israel, and on themselves in Lebanon.

It has been fashionable of late in philosophical circles to be much preoccupied with the idea of the myth--a word which Webster partly defines as "serving usually to explain some phenomenon of nature, the origin of man, or the customs, institutions, religious rites, of a people." In the opinion of Joseph Campbell, the Irish teacher, philosoper and mythological expert, Hinduism and Islamism are two great

50

mythological structures and the state of Israel is, in his words, most certainly a mythological institution, "because the Jew has the mythology of the chosen race and therefore a land which has been chosen by God's grace, a land which they say is a gift from God: You cannot explain a people's feeling of having a right to land in purely political or social terms."

Often the question is asked, why does the Jew hold himself apart? Why is he so clannish socially?--in effect, why does he ghettoize himself?--and those who ask are well meaning. Perhaps the old query of the chicken or the egg is relevant--is he set apart because he is not wanted, or not wanted because he sets himself apart? Then, too, there are those Gentiles (not many I should think) who really believe the Jew has a special relationship with God, and they have ascribed some anti-Semitism to jealousy of that relationship.

Well, I know what the Bible says about the chosen people, but in all of my seven decades I don't know that I ever ran into any Jew who thought he was a special favorite of God. Oh, yes, I knew people who were comfortable, even full of glory in their Judaism, but *chosen* like Noah or Moses?--well, anyhow, not within miles of Broadway and Olive.

I have always felt that all religions were essentially alike, that their systems of ethics led to the same Golden Rule, but this same Joseph Campbell tells me I am wrong. I am somewhat shocked that he says Judaism and Hinduism are ethnic religions--one is born a Jew, one is born a Hindu, whereas Christianity, Buddhism and Islam are creedal religions: "I believe," and birth has nothing to do with it.

In any case he reinforces my theory that all of them are a little outdated in a contemporary world. And here I quote him directly:

"Go to any church or synagogue and you will find that clergy trying to support an archaic concept of the universe against the findings of science. Religion has been kicking against

51

science since Hellenistic times. Just think, the first chapter of Genesis was composed when the Greeks had already measured the circumference of the earth to within a couple of hundred miles. It presents a deliberately archaic notion of the shape of the cosmos and the way in which it came to be and then the religious system is hung onto that belief. When Copernicus published his formula for the Heliocentric universe in 1543, a persecution of scientists set in since the religions had tied their faith to a geocentric system."

Can we draw any comfort from the fact that public educational standards are low in the Middle East and in Ireland, and that as they improve, bigotry will lessen? Well, perhaps a little, but even if I am right in arguing that an enlightened atheist will be more tolerant of all creeds, I still believe prejudice would be around us were all humanity holders of doctorate degrees.

There are different levels of discrimination, economic, corporate, educational and--predominantly in America--social. Indeed, the stubborn failure of the liberal element, the Congress and the courts to distinguish the social from all the others is not only stupidly unrealistic but has made most of the trouble. It seems clear to me that the Congress can enforce "minority" memberships in a school or a private club, but it cannot prevent the process from wrecking the institutions; for humanity is gregarious, cliquey and loves social distinction. The great American social mistake in the second half of this century has been not in its attitude towards equal rights, which has been superb, but in the liberal belief that legislation and appropriations will change human nature.

*****

It is not easy to assess comparative ratings between the climates of various American cities as to the acceptance of and prejudices against the Jew. I have read that the Eastern Seaboard is the harshest, but that the sociologist finds milder, more acceptable situations as he moves west and south. There are experts at this sort of thing and I am not one, so about the only part of the subject I can explore is what I have seen happen in St. Louis.

What I saw and heard of, when I first came here, was a city almost completely segregated socially but one which was about to change, and I think it has, significantly, in the 50 years since then. It is always the most secure, most powerful, "best" people who are the leaders in social liberalism. The names of Ethan Shepley, Samuel Conant, David Calhoun, Russell Gardner, Frank Rand, Bishop Scarlett, Wesley McAfee and a score of others loom high in my memory. Not only were they active and effective in breaking barriers, they were secure enough in their own positions to be contemptuous of the little people surrounding them who objected.

I think now of the Veiled Prophet organization, of the St. Louis Club, of the Noonday Club, of the Chamber of Commerce, the Municipal Opera, the Shaw's Garden board and the boards of trustees of both universities--and of these there is some history to be recited.

I suppose that originally the VP was commercial rather than social, since St. Louis was, during the latter part of the 19th and early part of the 20th century, a wholesale center serving the South and great Southwest. Originally the prime object of the parade and its glittering ball was to attract the out-of-town merchants. And while the records were secret, it was known that Sidney Shoenberg, Morton May, Aaron Rauh and Louis Aloe were members of that early VP society. The atmosphere, however, had changed; the event had become more social in character, and for many years, the Order of the Veiled Prophet had been closed to Jews. But about a year before I arrived, the golden boy of the Jewish community, Benjamin Loeb, entered the business and civic scenes of St. Louis. Of this man, whom I was privileged to call friend, I can hardly say too much. I know of no one, in my long experience, who gave as much pleasure to his friends, did as much to promote the softening of bigotry, promoted the welfare of his fellow Jews or enjoyed life as much as he. A member of the respected Loeb family, which had already produced a dean at Saint Louis University, two other prominent doctors and a president, briefly, of the University of Missouri who later became dean of the School of Business at Washington University, Ben had family background indeed. But he was not an intellectual, brilliant as he was; his forte was common sense, on which it sometimes seemed he had a corner.

Ben had been at the University of Missouri when his uncle, Isador Loeb, was president. While Ben stood in awe of his uncle, his natural high spirits were not to be curbed by any such restraint as fear of an uncle in a high place. He was quickly popular at the university and his lifelong friendships with Wesley McAfee (who augmented his sparse income by running the floating crap game in his rooms), Richmond Coburn, Howard Rusk--later the distinguished authority on medical rehabilitation--and hosts of others who were soon to be the "Establishment" in St. Louis, started him on a career not to be equalled in the Jewish community.

Ben was rich enough when he died in 1962, and had had a fine and successful business career, but his genius, in my judgment, lay in his service to his town and to its Jewish segment. He was more effective in his efforts for the Jew partly because he was so well liked, trusted and respected in the community at large. Do I give the impression that he was some sort of saintly, quiet, Solomon-like, staid personage? Hell no! Ben was a hell-raiser, a martini drinker, a lover of horses, poker, bridge and gambling for substantial stakes. He was equally at home with bookmakers, senators, archbishops, aldermen, university deans and bank presidents. And equally they loved him.

When he died, I wrote a Saturday morning column for the *Globe* which I called, "On Being Diminished." Among other things I said, "He gave of his purse what he could, but he gave of himself immeasureably more. But there have been others who worked hard--this was by no means the full measure of the man as he gave much he received still more and he was radiant with life. He loved it, enjoyed it, and it was impossible for those around him not to live more abundantly because of him. Ben taught me more than anyone else how to live in the world, how to watch the wheels go round. And he urged me to be a part of it, to do some of the things that had to be done if the world is to remain civilized."

The Jewish philosopher Harry Golden, who edited and wrote the once prominent *Carolina Israelite*, had an uncommon and wryly humorous ability to get at the heart of the Jewish outlook on life. He wrote this truism: The Yiddish word for a big shot among the Jews is *macher*, but the word for a Jew who is a big shot not only among Jews but in the entire community is *shtadlan*. And he said further that while the Jews admire and respect a *macher*, nothing equals their rage and hatred of a *shtadlan*. Which is to say: It's okay to be a V.I.P. among us, but don't get too big.

The reason for this is not hard to see, for the tendency of the successful man to involve himself in the town at large civically, equally tends to draw him away from the narrower circle in which he started. Thus, the frequently heard comment, "He thinks he's too big for us. The hell with him."

But this attitude was no part of the feeling for Ben Loeb. He was a door opener, an explorer of new paths through the bramble patches of bigotry that lay around. He began, as I indicated, from a firm base. His close friendship with those at college, and earlier at high school with young men like David

Calhoun, made him believable from the beginning. Of course they wanted him in the Veiled Prophet organization, of course his dear friend McAfee would take him on the board of Union Electric, and of course in the late 30's, when Rauh died, he was the first of our generation to become a bank director, then at the Mississippi Valley and later at the Mercantile.

During the 30's and 40's, the question of admission of Jewish children to the three prestigious and (I use the word guardedly) "quality" day schools, Mary Institute, Country Day and John Burroughs, was a serious one in Jewish circles. From the beginning, all of them had admitted Jewish children; indeed a few of the Jewish women have celebrated their 50th reunions at Mary. The question was, what was the quota? Now those were the times when the idea of a quota was anathema to the liberal. The Rabbi Issermans argued that merit was all that ought to be considered, and that if the Jewish candidates for Country Day had 20 top scores, that should be it! I remember Donald Danforth saying that if you did it that way, on scholastic merit alone, the whole place would be Jewish, and he couldn't quite see that. But then this illustrates the exaggerated opionion that so many non-Jews have of the average Jewish intelligence.

Every Jew knows that if the resort hotel takes more than 10 or 15 per cent of Jewish patrons it will soon be all Jewish, that therefore balance benefits the Jew and is in his interest, even though he is furious if he is not a part of the small accepted minority. Thus, when Loeb, who had "helped" the admissions faculty officer, Hugh Johnson, at Country Day School, left the board of trustees, I was asked to be his successor and took on the job. I quickly saw that Hugh Johnson was as fine and unbigoted a man as could be wished for, but that indeed he needed help. We always said there was no quota, but in fact there most certainly was. I've no idea what happens now; but in the 40's we held it to be about 10 to 12 per cent. I can only assume that something of the sort went on at the other two schools, and, in any case, it seemed to me that the relationship of these three schools with the Jewish community was excellent. Further evidence of that is the record of the quite large number of trustees of our persuasion. And in 1964, when Country Day found itself without a headmaster--its latest having left under not the most pleasant of circumstances--Jim McDonnell, the school's president, and Dr. Arthur Compton, of Washington University, asked me to search for a new man.

This request did not mean that I was to make the final decision--anyone who knew McDonnell and his dynamic, dominating habits would understand that--but I considered the responsibility a serious one and spent some time and travel and built a substantial file. The denouement was not without its comedy.

Although we had a good list of candidates, I was unwilling to recommend a selection without considering a man named Ashby T. Harper, who was teaching at the American School in Peru--hardly next door. But although I had not met him, his name was mentioned too often to be ignored. The late, great Christian Gauss of Princeton had said he was the best student he had ever had, and that was high praise indeed. I called Harper in Lima on the telephone, and he indicated he was due for a vacation and would like to talk with us if we could pay his travel expense. I had already spent a couple of thousand dollars in my search efforts, and, at a meeting with trustees McDonnell and John Cella, I urged that we should have Harper in St. Louis for an interview, but said that I had used some of my money, and that this time someone else ought to pick up the airline bill. Cella thought this fair enough and suggested that this time the three of us should split the check. Now either of them could have bought me at breakfast and sold me before lunch without noticing the amount, but they seriously thought that was fair enough, and we divided the $1,500 or so. In any case, it must have been a good idea, for Harper was hired and became a very satisfactory school head.

The decade of the 30's, in many respects, was the worst during my lifetime for the Jews in St. Louis; and everywhere the sense of danger was very great. The country was slowly emerging from the great financial depression, but Hitler was waxing and his followers were legion. Father Coughlin was on the air, and about him the church seemed complacent; the Klan was stirring; Gerald K. Smith preached; Huey Long of Louisiana made like a dictator and obviously would use any demagogic weapon to suit his purpose. There was praise for the Germans, even from a national hero like Lindbergh, and altogether there was a feeling of uneasiness in the entire American-Jewish community.

And Sinclair Lewis wrote, "It Can't Happen Here."

There were, naturally enough, many defensive reactions. The National Conference of Christians and Jews came into being in the East and then nationally; Charles Rice and Robert Mayer were active in St. Louis in getting it started. The B'nai Brith, a sort of Jewish Defense League, the American Jewish Committee and others sprang into actions they deemed beneficial. These largely consisted of intelligence gathering about professional, rabble-rousing anti-Semites and publishing truth about Jewish activities while nailing such lies as might appear.

I do not consider that I was effective during this period, but I watched the activities of Loeb with something akin to awe. He ran the Community Chest, twice during the war, was in the councils of the Establishment, was tireless in the building of the community image. All the while his circle was enlarging, respect for him was building, and the problems with anti-Semitic angles were dumped in his lap. The number of such problems were legion, for although anti-Semitism was a real and vicious force, the Jews tended to be neurotic about it.

They had reason enough to be concerned, but many of them imagined slights that were not there.

Thus: Was Johnny turned down at Country Day or Irvin's daughter refused at Burroughs because of religion? See Ben; he'll find out, and straighten it all out too.

Was Max refused a loan by Walter Smith at the First, or Hemenway at the Mercantile? See Ben; he knows them all.

Was the Klan planning a demonstration at the steps of Kiel Auditorium? Better talk to Ben about it.

Was it OK for Cohen to buy a house in Fair Oaks? If Ben didn't know the situation, it wouldn't take him long to find out. (Incidentally, it was *not* OK.)

One more thought about the *shtadlan*, the man referred to above who is a big shot in the community at large. The word has an honorable history with a more serious and honorable connotation. At times and particularly in 14th, 15th, 16th and 17th centuries--generally the period of the Western European Renaissance--the word had the dignity of a title, one which implied an honorary, voluntary position. The post could be held only by someone who, by virtue of his wealth, business connections, eloquence and personality, was influential with kings, princes or other authorities. He was the sentinel of the Jewish community within the state, which was always in fear of encroachment upon its meager existence, and he frequently averted threatening danger or harmful regulations against the Jews.

Things have changed, and Ben never heard of the word *shtadlan*. If he ever went to Sunday School he probably was a skillful truant, but the similarity between his life in St. Louis and those of the famous Werthmeier and Oppenheimer of Austria, Isaiah of Vilna and ben-Michael of Presburg is, nevertheless, plain to see.

I speak of a period before World War II and before the full maturity of Alfred Fleishman, who in the 40's came to the fore as the most prominent public relations counselor in St. Louis, and along with that success became increasingly sensitive to the integration climate. A little later, he was the chief source of intelligence for the Civic Progress organization concerning the black community. There is more of Al Fleishman elsewhere, but it seems important to say here that, together, Loeb and Fleishman kept the cool among the Jews.

If the hotheaded American Jewish Congress wanted to counterdemonstrate against a proposed meeting with the Klan, Fleishman would point out that such action was just playing into the hands of the bigots, that the newspapers could ignore a few Klansmen whose meeting was attended by scarcely a handful, but make a "thing" out of it, create a brouhaha, and the media had no choice--could not ignore it. You could not deal with the bigots and the haters, but they could be fenced off by being ignored, and in explaining this effectively, both men were superb.

Some months past, Al Fleishman and I began to record some conversations--dialogues about St. Louis, and our experiences here--thinking that they might lead to a book. The effort did not jell, and I gradually realized that if there were to be such a document, it would have to be done without him. But we had done a few preliminaries, and one day had explored at some length the anti-Semitic atmosphere in St. Louis. Here's how it went:

HFB: "What you are now leading into is anti-Semitism, what the climate is, and I think we have to speak of two or three kinds of climate. Neither of us lacks experience. Would you say we can divide the subject into social and civil rights?"

AF: "Yes, I think so. I remember the time when Jews were completely out of luncheon clubs."

HFB: "And most civic activities as well."

AF: "Yes, except for the fact that we always had an Aaron Waldheim, but he really wasn't a civic leader nor was Sidney

Shoenberg. They were leaders more by virtue of energy and money than by leadership qualities."

HFB: "Yes, I get the impression that early in the century there was not much of such leadership."

AF: "The first Jewish president of the Symphony was Stanley Goodman and I was the first chairman."

HFB: "I don't take too much comfort from this, because symphonies all over the country have had Jewish interest and support and many officers--Stern in New Orleans, Otto Kahn in New York, Zellerbach in San Francisco and Guggenheim."

AF: "But there were few prominent civic leaders."

HFB: "There was, of course, the famed Hanau Loeb of Saint Louis University, his brother Isador of Washington and Missouri Universities."

AF: "But I don't think anybody regarded them as Jewish leaders."

HFB: "When I moved here in 1927, I heard at once of men like Charles Rice, Ernest Stix, Aaron Rauh, Irvin Bettman, but though these men were fine merchants, lawyers and the like, there wasn't leadership of the kind you and I would expect to see--oh, in Civic Progress for instance."

AF: "Recently the American Jewish Committee did a study which indicated that lack of membership in clubs, luncheon and others, had a bad effect on Jews not because of social anti-Semitism, but because of the deals which are swung over the table or on the golf course. That would mean the handicap was great if they were eliminated from that area of industrial social life."

HFB: "I think the study was right perhaps, but not for the stated reasons. Deals are seldom made over lunch, but it is true that at social functions, you run into people you would otherwise have to make a date to see. You can sometimes say, over a highball, 'Do you really think Joe Zilch ought to be on the executive committee of such and such?' You can get a feeling, an impression which otherwise might be difficult to obtain. So I believe the American Jewish Committee was at least partly right."

AF: "I believe that the lack of Jewish civic leaders was because the town was really run at that time by what some would call the power structure. I don't think there is such a thing today--well, perhaps there is, but if so, it's a much larger, more diversified group. But not then. Dave Calhoun had to be consulted. Now the younger generation knoweth not Caesar."

HFB: "Members of that generation are either gone or fast going. I believe that with Calhoun's death and, more recently, Jack Sverdrup's there isn't a single dominating man or even a small group. Let's explore the question as to whether there has been any improvement in the Jewish status."

AF: "I believe the Jews have done better here than in many communities. If Ben were the first of modern times in VP, you were next, and then you were president of the Chamber of Commerce, followed by Irving Edison."

HFB: "Yes, Irving was there a little later. A fine fellow but one of the careful Jews, never aggressive, did not take strong positions. But we must talk of Buster (Morton D.) May who has received a lot of kudos and deservedly so. Few know how unswervingly he supported Luther Smith in his work for the river front memorial. He did yeoman work for the Art Museum and a wonderful job for Washington University. He discovered and fostered Max Beckman, the great German impressionist, and has helped a number of other artists."

AF: "Traditionally, younger non-Jews accepted the denial of Jews from the entire social pattern because this was the way they were raised."

HFB: "But here's the question--do you think it still is as severe, or exists to that extent?"

AF: "No, it is considerably alleviated. My wife and I were sitting at lunch one day next to a prominent business leader, and I said that we had attended the wedding of Charles Guggenheim (the film producer) who married Doug Street's daughter. We heard his wife, who was further down the table, a little distance away, say, 'Charles seems a very nice fellow--too bad he's Jewish'."

HFB: "I don't think you should be surprised at that, and it's not true anti-Semitism. She probably would have said the same thing is he had been cross-eyed or lame. It's a kind of congenital defect."

AF: "OK, now you've said it. I think you're putting it in focus in a way I haven't thought of. There are people who think it is a great liability. He's a nice fellow--too bad he's Jewish, too bad he's only got one eye."

HFB: "And that goes for all the best people--even the true liberals."

There was more of this, much more, and the sample above is included more perhaps for emphasizing the ever-present sensitivity of the Jew on the subject than for any light shed.

*****

The St. Louis Club, beautifully ensconced at the top of the Pierre Laclede Building, was the first major luncheon and dinner club to be formed since the old Noonday downtown, the Racquet Club on Kingshighway and the Deer Creek, a dinner club in the county. There were, of course, the small, limited, male fraternities, the Log Cabin and Bogey Clubs, but these were inner, inner circles of Bellerive, Old Warson Country Club and the St. Louis Country Club. No one paid any particular attention to the formation of this new club, which was to occupy the upper three floors of the new office structure being built by Greg Nooney, real estate developer.

Now Nooney, a redheaded, pleasant, capable Irishman, was well known to the Jewish community, having originally been

63

employed by the long-since-liquidated Lesser-Goldman Cotton Company, after which he was in the financial department of the May Department Stores, then briefly with Stix, Baer & Fuller, and finally in his own realty company. He had been particularly intimate with the Charles M. Rice family and after the death of that prominent attorney had continued, presumably as a gesture of affection, to handle his widow's affairs. Whether Nooney conceived of the club as a space renter to augment the income of the building, or whether he had been approached for it, is not clear; in any event there was not much comment about it.

After all, Old Warson had but recently been added to the country club list and the Jews were pretty well used to being passed over. Then a press release appeared in 1962 and the feathers hit the fan. The release described the new club as a "professional and businessman's club," and this was infuriating to the Jewish defense organizations (B'nai Brith, etc.) which did not want to see another exclusive club formed. They were ready to ask--what was wrong with the Edisons, Mays and their Jewish colleagues? Fleishman thought a sticky and undesirable incident was in the making, especially as so many who knew Nooney's business history with Jewish firms felt that he was a turncoat having been, as it were, nursed to prosperity in their areas.

All credit to the decent people. Almost immediately after the news item appeared, Ben Loeb and I were called by Calhoun and asked to see him. With him were assembled Kent Cravens of the Mercantile Trust and John Wilson, then with Anheuser-Busch. The conversation went like this:

Calhoun: "You fellows know about the St. Louis Club?"

Loeb: "Sure, how could you miss it?"

Calhoun: "You think the Jewish community is upset?"

Loeb: (Shrugging shoulders) "Not much. There's nothing new about this sort of thing."

64

Calhoun: "We have told them they would not be allowed to exist on those terms. Those days are over. You guys will join."

Baer: "What the hell! No one needs the damn thing. As far as we are concerned, you can stuff it."

Calhoun: "No, Howard, that attitude is no good. We don't give a damn whether you and Ben want or need it. That's not the point. We simply will not have this kind of thing in St. Louis today. You can afford it, and we insist you both join."

So I put it to the reader that such a request, with all the good will and years of friendship behind it, could not be denied. Nor could it have happened 35 years earlier. There are, to be sure, some who will label this "tokenism" and say that it is of no value. I don't believe it. There must always be a beginning, someone to pave the way. There are now about 30 Jewish members in the St. Louis Club, of a total membership of 750, or 4 per cent, just as there are 30 in the Noonday Club, about 7 per cent of the 425 regular members; there, too, there were none in 1927 and but three in 1954.

Moreover, even the sacrosanct Racquet Club has three or four, and there are small signs in the country clubs, fostered, I believe, by the intermarriages that seem to be popping up all over. The Old Guards, both Gentile and Jewish, will deplore these actions, and since human nature does not change, they must be understood; for even the bastards, of which there is no lack, have a point of view, which if not ethically to be defended is nevertheless real. And if we are to believe in the art of the practical, we must agree with Jimmy Durante who has said most profoundly, "Dese are de conditions dat prevail."

*****

A half-century has passed, and while integration has made progress and perhaps there is a shade less contempt or pity for the general idea of Jewishness, still, attitudes are not easily

65

measured. No one has to be a historian to know that not since the days of Solomon did the Jews feel more secure than in "enlightened" Germany during the latter part of the 19th century. To be sure many of the poorer of them went to America both because it was the land of opportunity and because there was no chance for advancement in the military in which they were required to serve.

But the well to do were doing very well and the professions were open to them. Ah well, there is no real security under the sun. The earthquake, the plague, the tidal wave, the famine and sometimes the Hitlers finally drive home the inescapable point that there is no such thing.

But there is a Jewish society of sorts in St. Louis though it lacks the elegance and cohesiveness of the first quarter of the century, and to describe it seems difficult. Like quicksilver, its essence is not easily seized.

To find its leaders, to think of it in terms of social elegance, is nearly meaningless. This much, however, is clear. There are in public affairs, in commerce and industry, in civic activities more, many more, Jewish men and women of first rank prominence. Consider Larry Roos, a three-term county supervisor just at the time when the county has taken the front and center position away from the city. And now, as newly elected president of the St. Louis Federal Reserve Bank, he has broken new ground.

In finance, Elliot Stein stands not only high but perhaps far above any investment banker in the area. Head of his own substantial firm, member of the boards of a half-dozen of the area's finest corporations, his services and opinions are respected not only locally but on Wall and State Streets. Lee Liberman chairs the Laclede Gas Company; while Millstone and Sachs--self-made leaders in construction and real estate--are both university trustees, as is Joseph Ruwitch.

Women have been slower to emerge in prominence,

although for decades the energies of Jewish women's auxiliaries have been prodigious, but these efforts were largely in the cultural, health and welfare fields. Now at long last it is possible to see a Ruth Bettman as trust company director and trustee of Saint Louis University. No prophecies are allowed here, but there will be more women of prominence; that much is certain.

The philanthropists are still more than ever prominent in St. Louis, the wealth and numbers having grown, and the Mays, Shoenbergs, Waldheims have been joined by such men as Yalem, Weil, Sachs, Edison, Millstone and the late but almost legendary David Wohl.

There are scores of others who, wedded to their own religious community and emotionally affected by the state of Israel, have given generously--even sacrificially--of their means, but their interests have been secular rather than in the city at large. Without the support of those mentioned and many like them, it is not too much to say that life would be even more difficult for the Art Museum, the Symphony, the Arts Fund and for the cultural scene generally. And among the lawyers, doctors, teachers, the Jew is prominent and occasionally distinguished.

But his social structure has lost its *ton*.

Even more, the temptation to say that there is no social structure at all is strong. There are two country clubs; the old, original Westwood and the newer Meadowbrook, a well-run, even luxurious institution; but then many of its members-- though certainly not all--consider themselves as only waiting to get into Westwood. Westwood, then, one would think, would bear about the same monolithic relationship to the Jewish social structure as the St. Louis Club, the top of the heap, does to the community at large. Only it does not; it doesn't work that way. Certainly it did 50 years ago, but now the scene would not be recognizable to the leaders of those bygone days. Westwood itself has no quality of homogeneity. It has a dozen or so "crowds" and one knoweth not the other. It is common for an older member to say that he was at dinner there, and though the place was full, he knew only a half-dozen or less. He is bewildered, and many of his children have left the club. It is popular, has a long waiting list, is expensive, but does in no way constitute "society." There is no fortnightly, no dance class at which children can meet, learn to dance and get to know their peers, the sort of gatherings that may in the old days have created artificial values but also gave growing youngsters a feeling of belonging, of security. Its own party nights are well done and well patronized, but in the same manner as an "in" nightclub would be.

The reasons for all this seem to be varied. The generations immediately following our own, by which I mean those of us married in the 20's and 30's, have intermarried in surprising numbers. Of 10 of our own close friends and family members, all of whom married within their faith, their joint production of children has been 24. Of 22 of these now married, 14 have non-Jewish spouses. This overwhelming percentage would not apply to all the Westwood membership and even less to the entire Jewish community, but it does indicate a trend which is growing and can be expected to accelerate if the church means less in family life with the succeeding generations.

This, however, does not explain the lack of a cohesive social group, the sort of thing Birmingham attempted to describe in "Our Crowd." It might be reason enough had all those who married Gentiles become integrated members of other social groups, but this is not the case. The doors of the other clubs have not been thrown open--rather it would seem that many of the younger element, both single and married, have little interest in social clubs of the Westwood nature. In some measure I would venture to compare this attitude with the decline of interest on the part of those whose mothers, a

68

half-century ago, were breathless at their chances at the Veiled Prophet Ball.

Or it may be that the Jewish interest has shifted from a desire for any sort of social prestige to civic achievement. The community boasts two superb institutions: the Jewish Hospital and the J.C.C.A.--the Jewish Community Center Association. The hospital, of course, has a long and honorable history, and more recently, as an integral part of the Washington University Medical School affiliated group headed by Barnes, it probably ranks with the distinguished Mt. Sinai of New York and Beth Israel of Boston, which is to say with the very best anywhere. Members of its board of directors are numerous and are selected from those who are wealthy and are, therefore, prospective sources of contribution, or are good names in the Jewish community or, lastly, are the "doers," those who can carry the adminstrative burdens. It has been the prestige board in Jewish civic affairs.

In recent years the rise in importance of the J.C.C.A. has challenged the hospital's civic importance. It is, of course, a different institution, a welfare-cum-recreation organization, many-sided and almost unique. An outgrowth of the old YMHA, the Jewish equivalent of the YMCA, its main center sits in splendor on Schuetz Road although it has branches. Designed to bring a better life to the financially lower middle-class and poorer Jew, it offers housing, day-care centers, summer camps, recreational and educational opportunities and community social activity, in a manner never attempted by any YMCA in St. Louis. Heavily supported by both the United Way and the Federated Jewish charities, its staff is rated excellent and its lay board brings energy, ability and efficiency to a high peak.

The hospital board is now completely "integrated" in that it no longer looks with suspicion on those of eastern European ancestry, but it is still dominated by the old guard, those whom

69

the militants would term "the careful Jews" and the fresh breeze of the newcomers, the energetic, younger, newly well to do seems soon to challenge the prestige of membership on the board of the hospital in favor of the J.C.C.A.

So it is that the Jew in St. Louis is active, more prominent civically, financially, philanthropically than ever. He contributes substantially to the cultural, educational and medical environment of his city but has somehow lost, with the passing years, his own social structure. As the newer generations have not had the experience of an internal society nor the elegance of the old Columbian Club, so they do not suffer the lack of it; and those who remember its pleasant ambiance are now old, most of them very old, and their memories of its elegance are perhaps of something that never really was.

CHAPTER III

"The newspaper is of necessity something of a monopoly, and its first duty is to shun the temptations of monopoly. Its primary office is the fathering of news. At the peril of its soul it must see that the supply is not tainted. Neither in what it gives, nor in what it does not give, nor in the mode of presentation, must the unclouded face of truth suffer wrong. Comment is free, but facts are sacred."

Charles P. Scott, in the Manchester Guardian

The now and then love-hate relationship which I have had during the last 20 years with both the *Globe-Democrat* and the *Post-Dispatch* has puzzled me. At times I have been their darling boy, the subject of pleasant editorials, approving cartoons, feature articles, and in 1971 I was the *Globe's* Man of the Year. In between all this, I was castigated in *Globe* publisher Dick Amberg's day for putting the Henry Moore sculptures at the airport; by Martin Duggan, present editorial page chief, who accused me of lying to the public about keeping the Zoo free, and by the *Post* for pretty much the same reason.

I believe that St. Louis has been more fortunate than most cities in that it has been offered both the conservative and the liberal viewpoints in its two newspapers; but while in that respect we are lucky, I could wish for a little less arrogance and rigidity on both their parts. I think it was writer Martin Quigley, speaking at a convention of editorial writers, who said that it was not necessary to read the editorials--knowing the paper you had but to look at the editorial's headline and you knew word for word what it would say. There is seldom any changing of mind and never any meaningful apology for error.

Above I referred to Dick Amberg, the publisher sent to the *Globe* from Syracuse, New York, in 1955 when S. I. Newhouse bought the paper. He was its dynamic boss until his untimely death in 1967. Dick was one of those men of whom it could be said that he might be wrong but he was never in doubt. His opinions were wide ranging and far reaching, and it seemed that Goldsmith's verse might have been for him:

And still the wonder grew
That one small head
Could carry all he knew.

A Harvard graduate, he had apparently missed any contact with one of its great Italian art professors, Post, who had so stimulated me and so many others, but Amberg's opinions on the arts were nevertheless in no way tentative. Hence his editorial on the Moore sculptures, in December 1966, avowed that he thought they looked like "dinosaur droppings," a phrase which had evidently occurred to him as being devastatingly descriptive and satiric. While Dick could lay claim to being something of a dinosaur himself, I doubt that he had ever seen any such droppings. And he went on to say that "history, rather than pseudo-art, should adorn the airport." I remember that I was a little upset by it, but he was right about wanting them removed from Lambert, even if right for the wrong reasons. As I have always talked too much and often without thinking, I am not sure how I managed at that point not to answer the editorial, although long ago I did learn, and by the hard way too, that it is fruitless to argue with a newspaper, especially in its own columns.

It happened that a few days later I was to attend a meeting on some civic matter which he called in his office, but at the last moment I decided I could not go, because of an unremembered something which came up. Evidently he thought I was angry, in fact had mentioned to Al Fleishman that he hoped I was not, and said that I had been very much missed. Given that excuse I could not resist an answer, and having a reason I wrote the following:

"Dear Dick:

"I am sorry that I had to miss your meeting of the committee.

"I am moved to write this letter because in talking with Al Fleishman a few moments ago, he felt you thought I might have been upset and failed to attend because of petty resentment over your editorial on the airport and the Moore figures. Of course this was not the case. But since the matter did come up, I would like to say a word about it.

"I may be wrong, but I thought it was *your* editorial, because I think I recognized your style. I have absolutely no objection to the points you have made; and it may well be that eventually the figures should go to the Art Museum, but for reasons completely different from those you suggested.

"I will not argue with you about the artistic value or beauty (or lack thereof) of the sculpture. It should be enough to say that Henry Moore is generally regarded by people in the art field, such as museum directors, teachers, critics, etc., as the leading sculptor now living. If you want to put another and more crass value on his work, I might say that he has become very expensive, and that the figures at the airport are probably worth two and one-half or three times their original cost. The Modern Museum, for example, just bought another cast of one of these figures for its great sculptural garden. But that is beside the point because everyone is entitled to his opinion as to an individual piece of work.

"What bothered me more than anything else, was the derogation of these pieces as 'pseudo-art' from a great newspaper; and again the bother had nothing to do with me personally. You see, the *Globe's* editorial can't possibly hurt Henry Moore who is a giant in today's art world; and it hasn't hurt Isabel or me because in selecting these figures we had a very sound committee, whose judgment we think has been justified. But I was sorry about the editorial because the *Globe* does have national circulation and it does represent to a considerable extent, the city of St. Louis; and to have that sort of opinion expressed to the country at large would perhaps serve only to make both the newspaper and the city look ridiculous--not, I agree, to the multitude, but certainly to a great many people for whom I am sure you have complete respect. For example, the Fine Arts Department of your own alma mater would certainly not agree with you.

"So that is my complete feeling about it, Dick, and Isabel's too. We were not hurt by it, nor do we feel in the least vindictive. My friendship for you is in no way disturbed, even though I must admit that on this particular point we are miles apart. But no matter, we certainly think alike on most points!

"And that's all there is."

He would not retreat an inch and answered that he understood my point but that he still believed Henry Moore to be an artist of no consequence and that the figures were just plain ugly. But people, all people, are complex and not to be easily classified, and I could scarcely believe my ears when his lovely wife, Janet, told me a month later that he had brought my letter home to show to her and told her it was the finest he had ever received. He had told her that but he would not relent with me.

Amberg was something close to anathema to many of the Jews, not because of his aggressive, conservative--almost ultraconservative--Republicanism, but because of his obvious and frequent reference to his Presbyterianism. From the moment he arrived in St. Louis, he wanted it to be known that

74

Amberg was not a Jewish name. Humanity is strange and one thing we can be sure of is its inconsistency. Thus a great many of the Jews, who because of social and other discriminations have wished that they could rid themselves of what they believe to be a social and economic handicap, resent one of their own getting away with something, i.e., denying his background. They knew well enough that his mother had been a Godchaux, a member of an old and distinguished southern Jewish family, and while they did not recognize the Amberg label, they were suspicious of his paternal side too. Oddly enough, and again inconsistently, they had no such feelings of resentment about the Pulitzer family whose founder Joseph, of the defunct but once great *New York World*, never made any secret of his being a full-blooded Jew.

I always had the feeling that the principal difference lay somehow in the fact that Amberg was constructively involved in the community in all its aspects, was on boards, went to meetings, dreamed up projects (Herbert Hoover Boys' Club, Women of Achievement, Old Newsboy's Day, Man of the Year, etc., etc.) whereas the Pulitzers were above, rather than in, the swirl of affairs. Thus the present Joe Pulitzer has said that it was his duty to stay aloof and look impartially at the St. Louis scene in order that the paper might be more effective.

Well, maybe so, but it would seem that the *Globe* under Amberg and then Bauman has filled a vacuum by identifying with the middle-class community level and in so doing has prospered at the expense of the once untouchable *Post*. Some of my liberal friends would say that it has been despicable of the *Globe* simply to cater to the inevitable prejudices and middle-class tastes of the many. In any case, so far as I could see, there was among the Jews no resentment but rather pride about the Pulitzers.

My own quarrel with the *Post* would bother that establishment about as much as a gnat lighting on one of the

75

Zoo's elephants. Nor does it have to do with its liberalism, often mistaken as I believe it to be. After all, if the minority of conservatives, which we are in this country, were to be angry at the liberals and refuse to read the liberal press, there would be few places other than redneck villages where we could live; and we should have to forego the *New York Times*, the *Washington Post* and many others. Besides, a Jew cannot be a John Bircher, and I don't think of myself as a member of the right wing.

Rather my definition of a conservative is he who wants to conserve the values which mankind has so painfully shaped and carved out over the 5,000 years of organized society. Not that they must be preserved in status, mummified and unchanged, but that the best sharply honed elements be cherished and not lightly cast aside.

But back to our muttons: How and why do I quarrel with the *Post*? Well, I quarrel about the Zoo, the Old Post Office, the Arts Council and the Symphony--things with which I have had something to do.

On the other hand, I was totally in agreement with the paper's attitude about the airport, which means that except for two or three knowledgeable persons like John Fox, who had been on the Airport Commission with me, Walter Malloy of the city administration and the Commission's longtime chairman, and David Leigh, the then acting airport manager, we were in the doghouse. All business, labor and political outcries were against the East Side. There is more of this--a great deal more in another chapter.

There has to be a separate chapter on the Zoo and one about its concomitant Zoo-Museum District. In all but one respect the support for this institution has been strong and unfailing from the *Post*. It has, however, been its editorial policy that the Zoo must be free, that to have it otherwise is to defraud the poor, the underprivileged of their inalienable rights, and that such rights must take precedence over excellence.

More than once, and as recently as February 1976, they have editorialized that if the Zoo cannot be excellent without charging admission, then it ought to be content with something less; presumably that a little decay would not be amiss. Well, that's OK if you aren't the one possessed with some affection and even zeal for one of the good zoos of the world, if you are not charged with any responsibility for its mission or for the administration and growth of an institution which could be great, and for an attraction which draws more visitors than all St. Louis sports combined; and which gives pleasure, education and decent recreation to generation after generation of children and their elders who take them there.

On the other hand, the *Post* dotes on the Symphony, which has a total audience of perhaps 2,500 to 5,000 (the figure is the late, great Sol Hurok's, not mine) which spends about $3.9 million annually; incurs, in spite of unbelievable grants and fund-raising efforts, horrible deficits, and is each year at the brink of bankruptcy. I have nothing but praise for the good musical organization which I am sure the St. Louis Symphony is; but I suggest arrogance, the kind of arrogance that has no doubt of its own sense of values and will snort derisively at any comparison of the worth of two such varied institutions.

Apparently then (to the *Post*), poor children and their elders do not need good classical music or, if they do, it is not immoral for them to be required to pay for it--currently seats are priced from $2.90 to $9--but the Zoo must be free. Ah, but the Zoo (they say) is tax-supported and the Symphony is not, and the taxpayers have been accustomed to a free zoo and have been promised that freedom in perpetuity.

One would admit the validity of the taxing argument were it not for the fact that the Symphony is lately the recipient of tax funds in large sums from the state and Federal Arts Councils, from the State of Illinois, and from such foundations as the

Ford, which is to say about 50 per cent of such money is the taxpayers' subsidy. Nor would I accuse the Symphony of extravagance, although the manager, not the conductor, is reported to be paid more than $60,000 and has an administrative staff at a cost of about $400,000; but in the days of Vladimir Golschman, his manager Bill Zalken ran the show with a Girl Friday and a bookkeeper and drew a salary of $15,000 at his highest rate. Well, I'm sure the music is better now, and whether it is or not, there's assuredly a lot more of it.

Maybe I protest too much, but again I have no objection to, in fact am proud of, the St. Louis Symphony, but I believe its demands are out of all proportion to what the community has wanted--certainly what it has been willing to pay for. In its own annual report, which seems as full of obfuscation as a Humane Society dog is full of fleas, it is nevertheless possible to read nonmusical, or administrative or possibly "other" costs as:

Public Relations	$156,000
Other Production Expense	80,000
Overhead & Administration	317,000
Fund Raising	92,000
	$645,000

And this does not include the expense of Powell Hall, listed as $274,000.

I certainly have no intention of blaming all this on the *Post-Dispatch*, which is in no way responsible for the Symphony, and I list it here only to argue for a sense of proportion in which I believe the *Post* to be lacking.

Newspapers generally are not thought of as planners, as creators of civic assets and, indeed, it would appear, that since their roles are to provide reportage, opinion and vigilance, when they do attempt such efforts they mostly fail abysmally. I offer two such examples, both having to do with the inner city, and with reference to both I think the *Post*, or anyhow its publisher, can be charged with having failed the city.

In the exact center of the downtown area, occupying the entire block bounded by Olive, Eighth, Locust and Ninth streets, stands the ancient post office building. Constructed in 1884, it is an example of the Federal style of architecture. It had few employees, had become grossly inefficient, was and is, in fact, a pigeon roost. Since the government would need more office space in St. Louis, the General Services Administration proposed to remove it and construct on the space a modern office building, housing about 2,000 employees. In 1959, plans had progressed to the point that pleasant designs were available from capable architects. It was proposed to create on the eastern half or two-thirds of the block, an agreeably landscaped mini-park--the building to be placed on the west. The design and concept were influenced constructively to a considerable extent by George Hartzog, who during the critical years of the design and building of the Arch was the Jefferson Memorial Park superintendent, and had acquired considerable interest in and affection for St. Louis. Between his service at the river front park and his subsequent appointment as director of the National Park Service, Hartzog was employed as director of Downtown St. Louis, which was and still is a business and civic organization devoted to the promotion, growth and care of downtown. By this time he knew his way around bureaucratic Washington and was able to insure intelligent attention to architectural and landscape design.

The entire board of the Downtown St. Louis organization was in favor of the plan, since it was becoming increasingly evident that the old post office building was a cancer in the heart of the town. But it was not to be, for at this point there

79

entered into the lists opposing the project the *Post-Dispatch* and an *ad hoc* citizens committee headed by Austin Leland. The controversy raged in the columns of both papers--with the *Globe* favoring a new building--and the blockers were successful in causing Washington to withdraw from the razing of the building.

But successful in what? It was not so difficult to discourage the feds from spending money, as it is the common practice of Washington not to put its money where it is not wanted. And, as many congressmen and bureaucrats who were concerned with the decision felt that the influential and powerful *Post* might well be right in its opinion as to the value of the structure architecturally, aesthetically and historically, there was gradually a lessening of interest, interminable delay and in the end--nothing. There were put forward, from time to time, various schemes to remodel and use the structure, all obviously unpractical, all without any financial solidity and, at this writing, the building stands there forlorn and neglected.

Of late there are signs that the government, though reluctantly, is about to rehabilitate the structure, intends to locate several offices employing perhaps 500 persons therein, and will provide some space for private enterprise. But, at best, the dynamics thus provided for downtown St. Louis will be a puny fraction of what was envisaged in the original 1959 plan. Well, but the *Post-Dispatch* will retain its beautiful building.

Now it is no good saying that the building is ugly and that the best example of its style is the old State Department on Pennsylvania Avenue in Washington, because opinions as to beauty are just that. And there is no question that the *Post's* aesthetic opinion is weightier than mine. The point is that neither the *Post* nor Leland had any viable plan to substitute for the proposed living, breathing dynamic element proposed by G.S.A. So there it is, and no doubt the victory is a great one.

But most of us would say with the late General Pyrrhus, "Yes, but if we have another such victory, we are undone."

Then there is the matter of the adornment of the Kiener Plaza, a block bounded by Broadway, Market, Sixth and Chestnut. Now this is a very important open-space block facing as it does the Old Court House and the beginning of the Mall which ends at 20th Street. Its development has been pleasant enough--the designer was the late Gene Mackey, a good architect--but the principal figure, the Zorach sculpture, is worse than mediocre. It is simply lacking any element of quality or distinction. And this is how it came into being.

The source of funds was the will of Harry J. Kiener, an estimable bachelor who died in 1960 at the age of 81. I had the opportunity of knowing him in the last few years of his life, as he was a member of the Zoo board from the late 50's until his death. Harry had a great affection for the Zoo, but an even greater love for that marvelous period in his young life when he had been a track star. A star he was indeed, a high hurdler, good enough to make the American Olympic team in the year 1908. Captain of both the Missouri Athletic Club track and basketball teams, he was also an amateur boxer, wrestler, swimmer and professional soccer player. He served as boxing commissioner in St. Louis for 36 years. In his later years, as a Zoo board member, he was a close friend of Zoo director George Vierheller. With all his recreational and civic activity, he had nonetheless managed to build an estate of a million and a quarter, the amount he left at his death in 1960.

I had known him only during the last four years of his life, during which I also was a member of the board of the Zoo. When I became board president in 1960 and began to cast around for gifts, I thought of Harry as a donor. I did indicate to him the Zoo's need for capital funds; his enthusiasm seemed of such magnitude that my expectations for his will were high.

I admit to disappointment at his legacy of only $15,000 to the

Zoo, but we did pretty well with it. The architect William Bernoudy designed the arched main entrance at Government and Concourse Drives, and we were able, by adding an equal amount to Harry's gift, to build the graceful and rather handsome series of arches, now known as the Kiener Gate. I have always felt that we gave him his money's worth and that he was swindled downtown, for his gift to the city was a splendid $200,000.

This is how he thought of it in writing his will: "The sum of $200,000 to be used for the purpose of erecting a monument in some prominent place........said monument to be in the form of a fountain, to have as its motive "Athletics" and include an athletic figure........In the event for any reason actual erection of said monument has not been commenced within........five years........then........the funds remaining shall be paid over to the Shriner's Hospital for Crippled Children."

Now it does not take a genius to see that since Harry's consuming interest in life was in the field of athletics, what he wanted in his memory was a statue of an athlete. He said so in his will plainly enough to be understood by any schoolboy, or so one would think. He had left his estate in the hands of St. Louis Union Trust Company, whose president was David R. Calhoun, and Dave promptly did what was highly proper--he appointed a committee. Moreover, he appointed what seemed like a good committee, one for which in retrospect, he cannot be faulted. The members were Joseph Pulitzer, art collector of great capability and distinction; Aline Saarinen, widow of Eero Saarinen, designer of the Arch, and a prominent art critic in her own right; Edward D. Stone, at that time architect for the Stadium; Kenneth E. Hudson, dean of fine arts at Washington University, and Charles Nagel, director of the Art Museum.

So capable and well qualified was this group that one would surely believe it impossible not to achieve a distinctive and beautiful result--right? Wrong! It was not that the committee lacked ability, it seems that they had no leader or no interest. What they did for the first two years after appointment was nothing--anyhow, nothing about the sculpture or monument. Eugene Mackey, a fine architect with many good structures including the Olin Library and the Climatron to his credit, was selected to design the square itself but that was by the city. There was still no selection of a sculptor by the committee.

At length, Calhoun called attention to the lapse of time and indicated his concern that the gift might lapse in favor of the Shriner's Hospital. So the committee made a selection--picked an artist, a distinguished American, Alexander Calder! Stupidity in administration of the arts has never reached greater heights.

Calder was an important, perhaps even a great artist, but he did not do human, recognizable figures. I'm not sure how the Museum people catagorize him, perhaps as an abstract expressionist. At any rate, the public knows him as a creator of balanced, hanging, moving, graceful designs in metal, glass, plastic, etc., known as *mobiles* and of motionless figures called *stabiles*. They come in all sizes--some very large, even monumental--and his work, which is recognized worldwide, is in scores of museums.

When he was selected, Calhoun met with him, told him of the need and went so far as to say, "Now Mr. Calder, we require a runner." Strangely enough, Calder agreed to produce a design, and he did. I had hardly heard anything about the project, but one day Dave asked me, after a Trust Company committee meeting, to stop by his office. There sat a model, a maquette of a typical Calder stabile, an abstract design of perhaps considerable handsomeness but having by no stretch of the imagination anything to do with athletics.

Dave said, "What do you think of it?"

I said, "Let me see the will." He handed me the page referred to above and I read, "include an athletic figure."

"Well, Dave," I said. "Calder is a great artist and maybe this would be a fine example of his work, but you can be sued as a trust officer if Harry's ideas are to be so perverted."

End of Calder. And now the committee was ready to panic, for the hour was late--they were close to losing the gift. And quickly Zorach was selected.

How to evaluate Zorach? Well, he had been a man of some quality, an academician, but his best work was in small, organic pieces, often executed in wood, and he was also a painter. He had no recognition as a monumentalist, and had done little or nothing in bronze. Moreover, by now he was over 80 and no Titian or Michelangelo--both of whom were superb in old age. The result was what is there, and it is less than second-rate. To some extent, its harsh ugliness and its lack of any plastic virtue are obscured and softened by the water surrounding it.

The pool itself badly needs a filter, or at any rate some device to keep the water clear and agreeable. Assurances by the Department of Public Utilities of the city and the Park Department have been profuse that the matter was a small one and would be taken care of, but thus far action has been absent.

But what a waste of such a generous gift! A few months after it was first displayed in 1966, Katherine Kuh, the St. Louis-born art editor of the *Saturday Review* was our house guest. Her comment was, "But how terrible! For that kind of money you could have had a real Greek athlete from the classic age." Well, maybe, although I haven't seen anything by Phidias or Praxiteles come to the market in my time. The point was--they could hardly have done worse.

While speaking of bad sculpture, of which St. Louis seems to have more than its share, there are the two horrible examples--the Stan Musial statue at the Stadium, and the Vierheller one at the Zoo. I don't relish this confession, but I admit to being the culprit in the latter case.

When George Vierheller retired in 1961, Isabel and I wanted to recognize this remarkable man who had been our friend and kindness itself to our grandchildren. In connection with the cleaning up and reshaping of the waterfowl lakes, there was to be a small fountain adjacent to the juncture of the two bodies of water. The Zoo board had already decided to call it the Vierheller Fountain, and as the design seemed to cry out for a piece of sculpture at its center, we determined to commission a sculptured likeness of him, so that forever he could look over his domain. It really was not a very good idea, but our execution of it was worse.

Neither Isabel nor I were experts in the area of fine arts, but neither were we altogether unsophisticated. We should have known better than to give a commission to an artist simply because of friendship. The result was inadequate.

It was and is something of a disaster, and we have taken it away from its prominent position and placed it at the Zoo railway's main station where it bothers no one.

No such disposal has been possible for the equally bad Musial figure, an opus of the late Carl Mose. I was in no way involved with it, and the account of its coming into being has just been given to me by Robert Broeg, the intelligent, alert, literate, and exceedingly decent, sports editor of the *Post-Dispatch*. Bob, as were all sports writers and, for that matter, all St. Louisans, was an ardent fan of Stan the Man.

When the retirement of Musial from the diamond was imminent, Broeg had seen what had been accomplished in Pittsburgh in the form of a sculptured memorial for the immortal Dutchman--bowlegged Honus Wagner, the greatest all-round shortstop ever to play at Pittsburgh or anywhere else. It was well done according to George McCue, the knowledgeable art critic of the *Post-Dispatch*, the best of its kind in recent times. The project had been the dream of Frank Gustine, a many-talented infielder of the Pirates, and afterwards the leading spirit in a local Pittsburgh baseball association, a sort of rooter-fan group. Aided by the formidable Ben Fairless of U. S. Steel, they raised $50,000 and were fortunate or intelligent enough to hire a good artist, one Frank Vittor--a name unknown to me.

Broeg was familiar with it and wanted something of the sort for Musial, but he did not have Gustine's fortune with his artist. Rather than consult with an authority at the Metropolitan or Modern Art Museum or Rathbone in St. Louis, or even his own colleagues at the *Post*, he and the other sports news fraternity charged ahead.

Amadee, a cartoonist at the *Post*, had produced a pleasant sketch, Rockwellish in theme, showing Musial doing an autograph for a small boy hero-worshiper. Broeg liked that very much, thought it typical, the best about The Man and the sport, the hero example to the American boy. But, he said, the design was too complicated; they simply did not have the money. Like the Kiener committee, they were in a hurry; someone mentioned Carl Mose, a local sculptor and they settled for what they could afford.

The result is very bad, and does not come close to recording the unique batting stance that the great man used; the way he coiled at the plate, waiting for the pitch, would have been difficult enough, one would imagine, for Phidias or Bernini. It was completely beyond the efforts of Mose in this instance, although elsewhere he has done some nice work.

In all justice to Bob, he is no prouder of it than I am of the Vierheller--and, worse, he can't move it!

While we are on the subject of bad works of art, a comment about how to avoid it might be of some use. Art in public places commonly comes into being through philanthropy, by means of gifts. This is not always so; sometimes state or federal grants are used for the purpose, and there is a recent trend to budget small percentages of new buildings for adornment. But the vast majority of statues, fountains, murals, and the like, have been given by individuals or groups banded together to honor or memorialize something or somebody. Well and good! But not always. Beware of the donor who tells you what he wants, where it will be on your property, who will create it and what the inscriptions will be. His intent is fine, his soul is full of love, and the chances are his taste is terrible.

Tell him you have a committee which must pass on all gifts; suggest that the need is greater somewhere else--as indeed it will be, for you must have your own ideas as to higher needs for your garden, zoo, museum, park, library or whatever your institution is. And finally, if you cannot dissuade him from his project, and if it is as bad as you suspect, be firm and send him to your competitor. Of course, if he is offering you a Monet, a Rodin, or a Giacometti, grab it and ask no questions!

We have wandered in this discourse far from the newspapers about which we began, and it is time to get back to them. A. J. Liebling, the great critic and analyzer of newspapers for the *New Yorker* has been dead for a decade, and there is no replacement--certainly not here in St. Louis. I can only say what I and my friends think, which is in general that those in business, the Republicans, the admirers of capitalism, dislike, even hate, the *Post*; they like, but do not especially admire the *Globe*, which appears rapidly to be catering successfully to the likes, the prejudices, the beliefs of the middle classes, the blue-collar worker and suburbanites. Then, too, Bauman, the Catholic, has no use for birth control or abortion, and he also praises the heroism of Israel; as the combined Jewish and Catholic population of the area is perhaps 30 per cent, he thus does his paper no harm.

On their part, the Jews find it difficult to leave the left-wing liberalism and patent love of the *Post* for the Democratic Party, but are nevertheless grudgingly doing so. Both papers have excellent staffs; the differences lie with publishers, who could hardly be more disparate in life style, in background, in taste, in political beliefs, in concept of their jobs.

On the one hand Pulitzer, grandson of the original owner of the *New York World* and *Post-Dispatch*, is sixtyish, handsome, athletic, sophisticated as to amusement, the arts, society and social contact. He heads a wealthy newspaper empire, which unfailingly attacks corporations and is suspicious of capitalism. It boasts of its political independence, but, after much soul-searching, is nearly always for the Democrats and against the corporations. He does not believe in being personally involved generally with his city and has served, so far as I know, only on the board of the Art Museum, for which, as a brilliantly skillful private collector, he is eminently well qualified. That he considers himself primarily and permanently a newspaperman is certain--he says so--and it must, therefore, be painful to him that the paper is no longer considered, as it once was, one of the best three or four in the country.

Bauman of the *Globe* on the other hand, came up through the reportorial route and early was assistant city editor. Later he was switched to personnel and business matters. The public, upon the untimely death of the dynamic, controversial Amberg, did not expect that Dunc Bauman would be able to fill his shoes. No matter; the owner, Newhouse, thought Bauman deserved the publisher job, and his results have evidently confirmed his judgment.

About both papers I'd like to say this: If you are a left-wing liberal, supporter of ADA, of ERA, of teacher and police unions, of politicians like McGovern and Kennedy, you may, if you like, continue to sneer at and despise the *Globe*; and contrariwise, if you are a right-winger even unto Mr. Birch,

88

and see a Communist in every tree, a crook behind the desk of every Democratic senator, the enemies of the free enterprise system on every street corner, you will keep on snarling at the *Post*! But either way, you will be ill-advised to read only one at the expense of the other.

Both papers--like our Art Museum, Zoo, Symphony, universities, hospital systems--serve us as well, maybe better, than we deserve. We get healthy, mixed points of view, and not all towns are so fortunate. At times both the *Post* and the *Globe* have wished me well; I do the same for them. May they both prosper and continue putting the pressure on those they conceive to be the bastards--even though to each the bastards will not be the same. There are, in any case, enough for both!

CHAPTER IV

Twinkle, twinkle, little bat!
How I wonder what you're at!
Up above the world you fly!
Like a tea tray in the sky.

Lewis Carroll

I am sure that even the youngest among us will be familiar with the late Dorothy Parker's famous witticism which went like this: If all the girls going to the Yale-Harvard game were laid end to end, I wouldn't be surprised. In its time--the early 1920's--it was rated both hilarious and spicy. Today, well, I suppose it rates a yawn. Maybe I can offer a kind of analogy like this: If all the rhetoric, master plans, hypocrisy, self-serving political pronouncements, stupidity, waste, needless delays, viciousness and plain meddling involved in and surrounding the St. Louis Airport in the last 20 years were put into a witch's cauldron and simmered slowly over a steady flame of carefully nurtured misunderstanding, we should have, well, exactly what we've got, an airport which began with high promise but which is rapidly becoming obsolete and will sink to second- or third-rate status as the next decade or two goes by.

Serving in the Airport Commission for 16 years, from 1954-1970, I have had an opportunity to see much of the ill will and confusion which at this writing flourishes, and the end of which no man can see.

Lambert Air Field, or the first 246 acres of it, was purchased in 1928 from Major Lambert *at his cost*. Through the years, land was added until it now comprises more than 2,000 acres. Some was acquired by negotiated purchase; in other cases, condemnation was necessary. Capital improvement, i.e., buildings and other facilities, were paid for by general obligation bonds, but in 1952 this method of financing was no longer needed. In all, the city of St. Louis provided the first seed money of about $26 million.

Additionally in the beginning, all net operating losses were paid by the city, and it wasn't until the late 1940's that the airport took in as much as was being paid out. During the decade of the 40's, a few dollars of illusionary operating surpluses were turned over to the city--illusionary because the surpluses would have been deficits had Lambert been required to pay the administrative, legal and other services which the city furnished. So much for the start of things.

For years the airport was faced with the comparatively simple problems of city versus county, city versus airlines, civil service versus efficiency (the two are never synonymous) and growth patterns versus lack of funds. But, with the eruption of the proposed Cervantes-Ogilvy deal, mild controversy turned into a war between the states over the airport. As does everyone in St. Louis, I have a position (which has not changed since 1969 when the volcano erupted). I think the concept of a regional airport located in Illinois, or at least provision of the land for such a facility, jointly controlled, was and is logical--this from a man who is not anxious to break any lances for the sometime Mayor Cervantes. It's just that I think, in this case, he had something of value to propose, and I hope I may be forgiven for some degree of satisfaction that ex-Secretary of Transportation, William T. Coleman, Jr. thought so too.

But since the purpose of this chronicle is to present footnotes of what I have seen in St. Louis, I'll give small space to my opinions and concentrate on what I have seen at this point of airport matters. Although there had been a previous airport commission, small and inactive, the present commission began in 1954 when Mayor Ray Tucker and his Board of Aldermen were faced with a new, expanded airport. They realized that commercial aviation was developing from a rather short adolescence--during which it was considered a stunt for the reckless and rich--into a valid passenger carrier system and a major industry. As a result, they created a committee, or commission, within the Department of Public Utilities to operate Lambert-St. Louis Airport.

This commission was, however, not really autonomous, since its chairman was to be the chairman of the Department of Public Utilities, its contracts and appropriations subject to approval of the Board of Aldermen, its personnel practices conforming to the rules and wishes of civil service; while over all was spread the supervisory mantle of the mayor. Nevertheless, it did enjoy as much autonomy as Tucker could assign to it; and since his style was to let his appointees work out their own problems, the beginnings were good.

I suppose I ought to be ashamed to confess that membership on the commission is the one civic job I ever asked for. I was then 52 years old, but there was enough of the small boy in me to be fascinated with airplanes. I mentioned to Aloys Kaufman, the ex-mayor, that I'd like to be a part of the new activity. It was as simple as that, and without any hesitation I was appointed.

Conway Briscoe, St. Louis' long-time and perennial head of the water department, was also running the Department of Public Utilities at that time, and was, therefore, the airport chairman. Commission members were bankers Sidney Maestre and Walter Burtelow, machinery dealer John Fabick, investment banker Russell Gardner, automobile dealer Vincent McMahon and myself. Well, I can't say whether we were exactly equal to the trustees of Washington University, or the United Fund, but we were concerned citizens and not political stooges. Our early meetings were very much like those of any other civic activity. And I was not disillusioned about airplanes--they were and are fascinating.

Since it was all part of a new industry and technology, the problems were ever present, rapidly changing, and they grew in their complications. Still, the airport and its planes were as intriguing to many of us as electric trains are to small boys, which is to say that there was an element of just plain good fun in our commission work.

However, it was shortly apparent that the airport would also interest and appeal to politicians and some business elements for the usual powerful reasons--money, jobs and influence. The new industry--which has seemed nothing more than a toy a few years before--was growing so rapidly within two decades after World War II that everywhere airport plans were outdated before they could be implemented. There was cash flow from landing fees, from space rental to the carriers for counter, baggage, office and service spaces, and from parking garages, restaurants, news and gift shops, from insurance sales and auto rentals and from a host of fringe businesses which needed to be on or near the property. A new industry was coming of age as did the railroads in the middle of the 19th century.

Other cities were already generating income from hotels and liquor sales on airport land, but St. Louis was to allow liquor sales only years later and at this writing still has no hotel on the airport property.

What we did have was a good professional manager in Dave Leigh. I know of no man who has taken more abuse from politicians, irate citizens and uninformed but opinionated newspapers. In any case, in my view Dave is one of the good guys, honest, dedicated and knowledgeable.

He was beaten upon unfairly by the press, the politicians

and the bureaucrats; but not, let it be said, by his peers, i.e., his colleagues in airport administration across the country, who knew his worth. Indeed, it was hard to see why he stayed on the job--although there were some compelling personal reasons of no moment to this discussion.

Now he has gone; the present Mayor Conway, in his great wisdom of airport matters, having made it clear to Leigh that he must quit, after which he appointed a retired Air Force Colonel with no civil airport experience whatsoever.

In additon, we had the legal services of the then City Counselor, Thomas McGuire, a young lawyer of great energy who could express himself clearly and solve many problems. There is more about him elsewhere, but the point to be made here is that he was one of a team of sincere workers for a good airport. It is the general rule of city law department attorneys to be legal hacks, but McGuire was not of the general rule--he was very good indeed.

I have also, and perhaps to an even greater degree, to pay respects to Walter T. Malloy, who in 1957, upon the return of Briscoe to his water department, became Director of the Department of Public Utilities and, therefore, chairman of the Airport Commission. If there is such a thing as a perfect bureaucrat, Walter was and is the man. He was and is truly a civil servant in the best sense of the term, which is to say that he is unswervingly honest, straightforward, dedicated, hard working almost to a fault, intelligent and tough. He had what most of us would consider faults, right enough, but he is what he is, and in my view that is very good.

An engineer, he had what I have come to believe is the inherent engineer's attitude towards architecture and design, and, in fact, the humanities in general: He thought all these things a bunch of nonsense, dreamed up by people who stood in the way of real engineering values and progress. One result of this was that we were often at loggerheads because of my desire to protect the beautiful, basic airport design of Yamasaki. But, in Malloy's defense, he was very like the great Sverdrup, who had almost a contempt of architects.

I don't know when the more thoughtful members of this community began to be aware of the damage caused by the city-county schism; certainly when I first became a St. Louisan in 1927, no one was concerned about it. By 1954, however, when I joined the commission, nowhere was the mutual antagonism more strongly exemplified than in connection with Lambert Field. It seemed almost as if county officials took delight in injuring or at least gigging the activity, as though the city had the one asset of which the county was jealous and, therefore, somehow, it must be cut down to size.

Instances of this attitude are not lacking.

Although the city owned the property, the county refused to let the city police it. This meant that while Lambert was charged for security services, it had no control over police and guard personnel or procedures.

There can scarcely be any St. Louisan who used the airlines who did not know and frequently curse the fact that city cabs could deliver passengers but could not take return fares. Whether the county government was afraid of the county cab unions, or simply pleased to be a part of such expense and inconvenience, I am unable to say. I only know that I never heard that any county official was in the slightest bit interested in any correction of an absurd condition which helped to make the town look ridiculous to strangers. And at this writing, taxicabs are still under the control of the County Public Works Department; the airport has no authority over them whatsoever.

About 1955, a new system of fueling planes came into being at all major airports. Previously, large tank trucks drove up to the planes, hoses were stretched and tanks were filled. This clumsy, slow and sometimes dangerous method was replaced by an underground piping system with outlets at each plane gate and is, of course, now standard everywhere. When the commission, in company with the airlines, proposed to install such a system, the county authorities were interested to the point of blocking it for two years. The idea was that these engineers, in their wisdom, had to make sure it was safe in order to protect the public--something which the airlines, the commission and the Air Line Pilots Association, to say nothing of the Feds, would never have thought of, I suppose. When it eventually was installed in 1956, there were no substantive changes from the original designs.

Although the old original terminal building at the west end of the St. Louis field had six or eight rentable sleeping rooms, Pittsburgh was the first city, I believe, to serve the air traveler by putting a hotel right in the terminal building. Miami subsequently built a fine facility, and a great many major ports have incorporated such hotels as a part of their operation, but not St. Louis. There are, of course, a myriad of motels just off the property, but Lambert suffers financially through lack of income that the leasing of such an asset provides.

About 1960, all of us expected that a hotel would be built as an integral part of the airport expansion plan. Not only are such hotels profitable but this one would have been especially so, as the airport itself would have been able to influence traffic to its advantage. Now it can be, and was, argued that such a venture would provide unfair government competition for nearby but off-the-site private businesses, but then so do the airport news and gift shops, restaurants, bars and barber shops. It seemed to me and to other commission members that both the convenience of the traveling public and the financial need of Lambert outweighed any such consideration. Besides, a private operator would be selected for the hotel following the established pattern with parking garages, food, etc. No matter, the locals evidently had the ear of the county council, and the necessary zoning was denied.

There were, however, much more serious attempted blows, these either emanating from the county or abetted by it. In February 1958, the adjacent city of Berkeley decided simply to annex the airport, a ploy which, if successful, would allow Berkeley to cut taxes drastically by transferring such tax burdens to Lambert tenants and by taxing aviation fuel and various airport facilities. The city of St. Louis fought the annexation and won in the lower court, Court of Appeals, and finally the Supreme Court, but it failed in all attempts to get the county to join in the defense.

A more active harassment from the county was undertaken in 1963, when the county assessor sent letters to all airport tenants, announcing that they were to be assessed on their leaseholds from the city. If successful, such a tax would open the door to untold amounts of taxes and would lead to problems which were unimaginable. Again the city was a successful defender.

The list of harassments is long. There was the matter of liquor sales, and this ban was particularly galling to officials of the Chamber of Commerce. The traveler could imbibe in New York, Chicago, Dallas or Los Angeles, but not at Lambert-St. Louis, emphasizing again our historic provincial aspect. You might imagine that the county council members were afraid that airline pilots would go rolling and staggering into their cockpits, but I should be more inclined to believe that the council was effectively importuned by county saloon operators afraid of the competition.

After a few educational years, it began to seem to me, as it still does, that St. Louis ought to own an auxiliary or secondary airport designed to accomodate noncommercial or "light" aircraft. Such a field designed to garage and service executive, corporate and private recreational planes not only would relieve traffic conditions--as Lambert would tend to become congested in the future--but also would lessen the very real peril of the amateur flying the light plane into the path of the commercial carrier.

There was no evidence that the city was interested in the idea, so one day in 1960, feeling very strongly about it, I went to Ray Tucker to argue the point. As I remember it, the conversation went something like this:

Ray: "Well, damn it, I'm not going to do anything more about airports. The county has never done anything--let them do it."

Me: "But, Mr. Mayor, they won't do it."

Ray: "Well, let's give 'em a chance and if they fall on their faces, we'll show them up."

Me: (Reluctantly) "OK, I guess, but what do we do?"

Ray: "Maybe a joint effort. We'll see."

And he did go at it. What emerged was a conference with James H. McNary, the then county supervisor, and, in 1961, a joint city and county airport commission. Together with John Fabick, Walter Burtelow and Vincent McMahon, I represented the city while the county members were Councilman Maurice Stewart; Eli Goldstein, lumberman and philanthropist; Glenn Vatterot, attorney, and E. Holecamp. The city and county each appropriated a few thousand dollars to pay expenses (I believe we were paid about $25 a meeting) and we were in business. Fabick originally served as chairman, but was forced to resign by a later supervisor, Lawrence Roos, in a humiliating and completely unfair manner. Some eight years before, John had purchased acreage next to Weiss Airport in the southwest county. When Weiss was talked of as a secondary port, he at once offered to sell his acreage at his cost, just as had Albert Bond Lambert. The land had increased greatly in value, but the *Post-Dispatch* yelled conflict of interest. Roos demanded Fabick's immediate resignation. His resignation cost the city and the county a good man. What happened in the new commission was a big fat nothing. We met, we talked and the county members stalled--not all of them, Goldstein thought we were there for a purpose--but gradually the idea got through to me that the politicians were skillfully doing nothing and we, the city members, were being naive. We discussed the Spirit of St. Louis location, Weiss Airport, Columbia Bottoms, the East Side--in fact everything in the area, but there was never any specificity. Time passed and, in 1969, Roos was elected county supervisor, but nothing changed. The city members of the joint commission had lost hope, were disgusted.

So I asked Larry Roos for a lunch date and put it to him: "Larry, honestly now, you are never going to cooperate with the city on an airport, is that the case?"

"Yes, I guess that's it."

"OK then, aren't we wasting our time in these meetings? Why don't we dissolve the commission?"

He thought a moment and said he saw no reason to continue. That was the end of that and soon the commission was dissolved.

Ah, but when the proposal by Mayor Cervantes and Illinois Governor Richard Ogilvy for an East Side airport was made, then Roos and all his cohorts were Lambert devotees, aviation experts and Missouri patriots. Then it was their fierce loyalty to Lambert that was evidenced by screaming at the city politicians, who with all their bumbling had built the institution, had employed one of the country's best architects, had cost the taxpayers almost nothing and had given the area an agreeable, efficient port.

The old crossroads town, the inner city, tired, abused, sneered at by those living west of Skinker, had again made a contribution. Just as over the previous century it had established for all the area a fine Union Station, an Art Museum, a Zoo, one of the best botanical gardens anywhere, a

99

symphony orchestra, yes, and a complete sports program, so had it reached out into the county and built a major-league airport.

Now you might argue that it had to go out to the county. Where in the city of St. Louis proper could you put more than a thousand acres? That, of course, is quite true, but the fact remains that the city created the airport with no aid from county government or such sister cities as Clayton or University City or Berkeley.

Granted that the political and financial power of the county is a new thing, only two or three decades old, and that a major metropolitan aviation facility would then have been infinitely beyond its capabilities, still there was no evidence of the slightest interest by the county in any civic responsibility or cooperation.

The change of attitude is easily accounted for: Lambert has become an asset and not a liability. Consider that the Federal government pours billions into landing field aid, that property values have grown hugely around the ports, that merchants and concessionaires employ people, pay taxes and have influence, that the city skims 5 per cent off the top of gross revenue and that construction is never-ending. Altogether the time had come for county politicians to recognize that they had been missing out on a good thing.

If I give the impression that the city is the good guy and the county the slick con man--well, I'm way off base; for if the county can be accused of neglect and harassment, the city contributed its share of bumbling, bureaucratic stupidity, as well as greed and the always-to-be expected efforts to grab pieces of a good thing.

Illustrations of so nasty a series of allegations are harder to come by, for they are nearly always suspected rather than crystal clear, especially those of the greedy-grabbing type. The bureaucratic bumbling, since it has no element of illegality

100

is easier to pinpoint. There is, for example, nothing criminal in not having provided a secondary airport for private and executive aircraft, for not having hotel facilities on the property, for having a mayor's favorite as a generously compensated public relations counsel, for employing political favorites to handle real estate acquisitions, for hiring engineers and architects who are close to the city administration, and for using job patronage wherever possible. No doubt such actions, or lack thereof, are inherent in democratic governmental processes, but they hurt just the same.

When the new buildings were about to be opened in 1956, some of us expected that they would not, in the ordinary course of things, be very clean or well kept. One had only to look at the day-to-day condition of City Hall, the hospitals, or court buildings to see what the city's own janitors would do. So, since the entire administration was justifiably proud of the beautiful new tri-domed structure, we suggested that this might be the one really clean city-owned building if we contracted with a privately owned janitorial service company. In so doing we could demand performance, whereas there was no means of demanding any sort of decent work from city payrollees, protected as they are both by Civil Service and fatherly aldermen.

It was an excellent idea for a few moments only, for at once Elliot Scearce, director of Civil Service, aided by Comptroller John Poelker, claimed and demanded those jobs. We wilted immediately. I don't know *why* we had to give in, but we were told we must, and would lose if the matter went to court; and I suppose it wasn't worth a fight which, in any case, we should eventually lose, for when the chips are down, the city government owned us.

One member of the commission, automatically included by virtue of his chairmanship of the public utilities committee of the Board of Aldermen, was the estimable alderman, Ray Leisure, proprietor of Leisure's Lounge, a watering establishment at 13th and Chouteau Avenue. Ray was and is not a bad fellow, even though if his life depended on it he perhaps could not tell you where Shaw's Garden is located, nor why anyone would want to venture into Powell Hall or the Olin Library. His political thinking, so far as I could tell, was strictly one-dimensional, and his airport interests were unfailingly the same--how many jobs could he corral?

Ray is actually an anachronism, a throwback to the days of Boss Tweed, Crump of Memphis or Tom Pendergast of Kansas City, and I can see now the distain which would curdle the faces of many of our mutual friends who occupy the boards of our cultural institutions were they to meet him. And it is true that Ray with his cigar, his general air of slovenliness, his limp and his darting little eyes, gives something other than the appearance of an Adonis.

Yet Ray is in some, and perhaps many, ways a useful citizen; for he is an ombudsman to his ward, an employment agency to the unskilled, a vote getter for the Democrats, and for the Airport Commission he has usually been on the side of the good guys. He did not want to know the issues, the techniques, the problems of science, engineering or fiscal procedures. What he wanted to know was how to vote, which bill to route and which to stall or block at the Aldermanic board level, and he depended on the right guys, Malloy and Leigh, for the information. If there are more handsome aldermen than Ray Leisure, there also are many less useful to the city.

Let me here and now disclaim knowledge of any out-and-out stealing, although at times the city's image of purity would seem--well, a trifle fuzzy around the edges. It was not our responsibility as commissioners to act as anticrime agents, nor did we have the resources to bring to bear in order to scrutinize everything; about all we could be expected to guard against was blatantly evident wrongdoing, which generally involved political favoritism rather than crime. But, of course, since we were only partly naive we were often uneasy, and we tried to be fairly alert. In the beginning there was little even of favoritism, but as the makeup of the commission gradually changed, there was occasionally some suspicion, but as I have said, no evidence.

The newspapers from time to time wondered about real estate commissions and price appraisals on property acquisitions; but again in this area we had no authority nor would the commission or its staff necessarily be consulted as to appraiser or real estate agents.

The great Talleyrand is quoted as saying that war is much too serious and important to be left to the generals. In the same vein, matters having to do with financial patronage were evidently considered too important for the commission and its staff, and were handled at City Hall.

Shortly after John Fabick resigned, my phone rang and Ray Tucker asked me what I thought of his appointing Julius Garagnani, the famed "Biggie" of Stan Musial and Biggie's restaurant fame. Ray sounded slightly apologetic, which was understandable as Biggie was definitely not his cup of tea. But I answered that if he owed him something politically, I couldn't see any harm--after all, we could always outvote him. Of course Biggie, who had the appearance, diction and accent of a movie Mafia figure, was not at all a tough character, but he did like to think he had political influence. And I was wrong; we could outvote one Biggie but not his entire brotherhood, as it subsequently developed.

His first political patronage effort on the commission was in connection with the restaurant and general food concession at the new airport; and he did not bother to conceal his determination to see that Harold Koplar, of the Chase Hotel, would get it. Now the food concessionnaire was to run not only the main restaurant, coffee shops and snack bars, but, we hoped, would also be supplier of on-board meals to the airlines and eventually run the bars, when and if they became legal.

There was no way of insisting that the airlines use our food company, but if they did, it was that much more revenue, as the city would receive a percentage of all the contractors' sales. Among Koplar's deficiencies was the fact that his Chase Hotel, good as its food might be, had no airline catering experience whatsoever, and favorable consideration from airlines could not be expected.

Commission staff had asked for proposals from such experienced and presumably capable people as Dobbs House, Interstate Hosts and the like, as well as locals including Koplar and Schneithorst, the latter having for some years operated the inadequate food facility at the old airport terminal, an inadequacy that was not Schneithorst's fault, but that of the quarters available.

In any event, it was easy enough to block Biggie in this instance; presumably he could make the point to his good friend Koplar that he had at least given it his best effort. Moreover, he was always good-natured about losing. But it was difficult to be anything but uneasy about other transactions which now and then popped up. One day one of the staff, who shall be nameless, showed me the highest and best bid for the gift, news and general merchandise shop. The best bid, all other elements being equal, would be the one offering the highest percentage of net sales as rent to the airport. I don't recall the exact figure, but the staff man thought, and to me it was clear, that the percentage figure had been erased and changed; in other words, that the bids had been opened and looked at, that this bid had not been the best bid, and that it was altered so as to receive the award. But altered where?

Well, the bids ought to have been, and presumably were,

opened in the offices of the City Attorney--this was after McGuire's time in the job--but I pointed out that this in no way constituted evidence. Furthermore, it was not stealing. Revising a bid upward simply meant more money to the city, and perhaps we were wrong anyway. What we thought was a suspicious alteration may have been made honestly before the proposal went in. So there was nothing to do but drop the matter.

Looking back, it seems to me that perhaps the greatest opportunity for slightly illegit moneymaking was in connection with the physical growth of the field which involved continued real estate acquisitions and the construction to which I have already referred.

*****

In May 1968, Walter Malloy described the airport situation in the course of a symposium on airport planning sponsored by the Engineers Club of St. Louis (some nine years earlier than this writing). Among other things, this is what he said:

That FAA, the Federal Aviation Authority, had then recently indicated the need for:

Two major commercial airports,

Seven auxiliary general and private aviation airports,

An early search for the site for the second commercial facility,

That the second and new airport would probably cost $500 million,

That if all possible steps were taken to expand Lambert, it might last until 1985,

That Lambert was already becoming overcrowded on the air, terminal and land sites,

That while Lambert might handle 400,000 movements, it had in 1965 handled 375,000 and was close to saturation.

105

There was, of course, much more, but neither Malloy nor any of his commissioners had the slightest doubt that Lambert's limitation would soon become very real.

My late friend, Edwin Levis, used to say that anyone can play yesterday's horse races, so let's see what has happened to the assumptions in Malloy's report of 1968--all of which have considerable meaning for us, in view of the *Globe-Democrat's* confusion of Lambert with the national symbol, i.e., the Stars and Stripes and Lambert Forever.

At first examination, it would appear that the Missouri xenophobes, i.e., the *Globe*, Messrs. Persons, Roos, Symington, the Governor, and all the me-tooers, have been right. The air movements at Lambert, 342,000 in 1967, have not grown as fast as projected, nor is Lambert yet saturated, and they are the apparent heroes who have saved us from a fate akin to rape (which was formerly deemed a pretty lousy crime). But if they have been right, then the mistakes have not been made in St. Louis but rather in Dallas, Fort Worth, Kansas City, Washington-Dulles, Tampa and Los Angeles in their various elaborate preparations for colossal aviation futures.

Maybe so; and then again, maybe not. Let's look a little closer. If air movements at Lambert had continued to grow at a four per cent compounded rate as we confidently projected in 1968, this is what would have happened:

1968	355,700	1973	432,500
1969	369,900	1974	449,800
1970	384,700	1975	467,800
1971	400,000	1976	486,000
1972	416,100	1977	505,000

And if the number of passengers carried had grown at the same rate, the figures would have been like this:

1968	5,409,000	1973	6,612,000
1969	5,626,000	1974	6,876,000
1970	5,825,000	1975	7,157,000
1971	6,084,000	1976	7,437,000
1972	6,358,000	1977	7,734,000

By this time you will have already guessed that this is not what took place; instead the plane movements were like this:

1968	341,000	1973	342,600
1969	342,200	1974	331,000
1970	319,600	1975	314,400
1971	335,000	1976	321,000
1972	335,600	1977	334,200

And the number of passengers were as below:

1968	5,960,000	1973	6,432,000
1969	6,448,000	1974	7,155,000
1970	6,284,000	1975	7,192,000
1971	6,114,000	1976	7,600,000
1972	6,602,000	1977	8,430,000 (est.)*

* Now add 16 per cent intraline passengers not reported to the FAA--an additional 1,300,000.

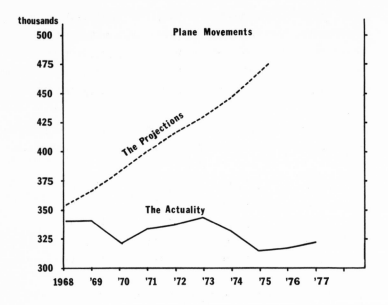

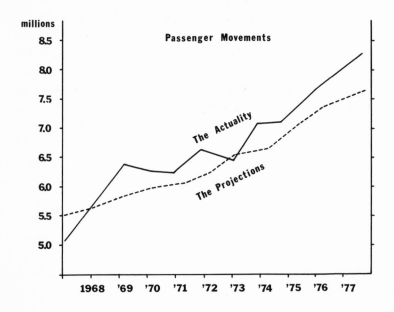

Or to put it more graphically, the curve as to plane movements, which the FAA, Malloy--and all of us--thought would rise sharply like the projected one on the top of the chart, flattened out like the one on the bottom. The passenger volume, however, will be seen to have far exceeded the predictions.

This at once raises two important questions: Why were we all so far from the mark, and what would have happened had we been correct?

First, as to our mistaken traffic forecasts and doubt about the airport's ability to handle the increase, the answer is in several parts:

1. Larger aircraft were put into service, the Boeing 747, McDonnell-Douglas DC-10 and Lockheed L-1011, which made it possible to carry the same numbers on fewer flights.

2. Somewhat more complicated is the change in the mix of flights at the airport. The commission, desirous of diverting private and executive flying to other airports, raised landing fees and generally encouraged the use of Lambert for commercial carriers. Thus, civil general aviation movements, which reached a high of 192,000 in 1966, by 1975 declined to less than 100,000. Additionally, the Air National Guard and Navy were cooperative in reduction of usage. Military flights which topped out at 25,000 in 1964 were less than half that number--11,800--by 1975.

3. Unanticipated also was the dramatic improvement, almost a breakthrough, in the area of electronic flight control. That is, less distance between arriving and leaving planes is now necessary, and the usage of a well-instrumented field allows for more movements without sacrifice of safety.

But does all that translate into the validity of "Lambert Forever?" It does not, but the voices of reason have not been heard, only the screams of the politicians, the self-serving cries of foul from some of the press and the phony expressions of concern from a county and state which for 25 years had used Lambert as a whipping boy.

Four hundred thousand air movements is still the saturation figure for Lambert. There were but 315,000 such movements in 1975, and of these, 110,000 were military, executive and individual, which presumably could still be lessened--not to zero but to less than 110,000. Will commercial traffic increase? Well, if not, why then do we have an active Chamber of Commerce (now the Regional Commerce and Growth Association)? The country's population growth has not yet ceased, and is not expected to do so within the foreseeable future.

Certainly there may be more and better technological improvements, though it is worth noting that some of these cancel each other out. The giant planes, 747 and DC-10, for example, must go back to a six-mile separation on approaches because of a dangerous turbulence which their wing construction produces.

And now a whole new ball game is in view because of one word--deregulation. Well, some would rather call it regulatory reform, but no matter, the end result is the same. Merely in anticipation of this, airlines have been slashing fares, and traffic thereby has risen and will continue to rise. And we must consider that the traveller has no common carrier other than the airlines, with the sole exception of bus service. Is not growth of air traffic inevitable--and is not deregulation only a hastening process? Witness the recent explosive growth of cut-rate charter fares.

The point is that those who talk of the Illinois site as though it were Siberia have no alternative to offer. In general terms, they talk of dozens of sites in Missouri, but independent studies have seen nothing closer than Cedar Hill or Foristell, some 30 miles away. Approach patterns to airports may not intersect without deadly peril and will not be approved. The argument over the location is, however, not so damaging as the idea that Lambert is all we shall ever need.

This is precisely the kind of attitude that made St. Louis lose the railroads to Chicago more than 100 years ago, an attitude which was the result of vested interests in the river steamboats which refused to look at the future. Before arguing this point, I have talked with those whose experience is considerable. I have asked them whether, in the light of what has actually happened, they have now decided that another major airport is not needed.

Without exception they admit the error in their timetable, but they insist, as do I, that all that has happened is a putting off of the day of reckoning, not its cancellation. So while it would be premature to begin building a major facility now, it would be neglect in the nth degree not to acquire property against that day--a day which will surely come.

Having said as much, I express no hope that St. Louis or St. Louis County or the State of Missouri will do so. If the land is to be "banked," i.e., held against the future, it will be acquired by the Illinois authority or it will not be bought. Planning is a dirty word in the United States today, because there is justifiable fear of federal planning, but if you are going to have airplanes you must plan for them as they need huge quantities of space. Only the city of St. Louis, through its Airport Commission, and the Federal Aeronautic Authority have had the slightest interest. In April 1960, Walter Malloy raised the question of the commission's responsibility and authority in that area. Questionnaires were sent out to county officials and to prominent individuals asking whether the commission should be responsible solely for the operation of Lambert or whether it should be concerned with developing and operating a system of airports which would involve duties including but not limited to:

111

1. Site selections
2. Purchase of land
3. Construction
4. Operations

There were precisely no answers of any meaning, and in June of that year, the commission could do no less than adopt the following statement of intent: "That, since there is no other able organized body to do so, the city of St. Louis must take the lead in establishing new airports for the Metropolitan Area *regardless of their locations.*" What a pity that there has been no implementation of this policy. Forgetting for a moment the possibility of another major airport, Lambert needs Weiss and/or Spirit of St. Louis and has said so for 20 years.

My part in the controversy which the community has been engaged in for about seven years, at this writing, has been only as an observer, but occasionally I have been quite close to some of the strange events.

It began, of course, when Cervantes and the Governor of Illinois announced in 1969 that they had come to an agreement that Illinois would build an airport for the St. Louis area; that St. Louis would contribute no money but would, nevertheless, have minority representation on the board of commissioners; that when the airport was completed and fully operative it would be merged with the Lambert-St. Louis facility, at which time the operating board would change so that Missouri and Illinois would be equal in both members and authority.

The news of the agreement burst like a bomb. The reactions were explosive, particularly from Senator Stuart Symington, from County Supervisor Larry Roos and from a few businessmen, including Wallace Persons of Emerson Electric who became a crusader, even a fanatic in his opposition. I suppose the members of the Airport Commission who pretended to any degree of independence from the mayor were, in addition to being surprised, somewhat chagrined at being presented with a *fait accompli*, of which they knew nothing. But when I thought about it a little, I found myself not only agreeing with the concept, but admiring Cervantes for his bold imagination--and this sort of admiration for him was not my habit. The values in the plan were solid, it seemed to me, and would greatly benefit areas needing just such a stimulus.

Although such communities as Belleville, Collinsville and Cahokia are quite acceptable, the East Side of the Mississippi River, from Columbia-Waterloo north to Granite City, with its miserable communities, including East St. Louis, Venice, Madison and Brooklyn, constitutes the most poverty-stricken, crime-ridden area in the State of Illinois; and located as it is, directly across from St. Louis, the East Side is a drag on the entire metropolis. It has taken the St. Louis business community a good half-century to revitalize the downtown area. Its gargantuan efforts for the Arch, the Stadium complex, Mansion House, the hotels and Convention Center have accomplished much; but still there sits, just across the bridge, a dank, gray, rat-infested, gangster-dominated 100 square miles, 640,000 acres of desolation.

Now Ogilvy knew that eventually something would have to be done for this cancer on the periphery of his state, and even a partial healing of the great sore would benefit the downtown area of the city just over the river. Airports are not only spenders and employers, but they tend to draw to their peripheries industries and secondary economic windfalls greater than the port itself. *Ergo!* Build a major airport in Illinois and benefit not only the East Side, but downtown St. Louis as well. This point has not been lost on those countians who denounce the possible loss of jobs in Missouri.

There were for me further attractions in the Illinois deal, not the least of which was that the initial burdens would fall upon Illinois perhaps for a decade or two during which

113

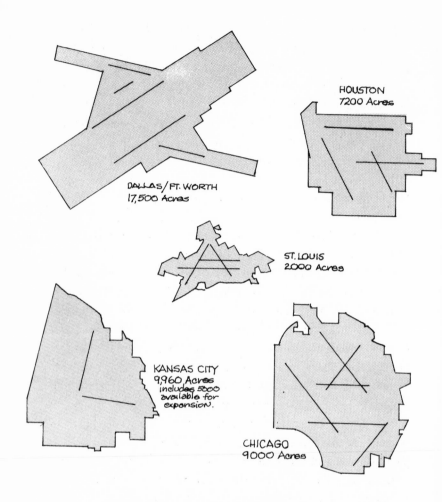

HOUSTON
7200 Acres

DALLAS/FT. WORTH
17,500 Acres

ST. LOUIS
2000 Acres

KANSAS CITY
9,960 Acres
includes 5000
available for
expansion.

CHICAGO
9000 Acres

If St. Louis is right,
then everyone else is wrong!

These four airports are not unfairly selected to prove a point. Some major ports as New York-Kennedy (5200 acres), Los Angeles (3000 acres), San Francisco (5200 acres), Boston (2000 acres) and Philadelphia (2500 acres) are not comparable because their approach paths and buffer areas are over water, necessitating lesser acreage.

St. Louis would be free to continue with the planning and development of Lambert.

Another reason for the project seemed to me to be an uncontrovertible one--there simply was and is no possible site in Missouri less than 30 miles away. A modern airport requires 10,000 acres and ought to have 15,000. The approach patterns or glide paths of planes must not intersect and this automatically places major airports 20 to 30 miles apart. Studies--many of them--have concluded that no Missouri airport closer than the Illinois site is practical. There are, of course, other considerations than distance--terrain, streams, existing structures, etc.--and the Coleman decision was quite definite about these aspects, too. Illinois is far better.

The distance from Washington University to Lambert Field is 8 miles, from the University to Wentzville is 33 miles, and from the University to Columbia-Waterloo is 15.5 miles, not as convenient as Lambert but certainly well in line with airport distances from other cities.

The reasoning of those who wish to keep Lambert forever as the sole facility, would make more sense if any reasonable action were added to the noise. Neither city nor county has been willing to acquire a general aviation field to lessen the noncommercial load at Lambert. They talk about the ability of the field to serve well into an indefinite future, a future so very infinite that we need not consider another airport, and they have listed auxiliary fields as one of the factors necessary to insure that possibility--but, as already recorded here, actions which began a decade ago have come to nothing. Indeed just now Mayor Conway proudly proclaimed Lambert would suffice for 50 years.

(In 1968 at the request of Mayor Cervantes, I headed a campaign for authorizing a $200 million revenue bond issue. We did not intend to issue the bonds until (a) the money for specific projects was needed, and (b) we had in sight the income to service the revenue bonds. The campaign was successful and the bonds are now being used, but I mention this only to indicate that Walter Malloy, our then chairman, clearly indicated the intention of earmarking $69 million for a new airport, including land acquisition.)

There now is a new argument that the development of the VTOL or STOL airplanes will alleviate the need for additional large ports. A word of explanation about these planes is in order. VTOL means vertical takeoff and landing, and STOL means short takeoff and landing. Both types of planes have been built and flown experimentally and indeed some military versions are quite practical for aircraft carrier use, as a carrier obviously provides short runways. The argument goes that because more than half of all commercial flying is on flights of less than 500 miles, and as these planes can operate on runways of 1,500 feet or less, airports can be built in downtown areas. Admittedly the planes, even jet versions not yet built, would be limited to 300 mile-per-hour speeds, but this would not handicap them because of the time saved in travel to and from the terminals, i.e., five or ten minutes at either end versus an hour or two at present. The theory is plausible except that it cannot work in this century. Neither the airlines nor the manufacturers can finance a new class of planes. With the giant 747s, L-1011s, and DC-10s, the airline debt is so heavy that in some cases it is approaching the disastrous. The prospect of an entirely new series is not just frightening, it is unthinkable.

Indeed at this writing President Carter has withdrawn support from STOL research, leaving the burden for future development to private industry. This action further emphasizes that, despite all promises for success over the past 25 years, the prospect is dim indeed.

Let us assume, however, that such planes could be built and financed. The airlines then would have to operate in two locations in St. Louis--both at Lambert and, well, let's guess at the Union Station area or perhaps behind the Convention Center on the North Side. Fine; but again the increase in cost of dual operation is dismaying to an industry which struggles from one crisis to another. And who will build the in-town port? Will it be the short-rationed city, or perhaps St. Louis County, which so far has spent on aviation not a thin dime?

In 1976 the other shoe dropped. At long last Washington--in the person of Secretary Coleman--made a judgment, in a beautifully reasoned and documented decision. And because it said the only reasonable things--that Lambert will not suffice forever and that Illinois is the best available location--the screaming began again, the lawsuits were filed.

That was to be expected, but they proved unnecessarry because, lo and behold, we got a Democratic victory in 1976; Carter received the Presidency and Teasdale the Governorship. The result; the intelligent, reasonable Coleman resigned, and Carter replaced him with Brock Adams as Secretary of Transportation. Discarded were all the facts so carefully considered by Coleman; "Lambert Forever" is the new federal view.

St. Louis has always had a peculiar talent for losing or shrugging off what would be best for its own growth interests. The pattern is here repeated.

And to make sure of that, the State of Missouri has just renewed its support of the so-called Missouri Airport Commission which, to this point, has confined its efforts to thwarting the Illinois project. What authority it has over or interest in Lambert--a city institution--remains a mystery, at least to this writer.

It seems probable that all elements in the airport control and management are not as comfortable with "Lambert Forever" as the public announcements proclaim. Word comes that the new airport director, Col. Leonard Griggs, has told his people not to push for additional airline service to St. Louis--no additional lines are to be encouraged! Saturation is evidently not an unknown word to him; but this decision is hardly likely to please the Chamber of Commerce, dedicated as it is to growth. Is he finally becoming educated to the underlying reality?

And further, deponent sayeth not.

CHAPTER V

"Who is Sylvia? What is she?"

Shakespeare

"Fie upon this quiet life! I want work."

Ibid.

What is Civic Progress anyhow? Is it the power structure, a mysterious group of puissant corporation heads, sitting in a remote dim cell, pulling the strings of St. Louis for their own benefit? Is it to be looked at with dark suspicion as the enemy of the poor, of liberalism, of labor, and as a long and somewhat evil arm of corrupt capitalism? Or is it, on the contrary, the horn of plenty from which all blessings can flow; a financial haven to which worthy civic causes can turn for manna from heaven?

Of course, it never was any of those things, but as it has labored quietly for the most part, with no desire for fanfare, the lack of publicity has generated both suspicion and confusion concerning its role in the town. This is how it came to be and what it was (and pretty much still is).

In 1971 William A. McDonnell wrote a short memo on the history of Civic Progress which he read to its members. From this memo the following is taken:

"In 1953 the then Mayor Joe Darst had reason to be concerned about his city, that St. Louis had been sitting on its hand for 20 years while others had spent tens of millions to stimulate growth and activity. Among his concerns were:

119

That no new office building had been erected in downtown since 1930.

That the St. Louis expressway program was not to be completed for 19 years.

That of St. Louis' 61 square miles, more than 50 per cent were blighted and that the Mill Creek area was a vast expanse of decay.

That except for the smoke abatement success by Ray Tucker and Jim Ford, nothing had happened for a long time, and there had been no progress on the building of the Jefferson Memorial."

Now Darst had heard of an organization called the Allegheny Conference in Pittsburgh, where dynamic activity seemed to be under full steam; and he appointed eight men to consider the advisability of a similar effort for St. Louis. They were Sidney R. Baer of the department store, Arthur Blumeyer of the Bank of St. Louis, David R. Calhoun of St. Louis Union Trust Company, attorney James Douglas, Aloys Kaufman, former mayor, J. W. McAfee of Union Electric, Powell McHaney of General American Life Insurance, and Ethan Shepley, attorney and Chancellor of Washington University. About then Ray Tucker succeeded Darst as mayor, and quickly there were added 10 other men, including August A. Busch, Edwin Clark, Donald Danforth, Morton D. May, William McDonnell, Sidney Maestre, Edgar Queeny, Edgar Rand, Tom K. Smith and Clarence Turley.

Naturally the first thing they did was to go to Pittsburgh. The Golden Triangle, at the meeting of the rivers, was already in being, handsome and impressive, and they wanted to see how it had been done. What they learned was valuable and definite and, in retrospect, was at least partly responsible for the Civic Progress success--a success of undeniably great value to this city. They saw and adopted three items of importance:

120

a. That the membership ought to be effective. It was to be a small group consisting entirely of the chief executive officers of the largest and most important companies. This was quite different from Pittsburgh where the organization had about 90 members, but was dominated by members of the Melon family. The decision regarding St. Louis was that since there was no family or individual that powerful here, the group would be kept effective through a small membership of only the largest companies.

b. That attendance at once-a-month meetings by the top executive himself be obligatory, with no substitutes allowed.

c. That the organization work closely with the top governmental offices. (It is for that reason that the Mayor and County Supervisor have been members, but only during their terms of office. And the same membership was accorded to the heads of both the major universities, again adding strength.)

The importance of this information and advice soon became clear. The usual order of things in creating a new civic body is to make sure that all community elements are included, i.e., labor, religious leaders, blacks, Catholics, Jews, etc. By avoiding such an approach, the closely limited fraternity of capable executives, with corporate power behind them, could talk to each other in confidence, without bombast, or fear of the press, and with the knowledge that their discussions would not be public property. And if they decided on a course of action requiring money, they could provide it from their own corporate treasuries.

Throughout its more than 20 years, Civic Progress has been a planner and a doer rather than an opposer. Its strengths, its list of accomplishments is formidable; its weaknesses are perhaps understandable--even inevitable.

McDonnell defined its function as a stimulator rather than a participant in civic matters; but as a practical organization, its members discovered early that stimulation was impossible without participation. The apparent paradox in that statement was resolved by the participation of its individuals, rather than the organization itself, in a given course of action, problem or situation. The idea of a professional staff was quickly abandoned. As McDonnell said, "We decided there was no particular reason to take on the expense of a full-time staff, in order to have ourselves pushed into this or that worthy cause by an eager staff anxious to justify its existence."

But though there have been no employees, two of the seniors of the public relations firm, Fleishman-Hillard, Harry Wilson and Al Fleishman himself, have served as secretaries, advisors and counsel--to the great good of the body.

Another definition might be that Civic Progress is a once-a-month discussion group composed of strong corporate executives, university and political heads, whose subjects are limited to the problems of their city, and whose discussions often lead to direct and indirect positive action. OK, so what have they done?

The first thing they did was to support, with leadership and money, the city's campaign for the urgently needed earnings tax in 1954. The overwhelming and quick success of the first venture convinced the members that they were on to something useful.

During subsequent years their contributions in expertise, in leadership and in money were effective in the passage of bond issues in excess of $750 million, in support of better (higher) tax rates for the Junior College District, public schools, the Zoo-Museum District and the City Sales Tax, and in the replacement of the old Community Chest with the United Fund, which since 1961 has reached its goal every year and been chaired each year by a Civic Progress member. More than once it saved the Symphony, and its blessing started the Arts and Education Council.

Intangibles too have been useful, as, for example, its long-standing series of breakfast dialogues with leaders of the black community, its studies of the public-school problems, and its influence for civic good with political leaders.

Above I have referred to its weaknesses. They stem from its policy of refraining, generally, from entering into controversial situations. To have done so, to have entered the arena of bitter political or governmental dissension, even when the proper course of action seemed clear, conceivably could have produced fatal strains in the smooth working machinery of its own structure and could have created public ill will and disastrously spotlighted notoriety. Thus, while it was concerned as early as 1961 with what some thought was the excessive proliferation of hospital building, and therefore sponsored a commission on hospital planning, it never undertook opposition to a specific project. Consider this example:

Few who could be considered knowledgeable or experienced in hospital care would want two city hospitals. The present and indeed historical setup provides a textbook case, a problem small but nevertheless expensive, the solution to which is so logical and so simple that it is highly divisive, and, for the present, impossible.

St. Louis owns two general city hospitals, one known as City Number One and the other Number Two, later changed to Homer Phillips. Before the 60's one was black, the other white. OK, this was unjust segregation at its most typical, a thing to be eliminated, which it was. Whereupon, blacks were not only freely admitted to Number One, but, of equal importance, so were black physicians to its staff appointments. This having been accomplished, we had two unsegregated city hospitals, except that Homer Phillips remained largely black because of its location and because the blacks liked it that way--felt it was their hospital.

123

Meantime the voluntary, i.e., nongovernmental hospital system in St. Louis grew apace and became one of the world's finest; and as both government and private health insurance became widespread, the demand for City Hospital beds shrank. Given the money and freedom of choice, the citizen had no difficulty in selecting better care. Neither of the two city hospitals is filled so why not consolidate? Both the black physician and his patient had wanted an end to separateness, here it was. Of course, if you wanted even more efficiency and still better care, you could abandon both and purchase the service from the voluntary hospitals.

No way! What the blacks wanted and thus far have got is the best of two worlds. They have kept control of their own hospital with full access to and enjoyment of the other. But Phillips, which at one time produced medical care of considerable quality and trained more black doctors than any other hospital in the country, has declined in quality. This too was probably inevitable as the younger, graduating physicians have naturally sought the superior education of the private system, and, like many of their black patients, they have left Phillips for greener fields in St. Louis and elsewhere. The fact that neither of the local university medical schools will any longer staff, teach or supervise Phillips unless given authority under minimum standards (something which the blacks will not agree to) simply underscores the impossibility of abandoning Number One in favor of Phillips, whose standards are probably barely worthy of accreditation by the American College of Surgeons, the certifying agency of the profession.

Should, then, this kind of problem be the concern of Civic Progress? The answer is probably not, for the controversy has now become social and political, which is to say that reason and science are out the window. The facts are readily available. There appears little doubt where the proper answer lies; but the black community evidently feels that to close Phillips

124

would be depriving them of something which is theirs, and it would seem that they have shown a lack of interest in arguments as to the quality of medical care.

As this is being written, the controversy has erupted into the public arena, because a reasonable recommendation has been made by an impartial body--a recommendation for consolidation as above. But the reaction again had been predictable, as noted, and the politicians show no evidence of bucking the black outcry.

In all fairness, there is no difficulty in understanding the viewpoint. Why should they lose the patronage involved? And as for quality, well, they can always go to a private hospital, that is if they have insurance or Medicare. The entry of Civic Progress into the argument would inevitably injure the carefully cultivated relationship with the blacks and would do nothing to change their highly charged emotional attitude. Too bad, when the issue seems so clear but, still, it's understandable.

Not so readily to be forgiven was the lack of action by Civic Progress in relation to the old post office building. This disastrous blockage is mentioned elsewhere, but it is to be noted that as early as 1956, the disposal of the building was discussed. When the proposal for the new federal office building was opposed by the *Post-Dispatch* and the Leland group, Civic Progress simply kept quiet. As the opposition was neither political, racial, nor from labor, this lack of action shows up in retrospect as a major error.*

Were those who founded Civic Progress in 1953 taller, more

---

* One of its members, Edwin Clark, president of Southwestern Bell, did, on his own, bring in a developer who was interested in an office building on the site, an interest which, of course, came to nothing--but this was an individual action rather than one by Civic Progress.

effective, more adventurous and aggressive in their crusade for the city than their successors--their latter-day inheritors? Yes, I think so, although it is possible that the fires of talent which were apparently banked in the late 60's may be bursting forth once more. I know what was written in Genesis, "that there were giants in the earth in those days," and that all oldsters (like this author) tend to lament today's dearth of heroes. Still........

Among the charter or founding members of Civic Progress were: Edgar Queeny, August Busch, Edwin Clark, Donald Danforth, Morton May, J. Wesley McAfee, Ethan A. H. Shepley, Sidney Maestre and Tom K. Smith. There were more, of course, but all of these were in positions differing in security, independence and freedom from those who now occupy their seats. Consider that Queeny had almost owned Monsanto and still dominated it, that his decisions were not defied with impunity, that others--Danforth of Ralston Purina, May of the department store, and Busch of Anheuser Busch--were nearly in the same secure positions, that the young men, McAfee of Union Electric, and Calhoun of St. Louis Union Trust Company, were so powerfully placed even in their early middle age that they could damn the torpedoes, and that the bankers Smith and Maestre and the utility head Clark had no worry as to their directors. Further, neither the federal government, the Securities Exchange Commission, nor the ever-ready-to-sue stockholders were then looking so closely over their shoulders as they now do.

There was less caution among these men. And they had known one another for a long time, so frankness was the rule in these monthly meetings. This is not to say that the newer generation is less capable; indeed the opposite may well be true. Those we now see--Hanley of Monsanto, Griffin of Brown Group, the younger August Busch, Bernard Edison of Edison Brothers, Liberman of Laclede Gas, Knight of Emerson

126

Electric, Lewis of General Dynamics, Thayer of Mallinckrodt and the rest perhaps have had training in greater depth, and educational backgrounds of far better quality. It is to be doubted, however, that they are as easy and comfortable with each other as were the others 20 years earlier.

The emeritus members, those who no longer head their corporations, are still welcome at the meetings. Some do attend from time to time and are occasionally asked to serve on special committees. Having been present at several meetings of late, I have noticed that the atmosphere is different, more formal, more polite--I can think of no better word--more careful. Nor is it hard to see why.

The newer breed of chief executive has been looking over his shoulder; he is not the bold entrepreneur common only a generation past. His directors have been told of their legal responsibilities and watch him closely; his stockholders are ready to sue at the slightest cause; the Securities and Exchange Commission lurks ominously; the NLRP, the EEOC, the EPA and the consumer advocates all are to be considered in relation to every action. The adjective, swashbuckling, comes to mind, and if Sverdrup, Queeny, Busch, McDonnell, Clark, *et al.*, were not the Carnegie, Schwab, Rockefeller, Morgan or Vanderbilt of the late 19th century, they were, nevertheless, stalwarts for their city in the mid-20th. I think of a glimpse or two.

It was and is patently illegal for a corporation to attempt to influence an election, even one for the public good, such as a bond issue for public works or education. So the fiction was arrived at that the members would assess themselves for special contributions to the Chamber of Commerce Development Fund which in turn would support the effort. There is now a new term, the "laundering of money," and I suppose this was just that. Perhaps the Attorney General might or might not have approved of it, but it was thought best not to ask him, just simply to go ahead. How else could the corporations have aided and supported the Metropolitan Sewer District, the Zoo-Museum District, the public schools and the library, the Junior College District and many other causes which were obviously for the public benefit?

When John Poelker, recently the city's mayor, but in 1961 the comptroller (and perhaps the best ever to have held the position), was at the end of his first term, he faced opposition from a candidate whose qualifications were rather less than adequate. In fact, the late Mr. Denney was reported to have had no experience in fiscal accounting or city government matters. The thought of his defeating Poelker was nothing short of alarming; for by this time the business community had learned both to respect and trust Poelker. Therefore, when Fleishman reported to the group that Denney was likely to win unless Poelker's very thin campaign fund was quickly bolstered, the action was sharp and immediate. Let me hasten to say that it was entirely proper and legal in that individuals present contributed, not the corporations, nor was there any assessment. Rather, it was simply a logical outgrowth of intimate discussion.

And again when Alfonso Cervantes was running for his second term as president of the Board of Aldermen in 1958, a similar report from Fleishman, that one Alfred I. Harris, an alderman, lawyer and real estate operator, might unseat Cervantes, resulted in immediate action. It was not that they were so infatuated with Alfonso, rather that, between the two, there could be but one choice.

Neither money nor corporate actions was involved in the rescue of the Community Chest--again it resulted from simple discussion. For a good many years following World War II, the Chest had limped along, failing to meet its budgeted quotas under such leadership as could be persuaded (or in some cases designated) to take the unwelcome job. I, myself, had led the campaign in 1948 and, in spite of hard labor, much time and excellent assistance, had achieved only 95 per cent of the goal.

Then in 1961 there appeared the young Ethan Shepley, a vice-president of the Boatmen's Bank and that year's chairman, and with him was B. B. Culver, the Chest's president. Their message was succinct, eloquent and effective. What they advocated and pleaded for was, in a word, strength. They said that while they, as all recent leaders, worked hard, they would not reach their goal; nor did they believe that any future goals, based on true needs, would be attained without more dynamic and powerful leadership. They argued that they did not have the clout to produce the kind of giving from labor, from corporate executives, particularly those of middle rank, that was so badly needed.

In short, they wanted the Civic Progress corporation to shoulder the burden. Nor should this be done by assigning a corporate officer to head the campaign, for this had been tried with only so-so results. They wanted the campaign headed by the chief executive himself. I listened to that plea and was both amazed and surprised at the complete lack of hesitation and the quick concensus of approval. Each year since, a member of Civic Progress has headed the drive, and each year the goal has been reached. Not bad, St. Louis!

Nor are the giants all dead. Only recently the brilliant young Charles Knight of Emerson Electric, having saved, at least temporarily, the public-school athletic program, undertook an analysis of the financial problems of the entire city school system. After presenting his study and conclusions, he ended by asking for financial support for the ensuing tax election. Again there was no hesitation; this time the redoubtable veteran, Jim McDonnell, said, "It's the right thing to do. Let's do it." That's all--and it was done.

*****

Like all humanity, Civic Progress has been composed of happy men and those not-so-happy. Life has been good materially to all of them--obviously few corporation heads suffer starvation. The unhappy ones are those who, for one reason or another, quit working; and about this I have developed a sort of theory. It has, for some years, been evident to me that work is the greatest source of happiness, although if pushed hard I might be willing to substitute the word "satisfaction." For the greater part of my life I would, if asked, certainly have answered that happiness and satisfaction were allied with family, love, sex, recreation, the arts, money--the so-called good things in life, as indeed they are. I have enjoyed them all, and I am grateful for them. But life is not truly rich without doing--striving, if you will--and not necessarily for money, though the lack thereof is misery.

This is what may be seen in viewing the careers of the men of Civic Progress. Does a Jim McDonnell at 77, a Sverdrup at 75, a Busch at 78, a Shepley at 78 work for money? A half century ago, when I was a student, it was the mode in some Ivy League circles to sneer at the businessman who know nothing but work, who slaved until he dropped, who knew not Michelangelo or Shakespeare, who represented the image of materialistic America to what we thought was the despising delight of the cultivated Europeans. We were told how they sneered at the hurrying and the single-minded pursuit of power and money.

The American businessman, the story went, had no knowledge of, nor time for, the finer things of life--he knew neither wine nor the ballet, and that he was rich only added to his vulgarity.

Baloney! What he was doing was having a hell of a good time. The harder he worked, the more he invented. The fatter his pocket, the more effective was his search for new antibiotics. The more durable his tires, the more convenient his frozen dinners, the faster and safer his jet craft, the better he slept, and the more avid was his waking and his appetite for the day ahead. In contrast, examine the plight of those who, by the ill luck of bad health or the vagaries of compulsory retirement, have nothing to do but--well, just that, retire. The general comment from those executives about to quit, or rather to be forced to do so, runs about the same; they have so much to do they scarcely know how to begin. Sounds good, but mostly it simply isn't true, though when it *is* the results can be spectacular. Could anyone have restored Barnes Hospital as did Edgar Queeny; was not Shepley a magnificent interim and then elected chancellor of his university, and could its board have a finer president than Charles Allen Thomas?

Retirement has to be prepared for, and those who have not, who have thought the world would beat a path to their doors begging for their services, are soon disillusioned. I name no names, for that would be not only unfair, but cruel to the men who have been strong, vital in business and community effort, but who, in lonesome vacuity, play golf and bridge, eat lunch, travel and read a little.

For most people old age is anything but as Browning described it:

> Grow old with me!
> The best is yet to be,
> The last of life, for which the first was made.

It was a nice thought, beautifully put, but generally more on the mark is what my Kansas City attorney friend, Arthur Mag, says:

"Old age is not for sissies!"

Or consider what Anthony Powell's indignant character said, and quite reasonably, too: "You know, growing old is like being increasingly penalized for a crime you haven't committed." It takes fortitude to look squarely at the arthritic pains, the unwelcome and unexpected lassitudes, the morning views in the mirror, the lack of respect for one's opinion, the exclusion from consultations, the awareness that most of life is gone and that there is little to expect. But work is the antidote, at least in part, to the ails of old age.

Everyone, however, is not a Queeny, Thomas, Busch or McDonnell. What then of the great mass of humanity, those who do not control corporations and in retirement cannot guide a hospital, a university, a museum? Are they strangers to that satisfaction and happiness? Not at all--but let me, for a moment, digress.

The late George C. St. John, my respected and revered headmaster at Choate, each year would tell his favorite stories designed to inspire youth to effort and excellence. One was about a man who stopped at a building project and asked three workmen what each was doing:

The first said: "I am working for X dollars a day." (In those days it was about $3.)

The second said: "I am laying bricks."

The third said: "I am building a cathedral."

This was supposed to indicate that the third workman was the worthy fellow, humanity's pride, the example, I suppose, for convincing the schoolboy that doing Latin or algebra was building towards a career.

Well, I submit that it "ain't necessarily so." In the first place, the example never happened. The architect, not the bricklayer, was building the cathedral along with the church authorities. The bricklayers, not the architect, simply laid bricks. I have seen skilled masons, carpenters, ironworkers, engaged in Zoo projects of extraordinary design, things which had never before been attempted; and not one ever expressed interest in returning to see the finished product--the thing he and his fellows had wrought. Yet they were skilled, capable, happy and satisfied in what they were doing.

Every employer knows that the great majority of workers are not creative but achieve great satisfaction from repetitive tasks--jobs within their ability. The skilled fry cook, the production line worker, the nurse, the cab driver, the railroad brakeman, the meat cutter--are they not as satisfied in their work as the administrators and creators? No, not all, for some hate what they do, as do some lawyers, accountants and educators, and for these we must feel sorry.

Life for the square peg in the round hole is misery, and these, no doubt, are numberless. But for the majority, repetitive tasks have their satisfactions, and these persons are not to be pitied.

Ergo, do not feel sorry for the single-minded businessman, that is, unless and until he retires and has nothing to do. He must get ready for it; for not all, like Sverdrup and McDonnell, have enough power over their own companies to stay on forever, or, like Coburn and McRoberts, can practice law into their 70's and 80's. The ethic of the service concept is stronger in America perhaps than at any time in history, and the jobs are there for those who can alter their sights, whether they have been executives or not.

I can make no case that it's easy, nor can I argue that all who spend their days pleasantly doing nothing are miserable and unhappy. On the contrary, those of my friends, who, like the migratory birds, move to Mexico, Arizona, Palm Beach and California with the winter, are certain they live the best of all lives. Some are happy in the modern "retirement" villages or rest homes, and cannot understand those of us who do not relax.

I rest my contention on that of one George Whitefield who said, "I had rather wear out than rust out." It seems to me that those who live that way have by far the best of it--and of all I have known of that ilk, most of the members of Civic

Progress have been and are fine examples. Thomas Carlyle must have had them in mind when he wrote, more than 100 years ago, "Blessed is he that has found his work; let him ask no other blessedness."

CHAPTER VI

The camel's hump is an ugly hump
Which well we may see at the Zoo
But uglier yet is the hump we get
From having too little to do.

Kipling

Is there a real difference between luck and accident or only a
semantic distinction? I raise the point because for the life of me
I cannot remember when I first became interested in the Zoo,
an activity which was my chief occupation for 10 years and
which, after I had resigned from its board, drew me into the
heart of an effort which was the most difficult I ever
tackled--and that at the age of 68.

The Zoo, which was established by legislative act in 1915 and
began operation a year later, was a semiautonomous
department of the city of St. Louis. In fact, however, it was
almost entirely the creature of George Vierheller, who was its
first and only director until his retirement in 1963. In the
institution's early days, George was encouraged, aided and
apparently partly financed, by his close friend, Edward Lemp
of the old brewing family. Lemp, a shy, modest man, was not
much in the public eye, received no credit for his interest and
generosity, but must have been invaluable. But there was
nothing shy about Vierheller!

There was a board of trustees which met occasionally to
hear his reports, when he capriciously cared to give them, but
the board was content to let George run the show. The

chairman was usually the park commissioner--Palmer Baumes in 1956 when I arrived--and he, like his predecessors, took no active part. He was happy that George was the be-all and end-all.

Above, I purposely used the word *show* because there is no question that Vierheller was the greatest zoo showman America has ever produced. He must have equalled the legendary Carl Hagenbeck of Hamburg. It was David Calhoun who suggested to the board that I fill a vacancy. As it was 1956 and I could sense retirement from business within a few years, this type of activity seemed a good idea, sounded like fun. Also there were good fellows on the board; Vierheller himself, Russell Gardner, John Poelker, then City Comptroller, Harry Kiener and, of course, Dave Calhoun.

And quickly I found that it *was* good fun. I never pretended, and still do not, to any consuming interest in nor love for animals, but the Zoo was and is much more than that. What did excite me was the marvelous effect the animals had on children. Watching the chimp show for the first time is the best of innocent amusement, but turning away from the stage and watching the *children watch* the show comes pretty close to the best earth has to offer. I was a pushover, quickly enmeshed and completely captivated by George and his single-minded love for the place.

Only once was he angry with me; for the most part I was his apprentice and he groomed me (without my knowing it) for the job of president. I had no idea how much there was to learn, for a good zoo is one of the most complex of all institutions because of the variety of functions, attractions and facilities which a complete zoological garden provides. Consider what these may be, and indeed should be, if top quality is to be claimed:

1. A collection of animals, birds, reptiles, etc.

2. A garden--note the term zoological *garden*.

3. A place for educating children and adults in a

136

smattering of zoology and nature as a whole.

4. Some scientific investigation to add to the sum of zoological knowledge, conservation and ecology.

5. Theatrical animal displays for the entertainment of the visiting public.

6. Facilities for public recreation, including food service, picnic furniture, conveniently located restrooms, ground transportation, parking, etc.

7. Guard and security services.

Obviously, not all zoos provide all such services equally. Some excel in certain areas in which they have elected to specialize. There is a wide array of personnel involved, including the necessary administrators, comptrollers, secretaries, bookkeepers, zoological curators, keepers, janitors, gardeners, maintenance engineers and mechanics, veterinary doctors and assistants, biologists, zoologists, graphic designers, scene builders, teachers, ground cleaners and more. A zoo's personnel problems tend to be complicated, even bewildering.

In 1960, after some 45 years of existence, the St. Louis Zoo did not include all of the above, nor does it today, in unqualified excellence. Indeed it never will. Probably there is no zoo which provides uniform top quality in all seven named categories, although in America those which probably rank highest are: San Diego, the Smithsonian (Washington), Bronx (New York) and Brookfield (Chicago); elsewhere Frankfurt, Regent's Park (London) and Tokyo (which I have not seen) are operated on the highest of standards.

In the 1950's the St. Louis attitude towards its zoo was a curious one, and fortunately still is. Again I refer to the showmanship of George Vierheller and to his salemanship as well. For while the typical St. Louisan was accustomed to deprecating and downgrading his city, to crying bitterly at the decaying downtown and at the lack of glory in its then fading symphony, he was almost to a man convinced that he had the world's greatest zoo.

When I was first elected a trustee and, in 1960, president, there was never a week that someone did not say, "but isn't it so that we have the world's best?" The fact was that we were not within a country mile of being best--what we were was pretty good. How could we have been the best when our annual cost of operation in 1950 was $446,000 and in 1960 $590,000? Even then, San Diego was spending $2.5 million, Washington $2 million, New York $3 million and Chicago $1.5 million.

Is it true that we were "best" in category number 5, listed above, theatrical entertainment. As conceived, built and developed by Vierheller, his lion and tiger and his elephant shows were the equal of any circus, while his chimp show was without equal anywhere. Without training, with small formal education, with no background in zoology or anthropology, on a salary of $8,000 to $10,000 a year, he made that corner of Forest Park a mecca for generation after generation of children who must certainly be grateful for his large contribution to their remembered happiness.

From the beginning the zoo had been financed almost entirely by the city, its operating expenses supported by the original 2-cent real estate tax and its capital addition by special bond issue money. In the 1950's a 1-cent tax in the city brought in about $175,000, so that the Zoo was receiving from its yearly 2-cent tax an income of some $350,000, an amount which held fairly level.

During the dark, poverty-stricken days of the 1930's, the tax was more than adequate and made the Zoo one of the best financed in the country. Other zoos dependent on yearly budget allotments from city or county administrations were cut to bare bones, but the St. Louis Zoo had its own untouchable mill tax. Louis Nolte, the then comptroller and a notoriously tightfisted one, was known to complain that he could not buy sheets for the City Hospital, while the Zoo and Art Museum were living in luxury. So far as the Zoo was concerned, no one seemed to mind.

Although Vierheller was untrained in economics, he proved to be something of a financial genius in his control of expenses, his ability to provide extraordinary values for his expenditures and his building of additional income.

For he was a natural entertainer and was expert in the extraction of loose change from his public--all of whom were free guests as there was no admission charge. In another milieu he would have been a successful carnival proprietor. Not only did he build the sale of hot dogs, hamburgers, popcorn, snow cones, soft drinks and novelties (for which the carnival name is "slum") to substantial figures, but he steadfastly resisted the suggestions of his well-meaning friends to put in a real restaurant.

By 1955 he was netting about $230,000 from such sales to the public, so that income for that year was:

Taxes	$340,000
Earnings	230,000
	$570,000
Expenses	510,000
Net Gain	$60,000

It is difficult to see how he could operate an 80-acre zoo, accommodate two million people, support 4,000 animals, birds, etc., and provide three first-rate animal shows all summer long on the pitiful sum of only a little more than half a million dollars. Moreover he had created reserves by saving money during the previous decades so that when his first real deficit year, 1960, occurred, he had a cushion in cash reserves of about $450,000.

139

He was able to run the institution at such low cost only because he was a combination of Scrooge and the fabled sweatshop operators. The animals, you may be sure, had plenty to eat--there was even beer for his beloved chimps and gorillas--but his animal keepers had to make do with hard cheese. And his gardens and building maintenance were deplorable.

He knew it well, but he was as hard on himself as on his staff and employees. The records are not clear, but I'm sure that he never drew more than $13,000 and he was shocked at the salary we agreed to pay Marlin Perkins who succeeded him. But then it will be remembered that in 1955 the mayor's salary was only $10,000.

It could easily have been otherwise. Above I referred to his resistance to the suggestions of many of his friends. These generally were to the effect that the Zoo which gave so much pleasure to so many ought to have at least one pleasant restaurant; but he felt, and quickly I agreed with him, that there could be no more damaging blow to the Zoo's income. One of the best lunches I ever ate in Paris was at the Vincennes Zoo, and the chef beamed when we told him so, but that was Paris. However, though Forest Park is pleasant and the prospect of lunching or dining leisurely in such an atmosphere seems sensible and irresistable to many, the conditions are quite different.

Such an eatery is invariably a financial disaster. The best return to be expected is perhaps 10 per cent of sales; the Zoo in its contemporary 1976-77 budget expects a gross profit of 76 per cent and a net after all expenses (except rent which is not charged) of 47 per cent. The importance of this is indicated by a net earnings figure of $1.1 million--more than a quarter of the total budget--which is expected at this time from food and novelty sales, etc.

In the Vierheller regime, the dollars from such sales were less but were an even larger percentage of his entire income.

140

In any case he felt that his vulgarian hot dogs, popcorn and snow cones were too important to be trifled or experimented with, and there is small reason to doubt his wisdom.

The Aloe Company, of which I had been president since 1929, had been merged with Brunswick of Chicago in 1959, and by the following year I knew that I would not stay with it for long. I was 58 and longed for freedom from an industry which was traveling on a very fast track. I knew that the new owners would demand higher performance; I had long been nursing a potential hypertensive condition; and I did not think I would be capable of or physically up to the demands of a growth company. And while he never said so, neither did my old friend and new boss, Ted Bensinger, the Brunswick chairman. I had refused a contract of employment and was ready to retire.

So when Dave Calhoun said to me in 1960 that Vierheller wanted me to be president, I thought the timing was providential. It was apparent that the complexities listed above would offer unending challenges and that there would never be boredom in that sort of job.

This was about 17 years past and the situation was, as I then saw it, about like this:

The staff consisted of Vierheller who was approaching 80; Henry Sanders, a general factotum with neither educational nor zoological background but a willing slave to his boss; Virgil Turner, an excellent but overworked maintenance foreman; Moody Lenz, the devoted general curator, and three showman of which the nonpareil was the late Mike Kostial, the trainer of chimps. There was also the experienced Hattie Ettinger, who had been briefly married to William Conway, now zoo director at New York. She was a general assistant, produced the Zoo's brochure and other literature, and was its public relations manager.

The financial picture was gloomy. The Zoo still had some unspent bond issue money and its own small reserves, but was, by then, unable to live within the small income and would at once need new operating funds.

Its grounds and buildings were in deplorable condition and obviously required large amounts of rehabilitation; no one knew how much.

There was controversy over the actual acreage--both Zoo and Park Department claimed some of the property.

There were glaring deficiencies--i.e., no veterinarian, no real gardeners, no attempt at any sort of education, no friends' or other auxiliary organization.

And George was not *getting* old, he was already there.

One day John Poelker, who was then the respected City Comptroller, said to me, quite casually, "You know George has accepted the city's pension plan for the Zoo, and since this requires retirement at 70, he certainly has to quit. You really will have to do something about it." I thought George would take it very badly since I was reasonably convinced that he intended both to live and run the Zoo forever. But it proved otherwise. He readily agreed that the time had come to make the change and said he would help me find a successor.

I had for some time been thinking about that succession and had talked with Fairfield Osborn, the ancient, legendary and distinguished head of the New York Zoological Society, and with Dr. Shroeder, the brilliant director of the San Diego Zoo. It seemed to me that all indicators pointed to Marlin Perkins of Lincoln Park Zoo in Chicago. Perkins was a Missourian, had started by pushing a broom here in St. Louis, was respected and liked by George and was obviously ready for a major zoo; indeed it was surprising that he had not headed one long before. He was 55 and making about $13,000, a figure which might seem a pittance today, but which was respectable then in the zoo world.

Still, in retrospect, it seems that Marlin should have had a major zoo before his late middle age. He was ambitious, had climbed the Himalayas with Sir Edmund Hillary and was physically in superb condition. At that time he had been experimenting with television and was conducting a local Chicago show known as *Zoo Parade*.

The Lincoln Park Zoo was then, as now, a younger sibling of the large and really quite fine Brookfield Zoo, so Marlin was in effect playing second fiddle in Chicago and happy to be invited to St. Louis. But he wanted--

a. a salary of $22,500
b. a pension agreement
c. a membership in the Missouri Athletic Club
d. the right to do television

I thought this was all reasonable and was not bothered by any of the terms except the salary which was more than double that of the mayor--then Ray Tucker. Even though all St. Louis recognized that a $10,000 stipend for the mayor was archaic and ridiculous, still there it was, and no one in city government could be paid more. But suppose we were not precisely in that sense city government--what then? There was only one way to find out and that was to ask Ray Tucker. His response was a mark of the breadth of vision and the general quality of the man. When I told him of the salary demanded and the possibilites of a television show furthering a good image of the city, he said at once, "If you think it's the thing to do, go right ahead."

Conway of the Bronx Zoo said to me, not long after, that I had accomplished a salary breakthrough for all zoo directors and that they should consider themselves in my debt. And the 80-year-old Osborn of New York, upon hearing what we proposed to pay Marlin, nearly choked. He was choleric on the phone and said I did not dare upset the entire zoo world with such an outrageous salary, that no zoo man was worth it--but then he was as out of date as I suppose my contemporaries are now.

The television matter really was the asset that I thought made Perkins the best prospect for the job. I had met his producer, Don Meier, and believed that if the program were as successful as they hoped it might be, there would be considerable general value to the city. My estimates were partly right, but in some respects so wrong that the deterioration of our relationship was severe and painful despite the wonderful first two or three years of working together.

It was simply that the show *Wild Kingdom* became so good, the star, Marlin, so prominent that the tail wagged the dog. His contract with the Zoo clearly called for his entire time and permitted television and radio "providing that such engagements do not interfere with duties and obligations undertaken under the contract." That I thought he did not live up to his adminstrative obligations to St. Louis was, in all fairness, probably as much my fault as his. There is no question in my view that he was for a little while, and could have remained, one of the best--perhaps the very best--directors anywhere. He had all the tools.

He was personable, popular, had a charming wife, knew the zoo world from Aardvark to Zebra, was a splendid administrator, was experienced in zoo architecture and had a good enough working knowledge of zoology and anthropology to hire the right people. His only defect was that he became a star, and a big one at that. And I submit that while you may have great admiration for Enrico Caruso, Bob Hope, Stan Musial and Ty Cobb, you are not likely to have given much thought to their adminstrative abilities. But Marlin had the ability--he just did not have the time.

*****

About two years before the Perkins era, the fundamental

144

problems became only too evident, and nearly all were without solution unless there was to be more income. The Zoo simply was woefully underfinanced. Vierheller saw this clearly enough but hardly understood what I said when I deplored our lack of planning. Nevertheless, when I offered to undertake the attempt to double our 2-cent tax he raised no objection to getting a master plan. And strangely enough it proved surprisingly easy to persuade the voters of St. Louis to double the tax. On January 23, 1961 the increase was voted, and the following year the tax income thus increased to $650,000.

I had suggested to Gyo Obata, the gifted young architect at Hellmuth, Obata & Kassabaum, that he serve as the Zoo's supervisory architect; not that he was to get all its work, but that he must pass on its suitability, and this without fee except for any direct work. He, too, was strongly in favor of a master plan and suggested the landscape and city planning firm of Sasaki, Walker and Associates of Boston. Quickly this was pursued and about a year later, in January 1962, at a cost of $40,000, the finished plan was presented to the Zoo's board and to the public.

With its completion the Zoo acquired a sense of direction it had never had before. The workmanship was of high quality and while we did not accept every detail, it was our guide, and some 17 years later it still stands strong. Recommended in the plan, and at this writing accomplished, were:

A remodeling, reshaping and general overhaul of the central waterfowl lakes.

The rehabilitation of our famous bear pits with added pools and waterfalls.

The establishment of a recreational and practical transportation system (the Zoo railroad).

A Children's Zoo.

Rehabilitation of the 1904 Bird Cage--the Zoo's original and first structure.

An Administration Building.

A new lion, tiger, leopard and general big cat facility.

The construction of a wall-fence around the Zoo.

Rehabilitation and redesigning of the Primate and Reptile House.

Additional features not contemplated or described in the plan have been brought into being, some of which are the hydroponics building, the railroad office and the new restrooms, the massive redoing of the central pool chain and seal basin, the enlargement of the Zoo's two parking lots, and much underground water, sewer and electrical rehabilitation--none of which is evident to the visitor but is expensive, frustrating and very necessary.

When Perkins came to us we had already been working on the repair of the famous bear pits, and in so doing had introduced moving water into them. I had long thought that we in the United States had not attempted to imitate ancient or modern Europe in the arts and skills of moving water. Rome, Paris, Austria, Scandinavia, all, for hundreds of years, had produced fountains, pools, waterfalls, lagoons, and cascades and given enormous pleasure to their citizens. It seemed to me that we in America had, therefore, missed the boat not only aesthetically, but also, and perhaps more importantly, psychologically because of the cooling effect moving water has for the zoo visitor during the hot Midwest summers.

Each of the major bear pits now has either a fountain or waterfall, and not the least of the beneficiaries are the bears who love them. There also are jets in the big waterfowl lakes and pools in the Children's Zoo. And surely Obata's design of multi-level drinking fountains is one of the best to be seen anywhere.

*****

After Perkins arrived, our first joint project was the Zoo's railroad. Vierheller had long realized that 83 acres of undulating land was too much for many parents, grandparents and 3-year-olds who needed transportation, but he had not been sure what to do about it. With the advent of the master plan we were reinforced in our beliefs for a carrier system of some sort, and at once we agreed that its priority was number one.

At first Perkins argued for a rubber-tired train such as San Diego or Grant's Farm used; but, while I agreed that such a train was easier to install, was relatively inexpensive and required no road bed, I was determined to have a real railroad with tracks, stations, signals and, if possible, trestles, tunnels and the like. I had loved railroads as a youngster and was sure the kids would love them still. And there was a precedent in the Detroit Zoo where Walter Chrysler had built and given one to the institution. Marlin humored me (there is nothing like getting along with an amateur president!) and was at once in touch with Robert Heath, a designer and builder of such railroads, a hearty, carnival-type man. We had no difficulty liking each other.

The building of the Zoo railroad was the most successful financial move we ever accomplished--except, of course, for the establishment of the Zoo-Museum tax district in 1970. Moreover, it has been much more than a money raiser; it has already carried millions of children and adults and has given today's children innocent pleasure which they will look back upon as a happy part of childhood. Now when you can create such happiness and net $200,000 a year besides, then you've got something! And all without investing a thin dime. Here's how we did it.

Heath, the entrepreneur, had been told that we had no money for a railroad which we thought might cost $200,000 or $300,000, and that even if the funds had been available we would not gamble on the success of it. So he brought in the late Harry Batt, a successful New Orleans amusement park operator, and Robert Murch, a construction contractor in St. Louis. They proposed to build the railroad, own it, operate it and pay the Zoo 25 per cent of the proceeds for the privilege. Not bad, but the negotiations went like this:

Batt: "This is very generous--we have all the headaches, we do the work, and whether we lose or not you get 25 per cent."

HFB: "Fine, you agree to use our architects--we want control of any design elements in our own park."

Batt: "All right, providing we put a limit on such design fees."

HFB: "Agreed, now we will want an option to buy the road."

Murch: "That isn't fair. If it's losing money you would let us keep it and take your 25 per cent. If we make money you'll buy it."

HFB: "That's exactly right. But if we exercise the option, we'll pay you a good profit. After all, we admit you are gambling your investment and if we take it away from you we'll pay you cost plus 25 per cent."

Murch: "That's fair enough. But no option for two years; at least give us a chance at some operating profit."

The contract was signed, the road was built, the rolling stock came in and operations began in September of 1963. The cost was $395,000 and during the first full season in 1964 more than a million passengers were carried. At the end of 1966 it was evident that we had a small gold mine and that we had better buy it.

But Batt and Murch had a fat cat too, and they did not want to give it up regardless of their contract. So Murch wrote letters to the press about the evils of government ownership (Perkins and I were "government") and tried to appeal to a few in the legislature. This nonsense was not, however, our problem, which was where to find the money to buy it.

148

Borrowing a half-million to purchase an investment netting $200,000 annually was patently soundly conservative, but we could not do it since it is illegal for state chartered agencies to borrow.

It was at this point that Thomas C. McGuire, now Judge McGuire, made the first of his many brilliantly constructive moves which benefited the Zoo. He was then City Counselor and hence was the Zoo's lawyer. I had become impressed with him when he represented St. Louis at meetings of the Airport Commission. We became friends and he agreed that he could, as City Counselor, properly serve as the Zoo's attorney--without compensation, of course.

It was his idea that while the Zoo could not borrow, the friends' auxiliary organization, known as the Zoo Association, could do so; and that if we would arrange a bank loan we could lease the road to them for a period long enough to use the profit to pay for it, after which the Zoo would automatically recover the property.

There was no problem with the downtown banks who readily agreed to the loan, but McGuire and I thought that perhaps we could lower the cost by issuing the obligation as a tax-free note, in effect the equivalent of a municipal bond. After the Internal Revenue Service approved the tax-free rates, we asked and received from the banks a loan of $500,000 payable over six years at a rate of $3\frac{1}{2}$ per cent.

The loan could easily have been repaid in two or three years, but we now had a valuable financial tool and we used it in many ways. By paying off our railroad debt at only $100,000 each year we had matching funds for other gifts. Thus over the years the railroad has made possible--

Its own purchase,

Matching the Yalem gift for the Children's Zoo,

Matching the Busch gift for the Administration Building,

Matching the Friends' efforts for the Big Cat Country,

149

Matching the gift of William Schield and others for the rebuilding of the old bird cage.

I readily confess to some "creative" bookkeeping in connection with railroad affairs. In our annual reports we could have shown the income as part of our operating revenue. But we had a master plan calling for capital funds in large amounts and I thought if we held the railroad away from the main stream of operations, we could use its profits to match gifts. It did work out that way and an example of the process was the financing of the Children's Zoo.

Perkins and I felt this to be the next priority after the redoing of the bear pits and the lakes, but we had no money even to design such an addition. We believed then, as I do now, that in order to attract large donors--angels--it is useful and often essential to be able to show a model or picture to the prospect of what he is being asked to finance. Several times we commissioned architectural designs and more than once they paid off. Early conversations in 1962 with the nationally famous Charles Eames came to nothing, and we finally were able to persuade Obata to prepare a design.

But before he would begin we had to get the planning funds, and accordingly we approached the attorney, Edward Greensfelder, who had control over the trusts created by his late uncle, Albert Greensfelder. Now Mr. Greensfelder had been a very successful construction contractor (Fruin-Colnon Company) and had been a strong advocate of outdoor recreation, ecological protection and improvement; and in general had a fine knowledge of and affection for the natural beauty of the Midwest. We asked for $25,000 for preliminary designs and got $10,000. But a little later we received an additional and equal sum. We had a beginning even though a small one.

The period of conception was a long one. I had seen some children's zoos and so had Obata. We were both determined that this one would not be "cute," that it would not have Mother Goose elements scattered through it, nor be a barnyard zoo. It did have to include a contact area where children could touch and be intimate with small, safe animals; it had to have some elements of painless education and it had to be as close to nature as would be possible in a small space. Obata wanted no buildings at all, and managed almost to dispense with them in what I thought, then and now, was the best design of its kind I have ever seen. The one wintertime indoor structure is hidden beneath a small mountain, and the pools, streams, small valleys, glades and grottoes present to children the cave-like areas they love so much.

It was in 1964 that Perkins, Obata and I presented to Charles Yalem the model of the project. We were nervous, for we did not know where to turn in case of a refusal; but I had hopes because his accountant and great friend, Louis Tiger, had indicated to me that he had him in the mood.

When he saw it, he obviously was delighted at once with the model. After a few minutes he said: "How much will it cost?"

I said, "There's the architect. How much, Gyo?"

"I believe it can be done for $500,000."

"Well, there you are, Charlie."

He thought a moment. "If I give you $250,000 will that do it?"

"Yes, we'll match it."

"But where will you get the matching money?"

It was my turn, and I said: "Charlie, for the life of me I don't know. But you've known me a long time. If I say we'll match your money, I think you will trust me."

"Yes," he said, "That's good enough for me. Now let's go to lunch."

And later he gave me $25,000 more for the graphics which we added to Gyo's design. It is clear to all of us who work at the Zoo that it is a fine adjunct but equally satisfying is the unalloyed pleasure Charles has received. His millions had been given for the most part for hospitals, health and community centers, and, while he knew how necessary they were, they depressed him--made him nervous. In those places he saw the feeble, the sick, the downtrodden, the poor--here at his Children's Zoo he saw childhood at play and he was happy. More than once he has gone out of his way to tell me that more than any other gifts, this one has given him the greatest pleasure. Charlie had probably never heard of John Masefield, much less read him, nor have I thought of his couplet for 50 years:

> And he who gives a child a treat,
> Makes joy-bells ring in Heaven's Street,

but it comes in here loud and clear.

Oh, he's old and sick now--more than 80--and he won't last much longer, but it's nice to remember that he had fun. He started with nothing, was a poor dentist, found out how to finance second-hand cars and sold out for 60 million. And he had fun giving it away.*

A few years ago Shaw's Garden was conducting its campaign for the new Lehmann Library, and I was asked to take the Yalem card. I told them that they could not expect much as Charlie had not the slightest interest in gardens, and did not know the trustees. Anyhow, I asked him to lunch and we had a pleasant time for an hour and a half talking of his various interests, and nary a word from me about the Garden. Finally at 2 o'clock, as we got up to go, I said:

"Charlie, by the way, there's a drive for the new library at the Garden. You'll have to give a little--only a token, not much."

"What is it? I don't know much about it."

"Oh, well, it's a fine thing, but it's nothing to you. I wouldn't

---

* In March, 1978 Charles Yalem died.

do much--just a gesture; it is, after all, one of the town's important assets."

"What do you think?"

"Very little--I guess $25,000."

"Well, I was thinking $15,000."

"Oh, sure, if you like."

I had expected only $10,000! You think I'm smart? Listen. He went home and said to his wife, Jane, "You know, I had lunch with Howard Baer today. I figured it would cost me $100,000 to eat with him, but I only gave him $15,000. So I saved $85,000--that's how smart I am!"

I doubt that St. Louis will see his like again, in any case not for a long time.

William H. Schield was a friend of long standing--a little older than I; we had known each other for 40 years and in our younger days had been in the same golf foursome. Bill had for a long time been in the shoe business with the legendary Dave Wohl, but they had finally agreed to disagree, and he opened his own chain store millinery establishment. He had been successful--he and his wife had always had money--but he got really rich from an extraordinary investment in the Polaroid Company, the stock having ballooned from a low of $10 per share in 1960 to a high of about $150 in the 60's.

It was, therefore, scarcely to be expected, vulture that I was, that I would overlook Bill as a potential giver to the Zoo. About 1964 we were deep in our investigation of and planning for the redoing of the 1904 bird cage, but as usual we had no money. Bill then was about 72, active and cheerful, but he had developed a heart condition. The Polaroid stock was selling at about $65 to $67 as I remember, and we were together at a cocktail party. I said:

"There's no one I'd rather see real rich than you, you bastard, but if this stock keeps going up I want some money for the Zoo."

"Why should I care about the Zoo?"

"Why? Because everybody ought to, but mostly because you're so damn rich and because I ask you. And it will have to be a good gift, too!"

"Well, how much is a good gift?"

"I'll make a deal with you--Polaroid is $65, when it goes to $90 I want $50,000, nothing till then."

"The trouble with that, Howard, is that I've got this damn fibrillation; I might not live that long--would you take $25,000 now?"

He did live about three years longer and enjoyed the results of his gift, and his wife, our good friend Emma, persuaded another gift--this time to the Children's Zoo.

*****

The rehabilitation of the bird cage was one of the most difficult jobs I have ever undertaken. I have no idea who designed it, but it was literally the beginning, the first element in the Zoo, and it was impressive. The federal government through its agent, the Smithsonian Institute, had contributed it to the 1904 World's Fair as its prime exhibit. For its design and construction, it had appropriated $25,000. Sometime after the Fair ended the city purchased it for $6,000, and for the ensuing six decades it stood there. When the Zoo was established, the bird cage was an important part, but it was neglected and, of course, was deteriorating. Such was its eroded condition that our master planners recommended its replacement; but this was acceptable neither to Perkins or to me, both of us feeling that the structure had historic and sentimental values and that it was handsome and salvageable.

Having been impressed with the young Masao Kinoshito of the Sasaki firm in Boston, we commissioned him to study and design the needed changes. These included a walk-through bridge, waterways, and a waterfall. His work, which is now there for all to see, was easy enough; what was difficult was the rebuilding and repairing of the cage itself. The steel was rusty and failing badly, in places actually coming apart, the concrete bases and rooms below grade were crumbling, the wire screening was useless and no firm bids could be secured, as no contractor could tell in advance what decay he would uncover.

I sought advice from my friend Dink Frazier, as experienced and capable a building contractor as anyone in St. Louis. He said we must do it ourselves, that there were too many unknown pitfalls, and that any contractor making a firm bid would have to give himself so much leeway that bids would be astronomical. But he knew an ex-superintendent, eccentric, difficult, hard to work with but just the man to oversee the job for us--that was Lew Behnken.

Over the period of a year it was done--John Newman of the architectural firm of Hellmuth, Obata & Kassabaum, under Kinoshito's direction, supervised and placed every stone and boulder in the sculptural waterfall. The bronze plaque has a smattering of the history of the cage, and reads like this:

"This Great Flight Cage
was built by the Smithsonian Institute as an exhibit for the
St. Louis World's Fair of 1904. The cost was $15,000.
Its great size [228 feet long, 84 feet wide, 50 feet high] and
unique design as the first walk-through aviary attracted
world-wide attention. It aroused the civic interest that led to
its purchase after the closing of the Fair for $6,000 by the city
of St. Louis. This, in turn resulted in the establishment and
growth of the St. Louis Zoo.
It served for 60 years. Then $200,000 was needed for its
renovation, which was begun in 1966. A substantial
contribution was made by Mr. and Mrs. William H. Schield,

155

and the remainder of the fund raising was a project of the St. Louis Zoo Association which, in 1966, listed some 2,000 members. Reconstruction was greatly aided by the Frazier-Davis Construction Co. whose services were contributed.

Rededicated in 1967."

It is also something of a comment on inflation.

*****

Plaques are important, and they ought to be rather elaborate because generally they are the only means of informing the public about their buildings, monuments and public areas. Every structure, lake, fountain, statue, moat, planted garden in the Zoo--as well as in all our public institutions--represents hard thinking and planning, money collected, often with great difficulty, and, above all, someone's dreams of making life better, more pleasant or, anyhow, instructive. Should not the casual beneficiary at least have the chance of realizing that people in the past had taken thought for his welfare? Without such visible records how can he gain some feeling of the history of his city? Graphics, graphics--we need them so badly.

Graphics in one word are signs. Doesn't anyone--everyone--know how to make a sign? Nearly everyone thinks he knows, but in fact he does not. Finally graphic designers are beginning to be understood and more attention is being given to them by architects, planners and landscapers. There is more to sign making than meets the eye and to understand the importance of graphic systems requires the realization that signs ought to be integrated into a plan.

I don't want to get complicated, beyond my depth, about a subject in which I am neither a practitioner nor an expert, but

I am so convinced as to the need and value of graphics--graphics so sadly lacking in all St. Louis, that I'll go a little farther with it.

The basic, fundamental argument for them is this: when people know where they are, where they are going, how to get there, what they are looking at, they are at ease, comfortable. When they do not see their way, do not find the next step in their journey easily, have no idea what relation their present location bears to their destination, they are uncomfortable and uneasy. I know of only one city in America that makes any effective effort to put the incoming traveler at ease, and that is San Diego.

In Europe, driving into Milan, Padua, Auxerre, Cannes, you are assisted by legible signs which point to the center of the city, the business district, the prominent city features such as the frescoes of Giotto, the museum of Leger, the Last Supper of Leonardo or the Equestrian statue of Verrochio. What happens in St. Louis? Nothing. In Paris there are the famous kiosks on the streets with their circular posters telling of art exhibits, symphonies, theatrical events and the like, another form of graphics.

Not long ago I went to Philadelphia to see a friend who had an office in the giant Penn Center complex--a magnificently rebuilt part of the inner city. There are six huge office buildings numbered from 1 to 6. But the numbers are small, inadequate, and I wandered footsore over several blocks before I was finally set right. The numbers were too small.

When the Yalem Children's Zoo was nearly finished we were not completely happy with it. We had agreed with Obata's concept of a natural, simple environment with rocks, caves, streams, trees, shrubbery and as little evidence of man-made structures as possible, but it seemed to me he had sacrificed gaiety, sparkle and brightness. I thought the cake was fine, but that it needed some icing. Now Gyo has never been stubborn; he's sure of his talent, as well he may be, but he will bend so long as his integrity is not violated. He said the outstanding graphic designer was Ivan Chermayeff of New York and Boston, and agreed that perhaps he could add to the attractiveness of the basic design.

That's how I met Ivan. It is never easy to work with an architect or designer in another city, but his talent was worth the trouble. So in the Children's Zoo the flags, the strange and colorful water animals, the building block signs, all these are his. But the Zoo itself needed a graphics plan as we had no concept of any maps, directional signals, descriptive labels on individual exhibits, nor educational habitat maps. I had an ally in our employee, Hattie Ettinger, and rather grudging cooperation from Perkins.

Anyhow, after the completion of the Children's Zoo we asked and commissioned Chermayeff to do a master plan. This he did but the results were small. I had forgotten that no study by outsiders is of value unless it is wanted by your staff. The plan will always be torn to pieces, thrown aside, as this one was, if those who must implement it don't want it.

What every zoo ought to have is its own shop, a facility to produce labels, maps, signs and, above all, backgrounds for exhibits. The new materials, plastics, fiberglass, epoxies, lend themselves to infinite creative ideas but to purchase these display elements from outside sources is too expensive, and the outside artist or contractor does not have the day-to-day zoo contacts.

A few tentative steps in that direction have been made--but not enough. There was much talk about the plan but the Zoo is still a hodgepodge, though not as bad as the park itself or the city as a whole. After Chermayeff began on the Zoo plan, I was so carried away by the idea that I suggested to Cervantes a graphics plan for the city streets. I could visualize new signs, new street furniture (waste receptacles, newspaper stands, etc.) and possibly the French kiosk idea. I argued that he already had a shop to build signs and that the cost would be minimal. For peanuts he could make the city sparkle a little. To reinforce my argument I said I would put up several thousand dollars towards the plan.

He bought it. Chermayeff made some studies and came up with a document. But the Board of Public Service and the Streets Department yawned and my money was spent foolishly. We tried again on a smaller scale. In 1974 Louis Buckowitz was no longer Park Commissioner, Mayor Poelker having appointed Louis' wife Georgia to the job. She has taken it seriously, has learned much and, moreover, is willing to listen. Judge McGuire and I suggested that she get rid of her husband's fairly hideous signs in Forest Park and that she have a graphics plan created for the park only. We thought she could get cooperation from all the non-city-owned organizations in the park, i.e., the Zoo, Art Museum, Historical Society, Muny Opera, etc. And such cooperation was readily forthcoming. At a joint meeting each agreed to put up a thousand dollars towards such a plan, but, of course, most of the funds were to come from the city itself as the city owned not only the park but the public golf course within it, the Planetarium, and the Steinberg Rink.

Three years have passed and nothing has happened yet, as the city has dragged its feet. Still, it isn't dead and hope still lingers.

There have been other gifts, generous ones, to the Zoo. In 1963 we had begun the reshaping and repair of the large waterfowl lakes. These were and are the heart of the 83 acres comprising the area. We agreed with the planners that this project's priority was the highest. We had some unused bond issue money and lost no time in getting at it. Between the two lakes, almost at the exact center of the Zoo, and certainly at its crossroads, there was to be an ornamental circular plaza

159

containing both a bird cage and a pool. Obata had designed a stunning structure, contemporary, geometrical, and we had no money for it.

I asked my sister-in-law and her husband, Milton Tucker, whether they might like to give it in memory of her mother, Edith Aloe, who had been responsible for Aloe Plaza. They refused but then said they would do it in my honor. I was touched, but embarrassed. I said that as president I could not accept a gift with my name on it. So they went over my head, behind my back, to the board, the members of which had no such scruples, and the handsome cage is there.

The small pool was the gift of Sidney Cohen and has been, in my view, a failure. There is no reason for such deficiency, except a lack of design imagination, and it ought to be remedied.

In 1966 Perkins called my attention to an invention which was interesting to both of us. Working with agricultural people at Purdue University, a man in Indiana had developed a process for growing feed grass at a spectacular rate through the use of hydroponics. For the modest sum of $15,000 he offered a growing unit which automatically would produce, by using oat seeds, unjointed grass about 10 inches long at the rate of 1,000 pounds per day.

Hydroponics is, of course, the science of growing plants without soil by the use of chemicals in water solutions. Unjointed grass is any cereal grass about seven days old before the stem has thrown off joints, branches additional to the main stem. In such a fresh, youthful state it is rich, full of vitamins, extremely nourishing, and apparently delectable to grazing animals. The grain is automatically fed into trays daily, so arranged that one-seventh of the trays produce a matured mat of grass each day. All this is done in a sealed room, brightly lighted each hour of the 24, air-conditioned and nearly sterile. Each day the grass mats are harvested and fed

Vierheller: he gave ever to be remembered delights to generation after generation of children. (Page 135)

In Charles Yalem's children's zoo--his own best beloved gift, among many, to St. Louis.

e zoo's most famous exhibits--the bear pits.

Japanese gardens are designed for all seasons.

The Shapleigh Fountain at the Missouri Botanical Garden, designer, Eugene Mackey III.

The lake within Seiwa-En has its own particular beauty.

The greater of the two waterfalls in Seiwa-En, the Japanese Garden.
(Page 236)

Henry Moore, (Page 250) controversial to those who are cold to contemporary sculpture, but the art world considers Moore a giant.

The Angel Fountain memorial to John B. and Tillie Strauch in Shaw's Garden. By sculptor Romano Romanelli--1904, setting by Bernoudy.

Walker Hancock's
Indian at the Zoo--
corny, but definite-
ly honest and well
done.

Lorach's *Runner*--alas, poor Harry Kiener, we knew him well,
and he deserved better. (Page 81)

Stan the Man must shudder when he passes what
passes for him outside the Stadium. (Page 85)

The superbly beautiful interior of the Obata chapel at the Priory School on Mason Road. (Page 13)

The imprints of the great architects, Saarinen and Stone are in the Stadium. You might dub this Stone's variation on a theme by Saarinen--not one arch, but 96. (Page 10)

The architect William A. Bernoudy's gate to the zoo--a memorial to the late Harry Kiener. (Page 82)

From any angle the art museum is impressive. Cass Gilbert well understood the grandeur of Piranesi.

Again fine architectural design and clear, uncluttered display space--the remodeled Sculpture Hall at the Art Museum. (Page 226)

he Blue Cross building on Forest Park Boulevard. Maybe better
an a warehouse, but not much. (Page 216)

The controversial old post office. The *Post-Dispatch* deems it a
magnificence--downtown St. Louis a cancerous drag. (Page 79)

Where the Muny all began--the 1914 Pageant on Art Hill.

One of a group of individual medieval musicians at the Muny's box office.

The Muny, as do other St. Louis institutions, begins to offer the pleasantness of moving water.

into a chopper so as to be more easily eaten by the birds or animals.

The inventor's idea was to make fresh food available all winter long to farm stock so that the animals might be more healthy. We thought that at the Zoo it would also provide an interesting, scientific exhibit if one or more sides of the building could be glazed and opened up to public view. Charlie Thomas of Monsanto thought so too, and the hydroponics unit, therefore, was the gift of the Monsanto Foundation.

The concrete bridge in the lake system was a gift of Missouri Portland Cement Company, while the Freund Foundation, at the behest of S. E. Freund, a staunch friend of the Zoo, made numerous contributions both for educational projects and for animals. Then there was the matter of Gussie Busch.

Vierheller had almost worshipped the entire Busch family and especially Gussie; and when he retired Gussie and I had jointly given the retirement luncheon at which George's statue had been unveiled. I felt that some day, given the Busch love of animals, I could tap that source, and in 1968 the time had come. The Zoo then needed, and still does, a small mammal house, but it was desperate for an administration building.

So scant were its office facilities, that the board had no place to meet. Curators, accountants and, in fact, all employees had offices in dark basements, closets and any makeshifts that could be devised. We could no longer function, and it was high time to go to the brewery for lunch.

The ever-courteous Gussie was as great as ever, and, while I did not get the half-million for the mammal house, I did come away with a robust $120,000 for an administration building. It isn't large enough and ought to have a decent auditorium built on to it, but that, too, will come in time.

*****

Nor were failures strangers to us. Some were due to bad luck, others were due to lack of foresight on my part; others, well, we just weren't quite effective enough. Three come to mind at once:

The Washington University Center for the Biology of Natural Systems.

The great water controversy with the city.

The matter of the St. Louis Zoo Association.

The name, Barry Commoner, famous or notorious scientist of Washington University, was a large one in St. Louis in 1964. Botanist, ecologist, environmentalist, bio-physicist and, for all I know, much more, he had great imagination particularly in the creation of schemes to obtain federal grants for his research projects. It was in 1964 or 1965 that he conceived his project now known as the Center for Biological Natural Systems--whatever that is. This center was to use not only the laboratories of the University, but would require the assistance, cooperation and facilities of Shaw's Garden and the Zoo. As nearly as I could understand it, man's environmental perils were to be studied, and as all life is dependent on plants, and as all fauna is closely related to mankind, it would be desirable to put all these elements together, so that the research team would have at its disposal the material of both nature and science.

Commoner was a real pro at devising such programs and asking for grants. It was announced shortly that Washington was seriously considering the project. I was excited because David Gates, the then head of the Garden, and a capable, serious scientist, thought it had merit. So did Perkins, who true enough was not a scientist but had, nevertheless, a sharp grasp of these things. When a half-dozen of the big boys came to St. Louis from the National Science Foundation there was no one to represent the Zoo at the joint meeting, which Commoner held at the University, except me, Perkins having gone to the Antarctic for television purposes.

I hardly need to say I was impressed. I was surely the only non-Ph.D. in the meeting, but I spoke eloquently of the exotic animals we had to offer to science; told how medical research customarily confined its testing and experimental efforts to but seven animals, hardly an exhaustive search, and said that we were exceptionally able to help. The fact that I had no real idea of what I was talking about didn't seem to bother anyone. The University got the grant and I believe it still goes on. But the Garden and the Zoo were--well, shafted. Commoner and his people handled the money, as indeed they should have, but all grants carry overhead funds and so far as the two sister institutions were concerned, I understood these funds simply did not show up.

It was evident to me that Commoner was not able (or did not want) to work comfortably with Dr. Gates and Perkins, and that he was using the center for his own image and purposes.

Not long after this, there was a blowup at the University and Commoner was no longer head of the botany department. Perhaps the faculty members were jealous of his national prominence or, perhaps, they could see things not evident to the laity.

In any event, the Garden pulled out and so did the Zoo.

The water controversy with the city had elements of comedy, but it was and is serious as well. The Zoo, which occupies 83 acres in the park, feeds and waters several thousand animals and birds, has restrooms with accompanying plumbing, and is equipped with lakes, pools, fountains, waterfalls and drinking fountains. It uses, therefore, large quantities of water, much of which is wasted, overflowing into sewers and into the Forest Park lakes. This water is, of course, furnished by the city of St. Louis, but not for free. It always has been the practice of the city water department to furnish water without charge to all city departments, including city-owned hospitals, schools, buildings, and to charge a so-called "charity" rate to non-city-owned organizations such as hospitals, Salvation Army and the like. The Zoo received neither free water nor the more favorable charity rate.

Conway Briscoe, the longtime efficient water commissioner, was, for a while, head of the Board of Public Utilities, and as such was on the Zoo board. I had known Connie long before this as his Board of Public Utilities job temporarily had made him chairman of the Airport Commission, and I had a high opinion of him--still do. He was bright, hard working and devoted to his job, but like so many in the city government he was a trifle jealous of the Zoo which had its own tax income, not to be touched by the politicians. Of course his water department also stood on its own feet, had no connection with general revenue, and was fairly untouchable, but to him that was different. Water was his baby and he guarded it fiercely. There's no quarrel with that--he ran a good department and St. Louis had good water.

But his place on the Zoo board had no softening effect about the Zoo's use of water. Before going any further, let me admit to some degree of criminality. The Zoo always had stolen some water for the lakes simply by turning on non-metered fire hydrants, of which we had several. I thought we were being treated so badly, that we were discriminated against so unfairly, that I not only went along with the practice, I encouraged it! And I began to argue with Briscoe for the charity rate. I did not see why we were less favored than Barnes Hospital or the Salvation Army, as we were the city's own possession.

Finally in the mid-60's he agreed to a rate--a special rate--of 12.3 cents per thousand cubic feet. But the charity rate was then 7 cents and since the commercial users' rates began at 22 cents and went down to as low as 10 cents after usage achieved 4.5 million feet, the "special" rate was of no use, was actually more expensive than the industrial or commercial rate.

I fumed and fussed but got exactly nowhere. In some depth we explored the possibility of an artesian well so that we could tell the city to go jump in their expensive water; but all authorities told us not to try--we should only get unusable salt or sulfur water. Worse, Connie got the bit in his mouth, took some hydrants out and checked his meters. Then he raised his rates. We had paid during the 1960's the following water bills:

1960	$ 10,400
1961	13,500
1962	16,000
1963	16,000
1964	17,300
1965	19,300
1966	20,400
1967	22,000
1968	23,000
1969	29,000

In 1970 a crisis was imminent. The new rates would cost us annually between $40,000 and $50,000, about 4 per cent of our total income, and we simply could not stand it--or so I believed. I struck, simply refused to pay the new rates.

On July 20, 1970 we paid bills at the old rate and the checks were promptly returned. Briscoe told us to pay up or he would shut the water off. He would have too, but I knew damn well that the Mayor, Cervantes, would not let him. Could you imagine the political backlash were a city administration to stop water supply to the animals in its own most popular possession--the Zoo?! No way!

So Cervantes and I met. And, as always, the City Counselor, McGuire, was the compromiser and helped us work out a settlement. Well, neither of us "won." A compromise of $35,000 per year was agreed to, but that was to vanish if the Zoo-Museum District should come into being, as indeed it has. I agree that since the Zoo is both city and county owned that it ought now to pay a reasonable water fee. Its water budget this year, 1977, is $70,000, much, much higher, but we had done the best we could and did not foresee the galloping inflation.

The papers had made much of the controversy; it was meat for them; just the sort of thing they love best--a hot-tempered fight over triviality. To tell the truth I rather enjoyed it too.

The failure with regard to the Zoo Association can be charged mostly to the lack of foresight on my part. For that error I was neatly trapped, the Zoo suffered, and some 15 years later the problem has not been properly resolved. One of the first deficiencies of the Zoo which came to my attention, after I became president in 1960, was the lack of any auxiliary or friends' organization. Why was this? Well, it developed that there had been a Zoo Association, that early had been a factor in the founding of the Zoo, but that had fallen afoul of George Vierheller. The members had attempted to impose an idea or two of their own, whereupon George had simply dispensed with them. He had coolly informed them that they no longer had any connection with the Zoo.

Strangely enough, without any such connection, they had stayed in business, called themselves the Zoo Association, and had charged themselves $5 a year for membership, using the money to offer a lecture once or twice a year. Their president was a solid citizen, Roy Jordan, an easy man to talk to. In view of the Zoo's financial needs and the success of friends' organizations in St. Louis in connection with the Museum and hospitals, I believed that we could be helped substantially by such a society. Jordan was more than agreeable to a remarriage, but said that we ought to get new people and that he no longer would be president. So we went blithely into it, thinking that if Vierheller could not get along with them, we were more modern, more sophisticated and would have no trouble. Did not a small city, Toledo, have 18,000 dues-paying members of its auxiliary; San Diego nearly as many, and so on? It would be a bonanza for St. Louis.

We began by asking Jefferson Miller, a handsome young vice-president of the First National Bank, a socialite who was married to one as well, to be the first president and to undertake reorganization. It was my idea that whereas the Zoo was for all the people, poor, middle-class and rich, the new organization board should consist primarily of people who not only had money but were accustomed to raising it. And the younger generation of socialites, most of whom live in the county, in an area bounded roughly by Litzsinger, Woods Mill, Olive Street, and Big Bend Boulevard, were the workers, organizers, the doers in the region.

Perkins was somewhat less than enthusiastic from the start but Hattie Ettinger of the staff was as much for it as I. She volunteered to help get it started. And it went with a rush; there was no difficulty in getting board members and quickly they organized and wrote a charter. Our error--mine mostly--was that we had not examined the pitfalls, had not talked to enough sister institutions. I go into some detail about this, not to justify our own position, or to express any vindictiveness, but to record mistakes so that perhaps they won't be remade in the future.

Mistake number one was that we did not lay down ironclad rules, of which the first should be that the governing board of the institution should always be in control--control of money, of policy, of accounting procedures. In effect, the director of the Zoo ought to have the last word, although he should be able to delegate his authority to a staff member of the Friends. This we did not do.

Mistake number two seems trivial, was in fact major. There should be no question about the name--it must be a "friends" or "auxiliary" organization. In our case the new group insisted on the name "The Zoo Association." This had caused serious confusion which I think, in retrospect, they had in mind (and we had not envisaged). The public tended to believe that the board of the Zoo Association was in fact the governing board of the Zoo. Even the press has at times been fooled by the name.

Shortly after the formation of the auxiliary, two of the newly elected board members resigned in a huff when they found they would not be involved in administrative control of the Zoo. Both Henry Kendall and Martin Schweig considered themselves animal experts and suggested that one of them, I'm not sure which one, would do better on television than Perkins and that the other would be a better chairman than I. When they found that the institution would not (and could not) be turned over to them, they resigned in public--that is to say in the prominent columns of the papers.

This teapot tempest was of short and unimportant duration, but the impatience of the Association with the authority and "old fogyism" of the Zoo board remains.

Mistake number three had to do with money. The purpose of any auxiliary may include encouragement of volunteers, but its main objective should be to raise money--money under the complete control of the governing board. This is the way the most successful efforts are achieved at the Museum and hospitals in St. Louis and in other cities as well. But in the case of the Zoo, the governing board has had to stand on tiptoe and beg for both money and information from its own creation. Slowly and painfully most of the above has been corrected, largely because of the patient and difficult efforts of S. E. Freund of the Association, and Judge McGuire, the Zoo president, from 1969 to 1977--but the Association has a membership of only slightly over 5,000. San Diego now has 50,000 members--count them--50,000! An asset indeed!

*****

Early in his administration, Perkins pointed out to me the need for an enclosure, a fence around the park. Throughout its existence, the Zoo's 83 acres had been completely open, but the turbulent 60's were upon us and we began to be fearful for the safety of the animals. We knew that the building of a fence would be misinterpreted, that we would be accused of getting ready to charge admission, but that we would have to chance it. Both of us had agreed that, except in an emergency, we would build nothing that was not of good design. Excellence was to be our slogan.

I had a definite idea regarding fences, having but recently been introduced to Jefferson's serpentine wall, used both at Monticello and at the University of Virginia. This wall differs from all other brick walls in that it requires but a single thickness or course of brick, its strength coming from the series of alternate convex and concave curves which strengthen and reinforce it. Jefferson evidently had devised it to save expense since it required less brick and less labor; but in doing so he had created something of beauty. Although he thought of it as an economy, no mass-produced, cheap steel fencing being then available, it was not an economy for us. In 1964 ordinary chain-link fence cost us about $5 a running foot and the curved wall a steep $36. It also required very good workmen, more than ordinarily skilled bricklayers to build it.

It was my idea that we approach it gradually, that we begin modestly with funds available and add to it from time to time. We began with two walls flanking the entrance gate at the corner of Wells and Concourse Drives, and, at this writing, have gone as far west as the Children's Zoo parking lot and south to the 1904 Bird Cage. The vast remainder of the

169

enclosure has the ordinary chain-link fence. Admittedly there are higher priorities of need, but the serpentine wall is beautiful, and while it need never be used in those reaches closed to the public (such as the wooded west boundary adjoining the park) still, I would hope for gradual extension until the wall is finished. There will have to be an entrance gate included in it, off the south main parking lot, comparable in quality to the Kiener gate--which Bernoudy designed--already in existence.

*****

Somewhere I must have made a major mistake in my relationship with Marlin Perkins--but I can't see where it was. I have no doubt that one of my best moves was hiring him. I do not question that he is bright, capable and a good zoo director. Millions know that he is attractive, a major television star. What then?

When he came down from Lincoln Park in Chicago we were both enthusiastic, worked well together and had many, many plans for the Zoo's future. By this time I had retired from active business and began to see the Zoo as a major occupation. I read what I could, traveled to other cities and countries to see their zoological gardens--in a word became deeply immersed in the St. Louis Zoo. At the same time the television show was growing in quality and popularity--involving more and more of Perkins' time. At first I did not mind his absences and got into the habit of spending several hours every day at the park. The staff was thin--Harry Sanders knew about the operations, Moody Lenz about the animals, Virgil Turner, the maintenance engineer, about repairs and breakdowns, and Hattie Ettinger about everything else. And if our staff was thin, we were skating on very thin financial ice and really could not afford more salaries.

In effect I became a zoo adminstrator as well as a board chairman. I rather think, as I look back, that Perkins was satisfied to let the amateur president play at the work because Perkins was so busy with his journeys to Africa, India, Alaska, the desert countries and the like. Perhaps I should never have become so intimate with the job, as in doing so I may have taken away some of his responsibility.

In any case the situation intensified. His television popularity kept on expanding. Example: once we were high up over the Atlantic, en route to Rome and Nairobi, when an elderly gent (just my age) put down his work papers at cocktail time and said to me, "Can you tell me whether your companion is Marlin Perkins?"

"Yes, sir, it is. But I should know you, I've seen your face many times, and I think on the cover of *Time*."

"Oh, well, I'm a fellow named Dave Lillienthal. Do you suppose I could have his autograph?"

"Do you mean you are the man who was head of TWA and then the Atomic Energy Commission?"

"Yes, that's me."

"But Mr. Lillienthal, why do you want *his* autograph? It ought to be the other way around."

"Not at all. My grandchildren love his show--so do I."

We had given Perkins a five-year contract in 1961, when he joined us, and this contract was, therefore, about to expire in 1966.

Obviously, or at least it seemed obvious to us, things could not go on as they had been. The Zoo's only management, to all intents, was coming from me, and I was neither experienced nor sufficiently knowledgeable. With the consent of our board, McGuire and I informed Marlin that we would not renew his contract. He was shocked, could not believe it, and reminded us that he was within three years of retirement age and would lose his pension.

We countered with a proposal that he could stay until age 65 (and thus be eligible for the pension fund) provided we were to receive from his television sources sufficient funds to hire a working executive director as his assistant. For that we asked $25,000, a figure which we said was non-negotiable. We needed that sum and thought it reasonable as we had learned that Mutual of Omaha had budgeted more than a million a year for "Wild Kingdom." In all our negotiations Perkins kept telling us we should have to deal with Don Meier, his producer, but this was never wholly satisfactory to us for Perkins refused to admit ownership in the producing company itself. That he refused to tell us, however, removed all doubt in our minds that he was, in fact, a part owner of the producing company. All this added up to one fact: that his television was more important to him than his job at the Zoo.

Nor could he be blamed for this. If his salary of $25,000 would be considered moderate today, neither was it all that great 10 years ago, and while we had no knowledge of his television income, its potential had to be enormous. "Wild Kingdom" was and is a timeless show, with unlimited rerun potential.

The net of all this was that he could keep his title, as we knew he valued the St. Louis Zoo base for its use in his show; his employment until age 65 and his pension would not be affected.

It worked out very well, and he was particularly cooperative and helpful in our work with the legislature in the critical years of 1967-1970--the period of our efforts to increase our tax income. I regret that during the last year of his contract we had a disagreement, over the payments to the Zoo, which became so bitter that lawyers were brought in, and our parting was not amicable. I felt the Zoo had been taken advantage of--perhaps I was wrong. Of one thing I am certain; that I do not regret bringing him down to St. Louis.

A Zoo can be frustrating: there are too many things to do, too many acres to cover, too many animals that get sick, too many flowers that wilt, too many valves that leak, too many sewers that burst, too much litter to dispose of, too many motors that burn out, and on and on. But the challenges are unending as well, and if you like to build, to see things improve, the opportunities are infinite. I believe I enjoyed the hard, solid work at the Zoo as much as anything I have ever done.

But in 1969 I suddenly realized that I ought to quit. The principal reason was that I had begun believing no one else could supervise the Zoo--it was as though I owned it. No one told me that I was acting that way; but I knew it myself. Then, too, it came to me that I had spent 10 intensive years as president, had done the best I could. It was time to get out. Also, at about this time, Isabel and I were thinking of moving to the county and our residence there would make it unlawful of me to remain; so I resigned, believing that my services were at an end. In this I was wrong. Whether or not I had accomplished anything of much value up until then, the major service was yet to come.

CHAPTER VII

"There are few ways in which a man can be more innocently employed than in getting money."

Dr. Samuel Johnson

Since the mid-50's the Zoo had been chronically and increasingly short of money. Inflation was a small thing--not a matter of general concern as it soon became--but it was there just the same. Not only were expenses rising but tax income was static. The public was coming in ever-increasing numbers, a desirable situation but one necessitating increased expenditures.

In 1962 we had asked the city residents to double the property tax rate from 2 cents to 4 cents and they had responded nobly; but by the end of the decade it was becoming evident that even the higher rate would no longer suffice. In 1961, tax income had amounted to $341,000, and, after the 1962 election, it had risen to $650,000. In 1966 this reached its maximum figure of $700,000, after which it leveled off..

Expenses, which had been about $455,000 in 1950, were about $600,000 in 1960. Less than a decade later, in 1967, expenses were a staggering $1.1 million. Something would have to be done, and quickly. At this point Thomas C. McGuire, a new member of the Zoo board who was about to become a circuit judge, came to me with a suggestion that the legislature itself, without recourse to the voter, could authorize a tax increase. He made reference to the state constitution, Section 90.580 Subsection 2, which allowed the

General Assembly to delegate to a state chartered organization (such as the Zoo) the levy of a tax, provided the legislative body of the pertinent area (the Board of Aldermen) agreed to such levy. Such action, then, would be confined to the legislature, the Board of Aldermen and the Zoo Board--the voter could be bypassed. In using this method we intended no conniving against the public, no deception; it was only that the cumbersome processes of both legislative approval and city election were slow and expensive, and tax elections are subject to failure.

So we began. In the Senate the bill was to be handled by Lawrence Lee, and in the House by Paul Simon. McGuire, Perkins and I journeyed several times to the state capitol lobbying for our project, and once, at the suggestion of the veteran Senator Michael Kinney, we were accompanied by our chimp trainer, Mike Kostial, who brought the then famous performing chimp, Mr. Moke. The latter, if not an eloquent witness before the Senate committee, was nevertheless an effective one, dressed as he was in tattered garments of poverty. It made excellent copy for the press.

We gave a luncheon at which the ever-popular Perkins detailed his experiences with near-deadly snakebites, enthralling his audience and contributing to our eventual success. Indeed, we easily got through the House but bogged down in the Senate. It was before the Senate committee, to which the bill had been referred, that Senator Theodore McNeal said to me when I was testifying:

"But this is precedent, Mr. Baer. A tax without the consent of the voter."

"Yes, Senator, I know. But it is only 1 cent for which we ask. It means our very life."

"It seems small, but if we do this, will not schools and others want to go the same route?"

"Perhaps, Senator, but there is precedent in our favor. On

175

the national level the Congress sets taxes, does not go before the voters. If they had to, they'd never be able to tax, or not as easily. We don't think we could ask the public to support it--not now."

"Well, do you regard this to be a long-term solution to your problem? I should think it would not be."

"No sir. One cent will produce about $170,000. A fine additional amount, but it is only a stopgap."

"What then are your plans?"

"We have been thinking in terms of overall area support and are working hard at it."

"I'm glad to hear that."

Getting through the committee was not so difficult, but we lost the bill. The Missouri legislature's regular terms, held every other year, were limited by law to six months; and, heartsick, we saw our bill fail by only a half-hour. There was no substantial opposition but the bill was too far down on the calendar. The session adjourned at midnight June 30, 1967 with Senate Bill #7 within minutes of being voted on. Certainly we could not give up when success had eluded us by only a hair's breadth. We looked forward to a special session which it seemed Governor Warren Hearnes must call because there had been other unfinished business on major matters. We could not wait for another regular session two years later.

Now a special session of the legislature has certain advantages, the greatest of which is that no bill may be considered except relating to a matter which the Governor has placed on the agenda. Since he carefully selects but a few such items, the result is that they usually are given all necessary consideration; that is, they do not fail because of bogging down in a crowded calendar. About this Hearnes was very kind, and we went on to victory. He signed the bill, Senate Bill #7, into law March 18, 1968. It was the second tax victory, but this time we had gone alone, without the Art Museum.

There was, however, no gainsaying that Senator McNeal was right--we had plugged a finger in the dike, but we had not attacked the basic problem which was that the city's tax support was insufficient to support a modern zoo.

The more we thought about what must be done, the more it became clear that the solution was a district plan. The area was moving west, the county had become richer, more populous, more able than the city, and, so far as we could tell, its residents were the greater users of the Zoo. We began to send up trial balloons, to talk to the papers, to the rest of the media and to interested citizens. And we made in-depth investigations of the methods other zoos were using for income.

All major zoos, except Washington and St. Louis, were charging admission; but our studies indicated that an admission charge for us would not do the job. Besides, our charter called for a free zoo. At our suggestion, the Chamber of Commerce set up a cultural affairs committee which explored the possibilities of, and ended up by recommending, a district plan. Then, too, we were able to insert articles in the papers promoting the idea. By the latter part of 1969 it seemed the time was right.

One day in September 1969, without any conscious idea of a campaign, with no thought of a master financial plan, I sat down and began to write a "white paper" dealing with the Zoo's long-term financial problems. I don't know even now why I did it, I know only that there was a compulsion not to be denied.

This document of 24 typewritten pages discussed the Zoo's quality or lack thereof; it listed the things a zoo ought to include; it described the Zoo's financial history at great length; it forecast the financial difficulties to be expected over the ensuing five years; and it discussed possible solutions. These possible solutions were listed as:

177

1. Cut the suit to fit, i.e., reduce the size and quality of the Zoo.

2. Charge admission.

3. Charge non-St. Louisans only.

4. Gain district support.

One by one the paper then proceeded to demolish items one, two and three as either impractical or undesirable, and finally, at length, argued for a new district organization to be supported by both city and county and to include the Zoo, the Art Museum and the embryonic Museum of Science and Natural History in Clayton.

When we had doubled the city tax in 1962, we had taken the Museum along with us and again we included them in this document. Why? The Museum had always irritated me, much as I admired and valued the institution, because I had no use for its secrecy nor its smugness--its idea that no one should look at its affairs, that anyone in government was anathema to its well-being.

But Isabel, much to her surprise, had been made president of the Friends, and then elected to the Museum's governing board. She was completely devoted to the institution. Well, so what the hell, they needed the money too--put them in! In the case of the Museum of Science there was a double reason. Their small museum was the creation of one man, Stratford Lee Morton, who, great citizen that he was, had been indefatigable in creating it. And he had made a beginning, but it had little income, no endowment, no tax support. Worse, Morton had cancer, was a dying man. Who would see his museum into maturity? He deserved support, and St. Louis was a large enough city to need such a museum; but there was another reason. The Museum was housed in Clayton, the only one of the three institutions located in the county, and if we were ever to ask county voters to support the two city organizations, would it not be good politics to offer city support to the one in the county? When the paper was finished--it had taken about a week to work up all the material and to write it--I called Sally Bixby Defty of the *Post* and asked her whether she had any use for it. I was a little dazed when she took it and ran, a quite excited young lady. At once it was front-page material in the *Post*, and I was stuck with a project which occupied my time, almost to the exclusion of everything else, until election day on April 6, 1971.

Immediately Judge McGuire, now president of the Zoo Board, informed me that we must begin to create the new district, that I was tabbed for the job. We were, of course, successful in the long run, and there have been suggestions that the process ought to be recorded, as similar needs and opportunity could arise again. But much of the detail, important as it might be to a campaigner, is boring, so this discussion will be as brief as possible.

In the beginning, it was my idea that I would work at obtaining the enabling legislation at Jefferson City, but that if a miracle came to pass and we actually achieved that goal, some member of the Civic Progress organization, some V.I.P. would undertake the election. However, this second step seemed far in the future and was not yet to be worried about; the immediate task was to get a bill through the legislature.

Initial reaction in the General Assembly was anything but favorable. As was to be expected, we had no difficulty with St. Louis city members of the House and Senate, for after all our bill did not propose an increase in taxes for St. Louis, but only allowed for an equal amount from the residents of the county. However, I remember that Ray Howard, a black senator from St. Louis, was less than enthusiastic, but then he was reputed to be a chronic opposer, and we did not think his opposition would be significant. It was quite different with the county members. This was hardly surprising as they were being asked to pay for something, to be taxed for the support of

179

services which they had always enjoyed for free.

The membership of both Senate and House was, of course, heavily Democratic and that had to be taken into consideration, so we felt well served when veteran senators John Joynt and Lawrence Lee agreed to handle the bill in the upper chamber. In the House we had Paul Simon and Charles Valier, a young Republican.

But what was it that we proposed to create? What was the legal or governmental structure we wanted? McGuire and I discussed this endlessly and the bill which he wrote, while amended in the Senate, was essentially the one finally passed; House Bill #23 provided for the following:

1. That a petition signed by 1 per cent of the voters in the last previous election must be obtained for an election to establish the district.

2. That the tax so voted on be not more than 4 cents for the Art Museum, 4 cents for the Zoo, and 1 cent for the Museum of Science.

3. That a simple majority vote in *both* the city and the county was necessary.

4. That the governing board of the district should consist of eight members of which four should be city residents appointed by the Mayor, and four countians appointed by the County Supervisor, their terms to be staggered.

5. That the board would collect the taxes and disburse the funds to the respective institutions, with the board authorized to provide common services, such as audit, accounting, payroll, but in no event to spend more than 5 per cent of funds collected.

6. That under the district board, the individual institutions would be operated by subdistrict boards consisting of ten commissioners, five each from city and county, these members to be nominated by their respective boards and approved by the Mayor in the case of city members, and the Supervisor

in the case of county.

7. That the institutions would be "forever free" (an amendment insisted on by the Senate Committee).

This, then, was the plan, the essence of which was to keep the city tax at its then rate of 9 cents, of which 5 cents went to the Zoo and 4 cents to the Museum, and to ask St. Louis County for the same amount. In order to do this we had to reduce the Zoo from its 5-cent rate to 4, transferring that cent to the Museum of Science. A 1-cent tax from the city was then worth about $175,000 in revenue, and we guessed that 1 cent from the county would total about $225,000. The result for the Zoo would be an increase in income from $875,000 to $1,600,000; for the Art Museum from $700,000 to the same $1,600,000; and for the Museum of Science from zero to $400,000--a neat trick if we could pull it off.

We began with the House of Representatives, and the going was rough. Charles Valier, the young Republican member, was full of enthusiasm, but we had to hold him down a little. He was not only a minority member but had been a trifle brash as a freshman member, and was resented by some of the veterans. Paul Simon, the veteran St. Louis Democrat, was a powerhouse for us. The crux of the matter lay with the county representatives. As might have been expected, the outstate members of the House--and the Senate as well--cared little for the St. Louis institutions, and, as is always the case, their attitude would depend on how the members from the affected district felt. It was, therefore, essential to persuade the 42 members from the county to be with us.

Gradually we developed the theme that we were not asking those same county representatives to approve the project or even vote for it; but only to approve the authority from the legislature so that it might be put up to the voters.

We pulled all the stops we could. Once I had Al Fleishman take me to the legendary Lawrence Callanan, the supposed

181

big, bad boy of the steamfitters. He was old and sick then, but he promised support--he was reputed to control at least three members of the House. More than once when McGuire and I, or Perkins and I, were at the Capitol, Paul Simon would pull members off the floor to talk to us.

Some of the developments were bizarre. Example: at previous attempts, all successful, in Jefferson City, we had run into Buddy Kay, an esteemed member, a band leader in St. Louis and chairman of the House Municipal Affairs Committee. It was to that committee that our bills always seemed to have been referred, this time being no exception. Now we had had trouble with Buddy, or rather he had had trouble with us, and he had a right to be irritated.

The first time we had been before him was regarding an enabling act to purchase the Zoo railroad. After helping us, he gently suggested that as our Zoo Association was now conducting a yearly benefit ball he'd like to furnish the music for it. Well, why not? The dance band of social choice in St. Louis was then Russ David's, but Russ was not that important to us. So I said to Kay that certainly he could have the job, little knowing that the female members of the Association couldn't have cared less about our Jefferson City problem. They went their own sweet way and paid no attention to the president's request. Duly I apologized to Kay and told him he'd get the job next year. The next year we issued an order to that effect. It had the same effect--zero.

Now we had to go before Kay's committee on the most important matter the Zoo had ever been engaged in, and obviously there was a problem. But, ah, Buddy Kay was a--well, a protege of Louis Buckowitz, then Park Commissioner and lord of the 10th Ward in South St. Louis, and Louie and I were friends. You never know when a chance remark will come back to haunt or help you. Just a year before, when Cervantes had asked me if I would be Park Commissioner (meaning that he would like to fire Louie) I said to the press I was not interested in taking jobs away from my friends. It hardly needs to be said that I would not have taken the job in any event, but it didn't cost anything to say it that way. And Louie did not forget it.

So--I picked up the phone:

"Uncle Louie, will you do me a favor?"

"What is it?"

"I want you to ride up to Jefferson City tomorrow. I'll pick you up--we'll be there only a half-hour. I'll bring you back."

"What will we do?"

"Well, it's about Buddy Kay."

"What's he done?"

"Nothing, but the Zoo has a bill we want passed out of his committee and I think he's a little put out with me. I'll tell you about it on the way up."

"Well, I guess it's OK. What time?"

We drove up, and the committee had its hearing. Louie said never a word, just sat in the back row and looked intently at Kay. Within five minutes after our testimony, the bill was passed out favorably.

It takes about two hours to drive the 115 miles between the two cities, and about an hour out Louie said to me:

"What was that all about?"

"Don't worry, Uncle Louie, the bill is good for the Zoo. You did a good thing."

"I'll be honest with you. I don't know what the hell you were doing--but if you say its OK, I go along."

I make it sound too easy. It wasn't; but we had help. It was known that on the Senate side Clifford Jones, Maurice Schecter and Buzz King, all respected countians, were for us, and then, too, Senator Stone, a Monsanto officer, and Joe Frappier, an employee of Laclede Gas, Jack Schramm and Speaker James Godfrey were helpful.

183

On the first vote we failed. Then help in the person of Betty Hearnes, the Governor's wife, arrived via telephone. To say that I was low, discouraged and down would hardly describe my state. She was fighting angry. She said the vote was a disgrace and that, by George, no one was better than she at political infighting.

"Just give me the names of those guys who voted against you!"

God Bless Betty Hearnes--I've said it before, I write it now--again!

McGuire and I were there for the second House vote and thought we had failed again, but somehow we had misread the action. Tom Walsh, of St. Louis, the rough, tough but friendly member of the bricklayers' union came out of the Chamber and said, "What are you guys so unhappy about? You made it." We rode on air all the way back to town.

The Senate hurdle had to be surmounted, and we transferred our efforts in that direction. But meanwhile, back at the ranch in St. Louis, there were other developments. A lot of people had been watching us, people who were interested in other institutions.

The two groups who had been closely interested in our progress were the Symphony and the Arts Council. The Symphony, of course, was chronically stumped for money, always had been and, apparently, always will be; and the Arts Council, really a tool of the Symphony, while a successful fund-raiser since its reorganization, was obviously concerned. Neither of the groups had taken our ideas about a district plan seriously, but now that it became apparent that there was a chance, albeit a slim one, for success, they smelled money and wanted in. I was called for lunch by Ray Wittcoff, the brilliant young real estate operator, and he began by telling me that the board of the Arts Council had watched our efforts and supported them strongly.

"Well, thanks, Ray, but what else?"

"No, honestly, we do support you; it's just that we'd like to suggest some changes in your bill."

"Oh, like what?"

"Well, for one thing, the Symphony is not in."

"Certainly not, and for three strong reasons. One, it is not state owned and not eligible for the tax income; second, it is not of general appeal, has a small audience and would hurt us in the election; and third, it is heavily unionized and we can't imagine the legislature subsidizing a union to strike against the tax structure."

"You may be right and we would not insist on having the Symphony included. What we would like to see is a change so that some money would be undesignated--left, as it were, to the discretion of the Arts Council board."

"You mean to be handed out to the Symphony and to other institutions of yours, the dance groups, music educational organizations, theatre projects and the like?"

"Perhaps."

"I'm sorry to be blunt, Ray. It is not acceptable. For one thing, you are too late. We are through the House and working in the Senate. We should have to begin all over, and we'd fail. Besides, I don't like it. These three institutions are strong and are highly regarded--yours would hurt us. Sorry."

That afternoon their board met. There was some disgruntled effort to indicate opposition to the bill, but despite resentment they decided to remain quiet. Nevertheless, there developed an element of mystery which has never been cleared up. A rather powerful professional lobbyist was against us in the person of "Rube" Tapperson, a man who was pleasant and usually quite effective at the state level, whose principal employer was Anheuser Busch.

We do not know who his employers were in this instance, but it was clearly evident that he was buttonholing senators and talking against us. Lobbyists are required by law to declare their clients, but we could not find out his backer, even though I asked Senator Lee to ask him point blank whom he represented and was there when he did so.

"Who do you represent, Rube?"

"I'm a citizen, just myself."

That's as far as we ever got, and my promise to myself that somehow I would eventually find out who hired him has not been fulfilled to this day.

The opposition which later formed in the county was not yet evident. We began to feel that we would make it--but again we were trapped by time; which is to say that we lost the bill on the calendar. The session closed, and the Senate simply had not gotten around to us. However, this time we were not so discouraged as we had traveled that route before and looked forward to a special session. I thought Hearnes would readily agree to put us on the agenda for the special session, but he balked. Evidently he was irritated by his treatment in the Senate, and somehow did not trust our argument that we had a sure majority. He said:

"Look, Howard, you say you have a bill certain to pass. OK, you bring me a petition signed by a majority of the senators asking me to put this on the special session, and I'll do it."

"But, Warren, that isn't fair. We were so close; it was a matter of time only. Now you give me a hell of a job."

"I'm sorry--it's the only way."

I did think it would be a long, weary task, but it proved surprisingly easy. With Perkins and McGuire we went to the Capitol and got the signatures in two hours! Again our friends in both the Senate and House helped substantially. On April 9, 1970 I wrote to the Governor, presenting him with the signed petition.

The bill had to be reconsidered in the House, for this was a different session. Lost in the recesses of dim memory are the lunches, the several trips to and from the state house and thousands of words begging and pleading, but in May we had a bill and Hearnes quickly signed it.

It was victory, one which even our closest friends thought we could not win, and we were elated indeed, until we soberly began to realize that the hardest road was ahead of us--the election. In the back of my mind I always had the idea that should we ever get this far, we could put the election burden on a real leader, a corporation head, in the same way that Calhoun had led bond issue campaigns in the past. In this I was quickly disillusioned. It seemed that no one else was going to do it; it was my project, and I was stuck with it. I shuddered to think of it--there was no way that the county could be persuaded to pick up such a burden. We would be trying to persuade the old and retired, those who were skimping along on Social Security in times when inflation was daily reducing their buying power, to vote upon themselves a tax increase to support institutions which they had always had for free, and in which they were not much interested. And of the three, the only one for which they had ever evidenced real affection was the Zoo. Still, we would try, for having gone this far there was nothing else to do.

Already we had experienced difficulty with the Art Museum. The late Henry Pflager, its then president, had been willing to go along with our effort, but had been a drag too. Both he and most of the members of his board were suspicious and frightened of politicians and publicity; had never had open meetings with the press invited, and looked with horror on the prospect of a rotating membership on the board, as they still do. They wanted the money which the proposed district would make available to them, but more than that, they wanted their own little private empire.

Only a year or two before, Pflager had spent some $30,000 with the engineering and planning firm of Booz, Allen and

Hamilton for a study and report on the Museum's future and then had refused for months to show it to his own board and never had made it public. Henry had died, and the capable, realistic and respected ex-head of the accounting firm Price Waterhouse, Ben Jackson, was president of the Museum. Ben was and is in every respect a fine public servant. Self-serving pettiness would never have been any part of his make-up. But most members of the old board were still there, and they demanded that our bill must allow them to maintain the Museum's self-perpetuating status. Their stated reason was that they had been the recipient of important art collections, which had specified such self-perpetuation. As a joint effort, like a wartime coalition, always involves compromise, we went along, and we did get some excellent help from them during the campaign. We also had to contend with one stupendous error on their part, but that came later.

The time was then June of 1970, and we began to plan. As a special election in both city and county would cost the taxpayers more than $100,000, we thought we had better wait for a regularly scheduled election date so that we could not be accused of adding to tax burdens. It looked as though April 6, 1971 would be our target. This would give us ample time to prepare and conduct a campaign, and accordingly we fixed on that date--the day of our fate.

The next step was to get counsel, expert advisory help, and for that we turned to our old friends Fleishman-Hillard, the public relations pros who had been active in so many campaigns and who had talent to offer. Fleishman had never failed to help me. We did not see each other often, but we had great mutual respect and, at least on my part, real affection. Al, the proud, self-conscious Conservative Jew, proud of his heritage, verbose, rambling, spectacular, came from a completely different background, and we led different lives; but he was and is a friend, and his enthusiasm knew no bounds.

He thought the prospects for our success were slim but he knew we had to make the try and quickly assigned to us Bob Briggs, one of their men I had not until then known.

As we began to plan the campaign, Briggs initially wanted three things: a budget so that we should know how much money we'd have to raise; a moving picture film to be used at meetings and, if possible, in cinema houses and on television; and an opinion survey by a professional organization.

The detailed memorandum which Briggs prepared in July of 1970, could serve as a model instruction pamphlet for any civic-political campaign and touched all bases; nothing was left out; but the more I read it, the more I was convinced the job was too big; how could we possibly get it done?

The expense budget was prepared calling for a minimum of $150,000 and naming a more desirable figure of $189,000, a figure which we had to go to in the end. Where was this to come from?

Anticipating the financial problem, we had asked Civic Progress a year earlier to appoint a committee to study the matter of a district plan. While the committee did little other than offer words of encouragement, we had at least established the fact that they were involved. Nevertheless, when I asked for $50,000 from them I had very little confidence that I would get it, but I argued that, unlike some politicians they had supported on bond issue matters, I would undertake to match their grant two-for-one since the total budget would have to be not less than the $150,000 above mentioned.

Generously they voted to support us to that amount; and I set myself a quota of $1,000 a day to be raised. We also formed a finance committee. When the vote was finally taken and success was ours, the myth was common that I had done it all, that the entire effort was a one-man thing, all of which was flattering but simply not true. There was a working finance committee of six bankers and brokers, we had substantial solicitation help from Charles Buckley, the Museum's director, and Ben Jackson, its president, and I was soon close to my personal collecting quota of $1,000 each day.

As to organization, we had an overall campaign committee, and our working stalwarts were Gerald J. Williamson, a retired executive who had been so effective in implementing the non-partisan court plan, Mrs. George Whitelaw, Jules Campbell, the president of the Museum of Science, and Jackson. Nancy Schanbacher, a free-lance public relations professional, was added to our staff and was invaluable.

The amount of detail work was unending, some of which was like this:

Item 1. Organized petition drive. To get on the ballot, we had to collect thousands of signatures in both city and county. Whitelaw and her women handled this.

Item 2. Asked Paul Berra for endorsement of Democratic Central Committee. Success.

Item 3. Contacted all county throwaway papers, asking for editorial support. Did this myself. Fair success.

Item 4. Contacted most--not all--county mayors. Waltuch of Clayton, Brawley of Florissant, Kaufman of University City, etc., cooperative and favorable. Eagan of Ferguson, Cooper of Webster Groves, antagonistic.

Item 5. Attended town meetings. All at night. Miserable and tiring. Made headway though.

Item 6. Acted as narrator of the movie.

Item 7. Made trip to Washington to get endorsement from entire St. Louis delegation--Senators Symington and Eagleton, and Congressmen Symington, Clay, Sullivan. Very pleas-ant--got picture and endorsement. Also got lecture from irate Stu Symington on Cervantes' Illinois Airport proposal. Disclaimed responsibility.

Item 8. Debated with Mayor Eagan on television. Think OK.

And on and on. I lived for this, and nothing else mattered.

Much of it was bitterly disappointing, and it was hard to keep slugging. It was inconceivable to me that anyone in the city itself could not be for us, as we were asking city residents for nothing, only that they say they were in favor of their county neighbors bailing out their institutions. I was stunned when I learned Mayor Cervantes was against us.

"Why, Al, for God's sake, why?"

"Because you will take the best, most glamorous assets we have, the Zoo and Museum, away from us."

"Take them away! They're in Forest Park. We don't propose to move them--only to help them survive."

"Well, if the county wants to help, let them help my hospitals too. Let's have a hospital district."

"But, Al, you know damn well they won't."

"Well, that's it. I'm not going to let you do this. And, Howard, I lead from strength; I have political base; you are an amateur."

"Oh, sure, Al, I know you're too big for me. But what will happen to the Zoo? It's busted or damn near."

"It's always been there--it will survive."

This time I was really set back. What chance would we have if the city administration itself was against us? But perhaps the administration would not agree with his honor; anyhow, we'd see. My first stop was at the office of the License Collector (now Sheriff) Bennie Goins.

Mr. Baer, I know you; what can I do for you?"

"Mr. Goins, you are looking at a beaten, discouraged man. Do you know about our effort with the Zoo?"

"I do. It's great."

"But I'm licked. Cervantes is against me; I am ready to quit."

"Mr. Baer, you must not quit! It's too important."

"Oh, will you support us?"

"Surely I will."

191

"Publicly? You will endorse us and oppose him?"

"I will indeed; have no fear." *

Well, perhaps all was not lost--next stop the office of Paul Berra, head of the Democratic Central Committee, where I repeated the same sad story. And Berra's attitude was the same--all was not lost, and as reported above, the entire committee endorsed us. However, we kept after the Mayor. In October, when the Veiled Prophet parade was held, I, having been designated his escort, rode with him in an open car all the way from Kingshighway to the reviewing stand at 13th Street. We traveled, of course, at the usual slow parade pace, and I had a good two hours to work on him. No dice.

But as we went into 1971, and election day began to loom ever closer, his attitude changed. Bob Duffe, his executive assistant, sent word to me that at least he would not oppose us. The wind was blowing our way, and he wanted to change his mind. However, Al's general popularity had been slipping fast, he had made a number of goofs and it was clear--or so we thought--that now his endorsement might hurt us rather than help us. Very politely, then, we suggested to Duffe that, much as we appreciated the turnabout, we would rather City Hall stayed quiet. He understood that very well.

The problem with Supervisor Lawrence Roos in the county was a different one. Larry had been a banker, came from a wealthy, conservative family--in a word, was cautious. He knew that what we were trying to do was the right thing, but he did not want to back a loser--which he thought the effort certainly was. Although he had written me back in September of 1969, praising the original proposal, nevertheless, he was not present when I went before the County Council to promote the campaign and--well, he was at the height of his political popularity and we needed him. Nor did I want to wait until he

---

* Alas, poor Bennie--he has fallen upon evil days.

could see how the wind was blowing. Again luck came to our rescue.

From the beginning, Civic Progress had been in our corner and had started us off with that substantial financial contribution. I thought it time to make a progress report, especially as I noted that Roos was at the meeting and Cervantes was absent. The report was optimistic as to money, publicity and organization, and I wound up saying that we did not yet have the Supervisor's public support but that we still hoped for it.

Larry was on the spot. There he was among his biggest political backers and supporters, the 20 or so corporate heads of the biggest enterprises in St. Louis, and these men had supported us. They looked at him as he squirmed and rose to his feet.

"Of course, I support this. I could wish, with taxes as they are, it wouldn't come right now. But I support it and I'm very much for it."

He had said it in front of God and everybody, and he was hooked. So much for that--we had other things to do.

The League of Women Voters did not support us and I never knew why, but endorsements kept coming from many of the county mayors, from the Cardinal, from various church groups and from anyone or any organization we could think of asking. We even had a sports committee, the idea behind that being that the largest audience in St. Louis was for sports and we ran last minute ads on the sports pages in both papers, and radio spots by the ever-popular sports editors and broadcasters, Robert Burns of the *Globe*, and Robert Broeg of the *Post*.

The film which Briggs had produced was well done and effective. It showed the decay and deterioration of the Zoo, the leaking roofs and lack of climate control at the Museum and the total lack of proper facilities at the Science Museum. It argued pretty well and was undoubtedly a factor, more so than we had expected, because the major television stations ran it, and gave us prime time.

About ten days before the April 6 election date, the Museum, in its wisdom, announced the purchase of an Italian Renaissance painting at a price of something like $160,000, and it was front-page news for the *Post-Dispatch*. I could cheerfully have seen Buckley and his staff drawn and quartered. Here we were begging and pleading that the Museum was in decay, that the roof was rotting, that its very existence was threatened by abject poverty, and they were bragging of their splendid purchase. How would that affect the votes of a retired couple in Kinloch or St. Ann trying to get by on Social Security? Jackson, their president, was as upset as I was, but it had to be ignored; it had happened and that was that.

I was scared that we did not have enough money. Would it not be unthinkable after two years of effort to lose for lack of a few thousand dollars? We had realized our budget figure of $150,000, but what if, during the last week, we felt we must hit hard with more television and radio? Then, too, Fleishman and I had assessed the need for paying both Democratic and Republican poll watchers, and this came to $23,000--a sum for which no guarantees of value are available. All the pros can tell you that the party chairmen and workers probably won't help you; but they can surely hurt you if no money is forthcoming. The word for it all is blackmail--political blackmail, and like it or not, again it is a fact of life.

I had an idea. Naive as I was, I thought it might work; and I went to Joe Pulitzer's office. Now Joe knew what we were doing and, with his deep interest in the Museum, he was more than anxious for us to succeed. And he and his company were rich.

"Joe, I honestly believe we've got a chance. It's tough, and

194

the **pros are** shaking their heads, but I'm convinced we might do it. What bothers me is money--we may need $25,000 more at the last moment, and I have a proposal."

"What is it?"

"It's this: if I decide we need this the last week, I'll put up half of it if you will give me the other half. I'll split it with you."

"You're crazy!"

"Why, Joe?"

He got up from his chair and, obviously disturbed, paced the floor.

"You couldn't buy for any money the good publicity, the editorial support we are giving you, and we're going all out the last week. Isn't that enough?"

"Oh, come on, Joe. You'd do that anyway. This is your Museum, not mine. What kind of an institution will it be if we lose? How can you leave any part of your magnificent collection to it unless it's strong, viable? What I want is money--and even though you could buy and sell me--I'll match your amount."

"You really are demented." Then he sighed and rang for his secretary.

And he did ask her to make out a check, not for the amount I had asked for, but it helped. Nor is there any question that he was helpful and vastly useful--in person, in his newspaper columns and in his NBC television station which ran our propaganda film on prime time.

In retrospect, the major effort in the campaign took place over the weekend of April 3rd and 4th, the Saturday and Sunday preceding election day, when we telephoned nearly every household in St. Louis County, As you may imagine, this took some doing. First, we had to get the people to do it; second, we had to find a place with a multitude of telephones; third, we had to get the street and number information. Naide Whitelaw, our county chairman, got the girls, perhaps 50 of them, and they were nothing short of wonderful. Monsanto Corporation had the phone facilities, and the building was pleasant so the gals made a gala out of it. It was like a barn-raising, a community effort, and everyone smelled victory.

The telephone company has a private directory known as a reverse book, one which is not alphabetical but lists names and numbers by streets and blocks. They did not give it out generally; it was not available to solicitors or politicians, but we had it and it was torn apart, divided into sections, and the girls solicited votes. Surely that two-day period must have been one of the high-water marks of concentrated political effort ever expended in St. Louis.

So it was, as Macbeth, the thane of Cawdor, said "Time and the hour ran through the roughest day." And April 6 arrived. We awoke that morning to find a full-fledged snowfall in progress, and I groaned thinking that this was ruin. I now think I was wrong about that, and that probably it even helped us; that the elderly, the Social Security crowd, were discouraged from going to the polls, whereas the younger element, determined to save their Zoo and Museum, were not easily discouraged by the weather. In any case, the campaign was over; two years of solid work were behind us; either we had made it or it was all for naught. I was tired, exhausted, but anyhow the burden was lifted.

Buckley of the Museum had suggested a party, an election party at which we could get the returns that evening in the fine headquarters of the Friends of the Museum. Judge McGuire had arranged an open line to the County Board of Election. It was pleasant with an ample bar, but I was not much interested in whisky.

At 9 p.m. it was apparent that we were swamping the opposition in the city, but we had expected that; it was in the county where we would live or die, and they were slow in reporting. At 9:30 the Zoo and the Science Museum were ahead by a margin of perhaps 10 per cent, but the Art Museum was dragging. By 10:00 the picture improved; all three were winning--true, the Art Museum not by much, but then we knew all along that the Zoo would be the most popular. Each of the three institutions had to be voted upon separately, this having been the subject of heated discussion, some having felt that the Zoo could pull the others along if there were only one ballot. But we balked at this, both because we felt the voters were entitled to discriminate, and because we at the Zoo did not want to be handicapped by those who might be opposed to the others.

I had put on a bold, brave face, but deep down I hadn't dared to hope we could actually succeed until just that moment. The city desk at the *Post* was on the phone--"Will you make a victory statement?"

"By no means," I said, remembering Truman-Dewey. "We haven't won."

"Oh, come on, sure you have, Mr. Baer."

I drew a deep breath, took a drink--could it really be happening? At 11:00 the booze was flowing freely and I was still scared--until the contact man at the election board office in the county said to McGuire, "Look, what do you people want? We're going home because it's late and we're tired. You're *in*--good night!"

*****

The sequels were many and most of them were delightful. Before I was out of bed the next morning, Supervisor Roos called with congratulations. I was tired, it took me a week to get over that, but I staggered into the office of Fleishman-Hillard about 11 a.m. Shaking his head, Al said, "What damn fool was idiot enough to make you think you could do this?" And he grinned. I went to my office and passed the lawyer, Hy Stolar, in the corridor. He said, "I'm not your lawyer, but here's my advice anyhow--quit right now. You can't top it!"

And the following must be included too, although I'm not sure I can set it down properly. A month before election when things looked darkest, when the burden seemed intolerable, I had a strange--well, for lack of anything else let's just say a happening. I was in bed, awake, and there was a voice--a vision if you will, or perhaps it was the Biblical still, small voice. I am neither particularly religious, nor is my memory of it as clear as it once was, but I am very sure that it happened, that I was spoken to, that something outside me spoke. What came through to me was: Don't give up; this you can and will do. A grown man, an old curmudgeon, a hardheaded realist has no business making this kind of confession. I know that very well. It was such an experience that I did not even tell Isabel--for fear of I don't know what, for she would not have laughed. Never before this have I mentioned it and I do so now because--well, because without that help, we should not have made it, or so I truly believe.

I had borrowed $15,000 from my bank, the First National--the amount we were short in our expenditures--and it was time to pay. I asked Jackson, formerly of Price Waterhouse, and Kay Thompson of Arthur Andersen, the two largest public accountants, if there were any way I could get a tax deduction, and they both agreed it was impossible. So I paid off the loan. When I did, Barksdale of the bank said, "But this isn't fair. You should not have to bear this added financial burden." "What the hell, Cedge," I said, "that's a cheap price to purchase both a Zoo and an Art Museum."

*****

198

Six years have passed and the added income has helped them both immeasurably. But inflation has galloped apace and the Zoo's problems are not forever solved. It still has one hard nut to break--should admission remain free or is a change in order? The solution is the more complex because of an emotional air hanging over the question. Although St. Louis and Washington are the only two major zoos in America, and perhaps in the Western world, free of admission charges, the St. Louis citizenry is accustomed to that freedom. The major newspapers froth and sizzle when the subject of charges raises it ugly head, the *Globe* having gone so far as to accuse me of double-dealing when two years ago I mentioned that such action might be necessary.

And it is true that during the course of campaigning for the District Plan in 1970-71, we repeatedly boasted of our free zoo and begged votes for the Plan to keep it free. Moreover, House Bill #23 in one place says, "All of the subdistricts established under this section shall be forever free and open....." The implication and promise seem clear, but we did not imagine and could not know that the 70's would bring headlong inflation to our economy, that now, six year after, costs would be 50 per cent higher, and that continuing inflation would seem to be an acceptable fact of American life.

We did, however, give the Zoo an out. The bill goes on to say that it need only be free at such times as provided by reasonable rules, and that it may exact a charge "from any person in connection with the use, enjoyment......of the respective subdistricts." Can it legally charge? We believe so, at least we so intended; but, in any event, it is certain the decision will finally be in the courts. Assuming that the Zoo does have the right, the issue then becomes both a moral and a practical, financial one. As to both, I close with the following argument:

1. The best projections as to income and expense show

clearly that the crisis will come in two, three or four years. If income is not increased, the quality, or the scope of the Zoo's activities must suffer. Some, particularly the *Post-Dispatch*, have suggested this is what should happen to the best-loved, the best-patronized, the most popular possession the area has! In my view, this attitude represents acceptance of decay.

2. The need for additional income could be met if the tax rate were increased. This would involve the same major effort described in this chapter, i.e., a bill in the legislature to allow such increase, and approval by the voters in both city and county. Assuming that could be done, the question arises whether it is fair. The voters have already taxed themselves. Is it not equitable that the users bear some burden?

3. Admission fees would hold down vandalism, protect the Zoo, make it safer for children. Eleven years past, when the problem was discussed in the magazine *"Amusement Business,"* these statements appeared. "Vandalism has been a costly headache for all zoo directors; fees are apparently the best cure, but Denver had to put up fences to keep domestic dogs and undomesticated people out. Vandalism went way down when Chicago's Lincoln Park Zoo erected a fence. *That fees deter vandals was unanimously agreed upon at the recent convention in Milwaukee!* Gross, the Cleveland director, said, ' We have more lost children, more damage, more complaining on free days than on any other.' 'People appreciate a zoo more when they pay, and cleanup is easier,' said the Pittsburgh director."

Some 10 years ago in London, at Regent Park's great zoo, the director asked me what our charges were. Upon my telling him of our tradition of no charge, he said in amazement, "Free! But how do you keep the rascals out?" Good question, and a good place to end the argument.

CHAPTER VIII

"A doctor can bury his mistakes, but an architect can only advise his clients to plant vines."

Frank Lloyd Wright

If you live long enough, the wheel sometimes comes full circle--not always, but often enough to sustain a little hope. The transcendentalism of the 19th century was religious and optimistic--all was possible when Longfellow wrote:

> Though the mills of God grind slowly, yet
> they grind exceeding small;
> Though with patience He stands waiting,
> with exactness grinds He all.

Neither I nor the patient reader will believe justice is always meted out, that the weak inherit, that the wages of sin is as the Bible describes it, nor that, in the long run, the good guys necessarily win. Still, once in a while......

In the early spring of 1933, when the Great Depression was blackest, when all the banks were briefly closed, when the system wobbled on shaky legs, I was 30 and trying to run the 70-year-old A. S. Aloe physicians and hospital supply company. It had been a good, small company, had supported three or four Aloe families, employed maybe 150 people, and had lost, for the first time in memory, about $30,000 in 1932. It had, nevertheless, a net worth of about a million and a quarter. The problem was that while its gross assets were more than $1.5

201

million, we owed, not to the banks but to the open market, some $150,000 borrowed by means of commercial paper sold through Goldman Sachs and Company, the great New York investment banking house. Commercial paper was then, as now, a device whereby a firm with a sound statement and good credit could sell its own obligatory notes to any bank, corporation, or individual rather than borrowing directly from its own bank, and it had some advantages then as it still does now. The rate of interest paid tended to be fractionally lower than bank rates, and it took the borrowing pressure off the banks. The limitations, however, are definite and are basically that the maturity of the obligation is short, from three to nine months, at which time the notes must be taken up; and that the issuance of such paper is dependent upon bank credit lines to back it up. All of which simply means that if the borrower does not have the cash to pay the note when it comes due, he must be sure that he has bank credit to obtain the necessary funds to do so.

This was and is standard procedure. Nor would Goldman Sachs have purchased our own paper for resale distribution had they not been certain of our having such bank credit.

Our bank in 1933 was the same one my late father-in-law had done business with for many years, the Mercantile of which Lynn Hemingway was chairman, but we did have a secondary account with the old Mississippi Valley Trust Co. and a small, almost trivial balance with the prestigious First National of Chicago.

This then, is what happened. The $150,000 obligation matured, came due, during the bank closings, and the owners, therefore, could not present their obligations to us for payment. Actually they simply would have placed them with their own banks for collection through the banking system, but all were closed. We knew, however, that within a few days they would reopen, and we would have to pay our debts. This was to be a matter of no concern for us as the Mercantile Trust, having examined our year-end certified audit which we had presented to them in February, had written confirming that for the forthcoming year they had renewed their line of credit to us in the amount of $200,000.

Well and good, but these were difficult times and every precaution ought to be taken. A phone call was placed to Walter Rehfeld, a young officer with whom we customarily dealt, to inform him that we would expect to draw $150,000 to take up our notes.

It is almost exactly 45 years later, but I can remember with great clarity the shock that went through me when Walter said that there were to be no loans to the Aloe Company, that the line of credit so recently confirmed was withdrawn and that there was no appeal even to Mr. Eugene Mudd, the head of the credit department. Tom Paine was not the only man to live through the times that tried men's souls. There was I, having taken over a fine business when I was but 27, and I could readily see that only three years later I was about to send it down the drain. I knew the bitter cup of despair.

The worst did not happen, and while I draw a breath I shall think gratefully of the First National Bank of Chicago and its influence on the Mississippi Valley Trust and Boatmen's Bank of St. Louis. I need hardly say that our accounts at the Mercantile were closed immediately.

But back to old Henry Longfellow, time passed and in 1954 I was informed by George Berry, well-known automobile dealer, longtime pleasant acquaintance and fellow trustee of Blue Cross, that he thought I was slated to be treasurer of that organization to succeed Eugene Mudd. Now this was more than a score of years after my having been kicked out of the Mercantile, and I rather liked Mr. Mudd and really was not angry with him. In fact, I suppose I gloried a little at the number of friendly turndowns I had afforded Mercantile

203

officers when they, in their humility, had called on us and expressed regret at their 1933 decision--a decision, I had later found out, made by Messrs. Mudd and Hemingway.

Ah, but now I was a director of the First National Bank and here was an opportunity to do something for myself and, at the same time, correct a community wrong. In those times, about a quarter-century ago, the three big downtown banks dominated the community banking picture even more than today, and it was their custom, and by no means a bad one, to divide community responsibility. Thus public institutions such as schools, hospitals, Community Chest, Boy Scouts and the like would divide their bank accounts, and if loans or other financial services were needed, the three banks often cooperated on a proportional basis.

Now Blue Cross was a real plum. In those days its turnover of money was about $5 million annually, and nowadays it approaches $335 million, and while the increase is staggering, it scarcely surprises those at all intimate with hospital activities. Medicare was then undreamed of, and the patient's average daily cost in all St. Louis hospitals was about $12. Now it is $140, and where it will end no man knoweth. Small as the bank account was in comparison with 1977, it was still valuable, especially as it was not a community affair but reposed safely in Mr. Mudd's Mercantile Trust Company.

The annual election of the Blue Cross board was held and, as was expected, the old stalwart Scotsman, William C. B. Sodemann, was elected president, and I was the new treasurer. Nor was the reaction long in coming. But it did not come from Mudd, rather the phone call was from Hord Hardin of the Mercantile. Hardin was a man for whom I had enormous respect and considerable affection. He, William Braman and Walter Hein had been the supporting staff to Sidney Maestre at the Mississippi Valley Trust Company, and many people thought he was the best all-around banker in town. Apparently his never having made the top spot was due to an occasional flare-up of a hot temper, or perhaps his time never quite came.

In any case, the Mississippi, having been absorbed by the Mercantile and having far better officer talent, was running the new show--now the largest bank in Missouri because of the merger.

"Howard, this is Hord Hardin. May I come up to 19th Street to see you?"

"No, sir, Mr. Hardin. But I will come to your office."

"Well, but I want something from you. Let me come up."

"No, sir. You are senior. Anyhow, I have to come downtown."

When I got to his office the conversation went like this:

"Now, Howard, you are the new treasurer of Blue Cross. You can do anything you want with the account. But actually you know, Blue Cross is a community affair. The account ought to be spread around to the banks who are Blue Cross members as partners."

"I can see that--you mean the way Mr. Mudd handled it for the past several years?"

Hord was obviously embarrassed and impatient with himself.

"Look, Howard, I feel like a damfool. I know the position we're in, but they nominated me to talk to you."

"You know, Mr. Hardin, I asked your advice recently as to whether I should accept directorship on the First National Board, and you told me to take it."

"Damn right I did, and a good thing for you, too."

"Well, I'll ask your advice again. What should I do?"

He threw up his hands--"Whatever you want. I have no real standing."

I got up to go. "I'll tell you, Mr. Hardin, the account will stay here--somewhat smaller, and the First and other banks will get their share, but some day there will be other Mercantile officers in Blue Cross, and I agree with the community idea--it's just that with Blue Cross we're a little late getting there."

*****

I got involved with Blue Cross fairly early in its history. The work had a special value as well as interest for me because of our business which, of course, was hospital supplies. It was in 1940 that Leo Fuller of the department store family, who had been one of the original trustees of the St. Louis organization, asked me to take his place on the board. I was more than willing to accept because I believed that the more I could learn about hospitals, the more valuable such information would be to me at the Aloe Company. The experience was many things--interesting, dismaying, frustrating and, at the same time, exciting. We were, in common with other Blue Cross Plans around the nation, breaking new ground.

It would have been difficult, even impossible, for those involved in the business of health in those days--doctors, nurses, educators, administrators, trustees--to imagine the system as it is only 40 years later. To set the scene, nationwide there were some 8,000 hospitals, places generally feared (with good reason) by the public. For the most part they were frail financially and were often operated by preachers who had failed in the pulpit. They were but a few decades removed from the dark ages of medical ignorance, although, of course, some great ones had already emerged. These, such as Johns Hopkins in Baltimore, Massachusetts General in Boston, Mt. Sinai and Presbyterian in New York, our own Barnes, Pennsylvania in Philadelphia, and Wesley in Chicago could even then be considered distinguished. Associated with medical schools they were setting the standards for the brilliant future. The specialized training of administrators (then called superintendents) had not begun; wages were worse than sweatshop scale, and doctors were, with few exceptions, poor men. It was the popular conception that working for the sick was roughly equivalent to entering a religious way of life, that compensation was not to be thought of as a reward, that dedication was all. Indeed it had been only a few years earlier, in 1907, that Abram Flexner wrote his report on medical schools, which resulted in medical education itself being taken out of the dark ages.

In 1935, if you went to the physician with a problem, your chances for a proper diagnosis were about 50 per cent. It would have seemed insane to believe that just 30 years later the country's fourth largest industry would be the *business* of health, including hospital expenses, physicians' fees, medical school operations, nurses' income and auxiliary items. But all the same, it is true. Private hospitals are preponderantly operated by religious or community groups, not-for-profit, as a service to humanity. But there are a few others, as there always were, so profitable that some are listed on the stock exchange, a concept that would have enraged the early governors of the various plans.

In St. Louis, medicine is not our fourth industry; it is number one! Did you think our largest was McDonnell? Well, you're wrong. Consider that there are 57 hospitals employing 45,000 workers inside and 3,000 outside of these institutions. There are medical, dental and pharmaceutical colleges, schools of nursing and of hospital administration, and a huge supporting industry including Aloe, Sherwood, Affiliated Hospital Products, Mallinckrodt and departments in such giants as McDonnell and Monsanto.

The idea of Blue Cross had originated at Baylor University in Dallas in the mid-30's, when a group of school teachers banded together for the purpose of sharing the expense of illness with which they could not cope individually because of their meager salaries. What was different about the approach when compared to commercial insurance was that Blue Cross would not indemnify the insured with a direct dollar payment, but would provide hospital service for which it paid the hospital directly. Thus it made no financial difference to the patient that his doctor sent him to a hospital in Hermann or Perryville in outstate Missouri, or to St. Luke's or Barnes in St. Louis. The cost of the patient's care would vary greatly but in each case Blue Cross would pay. Limits were set, however.

It began in St. Louis in a very small way in 1937. From the beginning it was the creature of the hospitals, and in its early days, St. Louis University Medical School dominated in the person of its dean, Father Alphonse Schwitalla. There was nothing sinister about this, but those who can remember the brilliant Jesuit father will recall his dictatorial nature. There was, however, no exclusion of the other religious groups, and within a few years it truly was a community organization.

But it had elements of bigotry, as instanced by its refusal to pay standard rates for osteopathic hospital services.

The structure was tripartite. There were member hospitals whose cost per patient day was paid up to a set limit; there were employee groups, the insured; and there was Blue Cross itself, the third-party insurer and payer. The great commercial insurance corporations were peering at this new baby and wondering what it meant for them.

Also involved were the doctors who admitted and treated the insured. And pretty soon everyone was mad at everyone else! Some of the crosscurrents of irritation were these:

The hospitals, the chief beneficiaries of the entire concept, never felt they were getting enough money, and many were suspicious that they were being cheated. They excluded from membership osteopathic and proprietary hospitals if they did not like their standards, and they never did like them. No matter that the sick person had paid his dues and been sent by his doctor to such a hospital, his claim was not paid; or, if it was an emergency, such a hospital was paid a lesser than normal amount.

The doctors--well, not all, but the political types--were angry at both hospitals and the entire Blue Cross idea, many of them equating the organization with communism. They were fiercely independent, thought America had developed the world's finest medical system, and could see interference that might one day set and limit their fees and regulate their practices. The reader ought to remember that, while individual doctors have made important new discoveries and have advanced health care in general, organized medicine has fought every social advance. The early beginnings in group practice, the hospital practice of medicine, health insurance and corporate medicine, have each in turn been bitterly opposed by the American Medical Association, the local medical societies and other allies.

In a way it was to be expected that medicine would be conservative. Having but recently emerged from the dark ages of the arts of healing, a long period when quackery deluded and impoverished the sick, the new science of the 19th and 20th centuries had painfully discarded most of the witchcraft and had become severely skeptical of curative agents that could not be accurately demonstrated. These skeptical attitudes were more prevalent in England and America, incidentally, the two countries where the greatest progress had been made, and it was but logical to see that conservatism carried over into the economics of the profession.

Many physicians sincerely believed the liberties of their practices were threatened by Blue Cross, and some were greedy--simply felt that their fees might be fixed. Then, as it became evident that the public, the unions, the old, nearly everyone, wanted some sort of insurance, the giant commercial companies entered the field. They quickly became strong competition and threatened the very existence of the fledgling corporation. Their advantages were, and are, very strong.

Group life insurance had been very profitable for them and the idea of one package including both health and life was attractive to the employer and the union. Moreover, because the group life was so profitable, the hospital insurance could be (and was) offered as a loss leader, at cut rates. But their greatest advantage in rate quoting was their freedom in selectivity. They could quote different rates to preferred groups and refuse to sell to bad risks such as the old.

On the other hand, Blue Cross was stuck with its service concept, that all elements in the community ought to be eligible, and that their hospital care ought to be offered not only to employed groups in industry, but somehow to all. And as the early trustees were struggling with the problems of the retired, the unemployed, the old and infirm, in a spirit of true social responsibility, they were perhaps not to be blamed for wanting to control the quality of what they were offering.

As for the physicians, while some of their fears proved to be justified, one of them--as to their own earning limitations--was 180 degrees off the mark. They could not have dreamed of the enormous increases in income to be provided by Blue Cross, Blue Shield, and the private commercial carriers. Their free work and their bad debts decreased. As the patient saw his hospital bill taken care of, he could afford to pay the doctor--and as the doctor saw his $100 fee paid by Blue Shield, he could perhaps charge a little more, the coverage to be paid by the patient.

But this was all before Medicare and Medicaid. Then the benevolent uncle came into the act and all limits were off. Then it was that we began to hear of the ripoffs, the doctors with the $300,000 Medicaid fees, many of them phony, of the myriad of unnecessary tests, the unneeded hospital admissions, and the like. Just as power tends to corrupt and unlimited power tends to corrupt absolutely, according to Lord Acton, so does easy money do the same. The vast majority of all doctors, I am sure, are honorable just as are the majority of civil service employees; but a small minority can destroy the system.

The flaws of Medicaid, and indeed of all forms of medical insurance, are inherently in the concept. That we shall have to have health insurance in some form is evident; there is no avoiding it, with hospital costs more than $100 a day. But no insurance plan is sound when the insured can select against the insuror. To the uninitiated, that requires some explanation. To be able to select against a company means that the insured can decide when and under what circumstances he can collect. Thus, if you have life insurance, it is unlikely you will decide to collect by doing away with yourself; if you have fire insurance, the odds are against your setting fire to your house; if you have automobile insurance, you would be one of very few to steal or crash your own car. Ah, but if you have hospital insurance, that's different--both to you and your doctor. If he wavers, thinking that perhaps, or perhaps not, you belong in the hospital, and in any case it would be more convenient for him--well, you have insurance, so why not?

To illustrate: in the early 50's, it became evident that something was awry in Butler County, a poor area of Southeast Missouri. Suddenly payments to hospitals were being called for at the rate of 170 per cent of dues collected. For a while the situation was watched, and when it showed no signs of abating but looked steadily worse, a study was made. Putting Blue Cross patients into the hospital had become the county's chief industry. There was an investigation which uncovered a gross abuse of the plan. Again it was a case of a third party, the doctors, who had no financial interest in the plan but had nevertheless the authority to spend its resources.

Ma had walking pneumonia and the doctor prescribed

hospital care. "But," she would say, "I can't go. Who will take care of Pa?" "Oh, well," the doc would say, "You have Blue Cross, we'll put him in, too. A good rest and examination won't hurt him." So a penalty was assessed, payments were reduced and the matter was quickly corrected.

The abuses of those days were only small portents of the gigantic problems of today. Hospital costs have risen five times faster than the general rate of inflation, and while some of the reasons are understood, others are not so clear. It is easy to see that:

a. The wages of nurses, dietitians, x-ray technicians, cooks, orderlies, interns, security guards, janitors, laundry workers, pharmacists, etc., have had to increase like all others. There has been, however, this difference--that they started from a lower base.

b. Advances in medical, surgical and diagnostic methods have necessitated vastly more expensive equipment and techniques.

c. Insurance costs influenced by huge malpractice awards by juries have soared, almost unbelievably. In this year at one major St. Louis hospital, the bill for this kind of insurance alone is $1.75 million! Thirty years past it is doubtful that hospitals had any thought of such insurance. As this hospital (the Jewish) expects to render 187,000 days of patient care this year, malpractice insurance alone amounts to nearly $10 per day per patient. And in 1947 the total average cost of caring for a patient for one day in St. Louis hospitals was $9.13!

d. A not-so-mysterious increase in costs is the factor of many more laboratory, x-ray and other testing procedures which are done to safeguard both the doctor and hospital against charges of negligence. That many of these are unnecessary is readily admitted by most authorities, but, in view of the bitter experience of the recent jury awards, there is little choice.

e. Finally the hospital has become too popular. A

half-century past, a visit to it was regarded with justifiable alarm. Mortality was high, and anaesthesia was to be feared; surgical shock was not well controlled; the wards and private rooms were stark and cold, and the patient entered reluctantly. Many believed it only a place to die.

The pendulum has swung too far. Most patients are in surroundings more luxurious than at home; the food is vastly improved; the television the best obtainable, and the atmosphere, for those who are not miserably ill, generally pleasant. The public has been oversold on the idea that the hospital, with its doctors, nursing care and modern equipment, is the safest place to be in the entire world. So it is that they come in droves. But the hospital is by no means all that safe. True enough, if the patient needs the attention of the surgeon, the neurologist to treat a cerebral accident, or the cardiologist for the acute heart case in intensive care, then the American university hospital is unequaled in the entire world. Overlooked, however, are the matters of cross-infection, inevitable mistakes in nursing care and the hospital-caused diseases.

In summary, the American hospital is wonderful, but to be avoided unless needed. It is not a resort hotel.

*****

The two great unsolved problems facing health care in this late 20th-century, affluent age are common to the entire country, not only to St. Louis. They are the rising costs of which there seems to be no limit and the wasteful governmental approaches, which are obviously out of control.

The rate of increase in the expense of operating a hospital has been geometrical or worse. A check of Blue Cross annual reports shows that in 1940 the average per diem in St. Louis hospitals--i.e., the cost of caring for one patient one day--was

213

$7.30. In 1947 it was $9.13. In 1953, when I was chairman of the plan, I called attention (with alarm!) to the previous year's raise to $12.22. In 1955 it had jumped to $14.47. But now see the recent years--in 1974, $106, and then in the following year, the unimaginable $140! Nor is the end in sight.

But in 1940 we members of the executive committee debated long about whether we should allow the hospitals 15 or 20 cents a day for pharmaceuticals, and finally settled on the lesser figure!

All admit that something must be done to stop this steep, continuing increase, but the solutions have not yet appeared. Nor has this writer anything constructive to propose.

As to the Medicaid and Medicare ripoffs, the easiest thing to say is that they are Federal giveaway programs, and like food stamps, and most other welfare programs, are wide open to stealing by the recipients, the administrators and the third-party admitting and treating physicians. I agree with the *Wall Street Journal* which said recently in discussing the subject, that the fundamental flaw in the so-called War on Poverty is that it was not designed to give money to the poor, but rather to *people who provide services* to the poor. Certainly, then, support comes easily from organized medicine, the unions, contractors and, above all, public employees. The politics are good, and helping the poor has become a large industry.

Medicaid alone in the Bicentennial year of the Republic, 1976, cost $15 billion--and, while the St. Louis Blue Cross plan is innocent of wrongdoing, it is not too farfetched to say that some of its more than 1000 employees are part of that cost. Remember that in 1940, when the plan was young, there were nine employees and the sum paid hospitals was $712,000. And in 1975, 35 years later, the 1000 employees paid out to the hospitals $326 million.

St. Louis' largest industry, indeed!

*****

As the plan grew in volume throughout the years, so it outgrew its space limitations. I had resigned from the board upon entering the Army in 1942, but was reelected in 1947. In 1953 I was its secretary, the following year was elected treasurer, and in 1957, president. In 1959 I retired in favor of Eugene Williams of the St. Louis Union Trust Company, but agreed to remain on the board to oversee the building of the new Blue Cross headquarters.

The organization had, under the capable administration of William Sodemann as president and George Berry, treasurer, moved in from the old Continental Building on Olive Street to upper floors in the General Van warehouse building in the 4900 block of Delmar. For some 15 years the quarters had been both inexpensive and adequate. By 1959, however, it began to be apparent that Blue Cross would have to move. Its volume of claims was approaching 20 million, its quarters were becoming crowded, and the neighborhood was such that the female employees, who predominated, were uncomfortable.

Further, we had seen that in many cities Blue Cross had its own building with the attendant publicity that a separate structure affords. So it was that I proposed to the board a new building of our own; and indicated that because we would use some of our total reserves which were invested in government securities, then returning a very low rate of interest, I thought our annual cost of occupancy would be less than $2.80 a square foot. The board agreed, and we acquired, from the first Urban Redevelopment Corporation in St. Louis, the site on Olive between 14th and 15th Street near the Plaza Square apartments.

Because this was an Urban Redevelopment project, we would pay no real estate tax for 10 years, and only half the normal amount for the next 15. Thus we would more than save

215

the cost of the land. We employed the brilliant young Gyo Obata to design the building, but were definite in our instructions that it be held to spartan simplicity. We were a public corporation, using public funds and the last thing we wanted was criticism of luxury.

In 1962 the building was finished, and we were certain that with the extra two floors that Clarence Turley, our real estate consultant, had persuaded us to add, its 80,000 square feet of space would suffice for many decades to come. Well, we had no idea of Medicare and Medicaid and could not see that some 14 years later the volume of claims would be 10 times as great. Recently the building was abandoned and sold in favor of the new, adequately huge 250,000 square-foot structure on Forest Park in the Central West End. So the moving finger writes and moves on.

*****

But why such an ugly structure, built without an architect? In a way it is the same old story of the Stadium complex that was about to be designed by an engineering firm, the same one that has handled this project. St. Louis corporations, public ones who profess responsibility to the public, do it time and again. It has been but a few years since the telephone company put the shapeless mass on Twelfth Street at Olive, a building which put the dismal finishing touches on what had given promise of being a fine thoroughfare.

At one time Ma Bell built good buildings; the headquarters on Pine Street is respectable and really quite good for its time; but in the prominently located Olive Street building, the company simply abdicated all thought of design excellence. When they were planning it, I spoke to Richard Goodson, then company chairman, but he indicated that as the building was being built for them by a contractor, they would have no say.

216

But, of course, William Cunliff, his builder, would have built anything the company wanted and the argument was specious--simply a shrugging of shoulders.

There still are businessmen who believe that decent design is expensive, that architects are impractical people who want to build fancy monuments, that fine buildings are not good business. And there are ignorant politicians like those in the St. Louis County Council who, in order to placate a handful of householders, recently prevented Mallinckrodt from establishing a finely designed headquarters park on Highway 40, west of Mason Road; and then a year later let a shoddy and paltry little commercial complex be built a few hundred yards from the same site.

To be sure, there have been good buildings in the St. Louis area of late, those of the Pet Company, the Equitable Building, the General American-Philip Johnson edifice, the Wittcoff Number One Memorial Plaza, the Boatmen's Tower, the Mercantile, the magnificent Emerson Electric headquarters and even the Breckinridge conversion of the infamous Spanish Pavilion. For the most part, however, good modern architectural design in St. Louis has not been in the hands of government, excepting only the Arch. The private and non-profit sectors have done somewhat better.

I realize that this unhappy criticism comes from one who, having built one building, is a little unhappy to see it discarded after so short a time in favor of what looks like a rather dismal warehouse. Well, perhaps it is the carping of an old man and, in any case, I am glad to see the vitality in that Central West End. Even a good warehouse is better than the decay of slums.

*****

One final word about Blue Cross. I have already boasted of constructing the Olive Street building, and I have one more triumph to declare. I hired Oscar Rexford. It has, by some odd chance of fate, nearly always been my lot when leading any civic organization to be faced with the retirement of the old and the securing of a new director or manager. The best of all these judgments was the seduction of Oscar from the Public Service Company to be the manager of Blue Cross. He retired about a year ago, after some 18 years in the job; and during that time he guided the plan from a $19 million volume to one of more than $300 million, and there has never been a breath of scandal about its actions. He served under a multitude of chairmen and I have yet to hear a word of dissatisfaction. His was a job well done, and the difficulties were many. I am grateful to him.

CHAPTER IX

"If that's art, I'm a Hottentot."

　　　　　　　　　　Harry S. Truman

"Buy old masters. They fetch a much better price than old mistresses."

　　　　　　　　　　Lord Beaverbrook

The trustees and board members who manage civic institutions are, for the most part, convinced that their institutions are democratically operated; most believe that what they do is selfless, that their motives are pure and that all is for the best interests of the public they serve. These honorable opinions are, however, not always shared by others on the outside of such management, some of whom occasionally feel shut out, believing that some of the most prestigious organizations are closed corporations in the hands of self-perpetuating, elite, small groups. Which brings us to consideration of the Art Museum, the Missouri Botanical Garden, the Symphony and the Arts and Education Council, which is a comfort, aid and supporter of the Symphony; indeed, some have been unkind enough to call it the Symphony's tool.

Except for the political effort in accomplishing the Zoo-Museum District, I had never been active in the affairs of the Art Museum nor have I been involved with the Symphony, although for a long period I was, along with a hundred others, a board member of the latter, and I have been very close to the Museum, which has been of deep interest to Isabel. She has gained much satisfaction from countless hours spent as board member, president of the Friends Society, and docent-guide. Moreover, we have been in varying degree, friends of Rogers, Nagel, Rathbone, Eisendrath and Buckley, five of its directors, and were frequently and pleasantly associated with the late Vladimir Golschmann, conductor of the Symphony.

All of this is to say that no sour grape is in my larder.

I do, however, hold strong, critical opinions of both for different reasons: of the Symphony, not for exclusiveness or secrecy, but rather for its complete disregard of all the game rules; the Museum in contrast, for its furtive and at times murky actions, and its utter lack of candid disclosure of its operations. Strong statements, and they will require some proving! OK, here we go!

As is well recorded in the history of the Arts and Educational Council, *Persuade and Provide*, written in 1970 by Newton and Hatley, the Arts Council was founded in 1962 to succeed the unsuccessful Spirit of St. Louis Fund. Some seven small cultural agencies had been bounced out of the large, well-supported United Fund in 1969 on the grounds that they were neither health nor welfare agencies, and, gasping for the very breath of survival, they turned to Mrs. Morton May. With the never-failing help of her husband, she formed the small, separate Spirit Fund; but after two years it was evident it could not work.

In the meantime, the Symphony was deeper in its perennial mire. Always a deficit producer, it had struggled throughout its existence from one financial crisis to another. For many years, especially during the 1930's, Oscar Johnson had been its savior, supplementing substantially its own campaign which produced some $75,000 to $200,000 annually. Now this would no longer suffice.

The musicians' unions were restive; a desire was expressed for a bigger orchestra and for a better place to play than the huge barn-like Kiel structure on Market Street. It was again a time of crisis--and, as was the custom in those days, the problem was handed to Civic Progress. A committee was designated to look for solutions, and I was tapped for the chairman's job.

The upshot was a strong recommendation for a true United Fund of the arts; the fund, in essence, to pick up the seven agencies already in the Spirit Fund, and to add to them the Symphony and the Missouri Botanical Garden. The idea had appeal for the business leaders who composed Civic Progress. The United Fund had worked well, the institutions were needed, why not one campaign instead of many? It was launched with gusto, with strong leadership, and at once was successful. The first year it raised $560,000 and by 1970 $925,000--amounts which, to be sure, were a small percentage of United Fund efforts, but which compared favorably with similar arts funds elsewhere.

By 1970, the Symphony was getting about $450,000 and, in addition, $70,000 from the Camelot auction activity, or more than half of the entire fund. All of this was very much to the good, a splendid effort had been made, but it was not enough; for the Symphony had decided on excellence in the first degree. Stanley Goodman, the brilliant department store executive, an intellectual and a more than amateur musician, had become its president. William (Bill, Willie) Zalken was now manager of the Muny Opera, having been replaced at the Symphony by Peter Pastreich, certainly one of the most capable music managers anywhere or at least one of the most ambitious. And there was Powell Hall, the Symphony's new home.

All of this had uplifted the orchestra from what I suppose was a mediocre plane to a considerably rarified level. It is not yet spoken of as the equal of Philadelphia, Cleveland, Chicago, New York or Boston, but no one doubts that it is vastly improved.

221

And with its improvement have come increased costs--from $400,000 in 1960 to $4 million in 1975. There is, of course, no way of putting a price tag on excellence. Who shall say that St. Louis needs only an orchestra of X quality instead of Y? I, for one, who have always believed that architecture should be the finest, education the best and medical care the most advanced that science has to offer, would not quarrel with quality in an area foreign to me. But, it seems to me, as it has to many, that the orchestra should pay some attention to Polonius: "Costly the habit as thy purse can buy." My quarrel, then, is that the Symphony managers decided on the quality and went ahead, damning the torpedoes, forgetting the rules of Community Chest fund raising.

The Arts Fund does not raise enough money--OK, then it must be supplemented, no matter how. First there was Camelot, the clever idea of Evelyn Newman, an auction that has become a substantial fund-raiser of more than $100,000 each year, most of which goes to the Symphony. Then there was the Green Room fund, an association of board members and others who pledged $1,000 a year directly to the orchestra. Also, there were special campaigns to solicit selected prospective givers and to establish an endowment fund.

The Missouri State Arts Council came into being, and all credit to political expertise, the lion's share of its funds went to music. The Symphony also received special payments from city and county and from the festivals at Edwardsville, and a magnificent Ford Foundation gift. No question that the energies and ingenuities of Pastreich were fabulous. The emerging pattern, however, was that the federated campaign rules were observed by the other members of the Arts Council while the Symphony did what it pleased. Worse, certain of its most enthusiastic supporters were so-so givers to the combined campaign and generous with direct gifts to the orchestra. It has had the best of two or, more accurately, three worlds--a united campaign, various tax subsidies, and noninterference with its own special fund raising.

To any who complain of its rule breaking, the answer of its loyal and sincere advocates, such as Buster May, has always been, "What can you do? We need the money." It seems to me that Pastreich, Goodman, and Wells, *et al.*, have been ruthless in their zeal for a superb musical organization. Perhaps ruthless is an unfair word, but I don't regard it as such.

I must say here in their defense that having admired Goldwater's statement that extremism in the pursuit of justice was to be admired, I am scarcely in a position to attack their pragmatic approach to securing a fine orchestra. Nevertheless, I am doing so.

In spite of all their assiduous and multifarious money-raising efforts, the Symphony lies deeper in deficit than ever. The costs of administration and operation of its building approach a million, and that is before any musicians' salaries which are now comparable with the best in other cities. Some opinions have been voiced that, rather than a St. Louis orchestra, there ought to be a Missouri State Symphony, so that the nearly intolerable costs could be shared with Kansas City, and it is understood that tentative moves toward such a solution have been made. On the surface, and to the layman, the idea seems sound, but the objectors thus far have been in the majority, and it may well be that there is no validity to the concept.

It is certain that the unions would oppose the loss of about 75 jobs in combining the two orchestras, that Kansas City would fear the domination of the larger sister city, that those in charge would oppose the divided authority--in short, that small empires value their autonomy. For the present there is no prospect for such a merger.

There is also the matter of Powell Hall. By the early 1960's, the auditorium facilities at Kiel had become obviously unsuited to the Symphony. The hall was too large, the acoustics left much to be desired and the St. Louis audiences were bored with it and resented the parking difficulties. If the Symphony was to embark on a new look, it had to have a home of its own. The selection of the St. Louis motion picture theatre on Grand Avenue, which had shut down its operations, was considered superb by urban planners, by acoustical experts, by *Time* magazine and the *New York Times*: It indicated confidence in the inner city; the theatre's interior was basically handsome; the sound possibilities were rated superior. Besides, it would be much less expensive to buy, remodel and redecorate than to select a West End location and start from scratch. Moreover, the University Club was across the street and would offer luncheon and dining facilities to the afternoon and evening audiences. No matter that the neighborhood had been on the decline for years; the hall would turn it around.

I know of no one who opposed it with any vigor, and Goodman and his forces charged ahead, although there were those who were doubtful about the future of the area. The hall was purchased for $365,000, and $2.5 million was spent in the splendid rehabilitation. The naming of the hall was not without its irony. Helen Powell was a pleasant widow, reputed to be worth a million dollars, and she agreed that her fortune would, upon her demise, go to the Symphony. The gift appeared so substantial, so important, that her name was at once chosen for the building. Apparently what the Symphony people had not quite realized was that (a) she had no intention of undergoing an early death; (b) that she would remarry; and (c) that she had the right to encroach on her estate. More than 10 years have passed since the "gift" and though there has been no cash to be seen, still its promise was perhaps the major factor in the financing of the hall. Now it is not particularly important that, when and if the million-dollar gift comes to reality, the cost of interest on the loan for which it has been security will have been far more than a million; that, in fact, the million will have gone for interest rather than for the building; for without the pledge, it is doubtful that Powell Hall would have been a reality--anyhow, not at that time. Had it been delayed for a few years, it is probable the location would have been abandoned.

The removal of the University Club was a severe blow to the area, and though there is a strong likelihood of a new Missouri State office building two blocks away, those who will occupy it will hardly be Symphony supporters. The audience for music is small. When the knowledgeable musical entrepreneur Sol Hurok was in St. Louis 10 years ago, he told us he thought the New York City audience for ballet and symphony was not more than 25,000. Let's say, generously, that the St. Louis number is 5,000--OK, 7,500. Who are they? Would you not suppose they are the educated who live in West County, in Webster Groves, Kirkwood, University City, Ladue, etc.? You might also include the young who are at the universities and the young marrieds, some of whom are in the city.

Anyhow, the trip to Powell Hall for most clients is not convenient; it is, in fact, something of an expedition.

The corporate support of the activity has been not only superb, it has been nothing short of amazing. For those executives whose attendance (and I'll wager substantially on this) averages less than once in 10 years have, nevertheless, given financial support to the Symphony in generous degree. Well then, wonderful! Why do I criticize an effort which has been so monumental, so successful, so quality-producing?

I do so because I believe the judgment has been erroneous and self-defeating. The multiple fund raising will shortly cripple if not destroy the Arts Fund concept, the physical location will not suffice, the operating deficits will finally be too much to cope with. In the meantime, the orchestra is a fine one, and there is no denying that Mr. Micawber for years must have been a member of its board, though his name does not appear. Something has always "turned up." The crises have been passed, and the ensuing season is always announced. The present accumulated deficit of $1.5 million is worrisome, but no one loses any sleep. And it's part of the passing scene, the modern *Perils of Pauline*--what will happen in the next episode?

As this is being set down, the news comes that Pastreich has resigned to accept the position of manager of the San Francisco Symphony, an orchestra of great quality and the darling of the Bay Area. It was inevitable that capability, imagination and vigor would sooner or later invite an offer from a wealthier and more important musical community. All power to and respect for him--the gap here will be a large one.

The case of the Art Museum is, as has been said, quite different. The problem is not financial, or at least the finances do not constitute an operating problem. From 1907, when the Museum came into being, until 1962, it depended upon the 2-cent tax which the city had originally provided for its maintenance. When the Zoo doubled its own 2-cent rate in 1962, the Museum in a joint campaign effort benefited equally. From the following year until 1971, its tax income averaged about $700,000, a sum which, together with its additional income from Friends Society dues, contributions, and the like, enabled the Museum to operate sufficiently within its income so as to have small surpluses for acquisitions.

But the beautiful building, the impressive work of Cass Gilbert and the sole relic of the great 1904 Fair, was showing signs of wear. Rehabilitation was urgently necessary and in addition to such repairs, modernization was eminently desirable. The Museum needed climate control, better lighting of display spaces and improved laboratory facilities for conservation. As was the case at the Zoo, the Museum of Science and Shaw's Garden, more skilled personnel as well as added storage and display space would be required to handle greater attendance, to care for the growing collection and to serve the increasing demand for expanded education. The area's population was growing and its interest in the humanities was in proportion, happily producing ever greater demands on the Museum.

Throughout the years, the board of control had been a closed corporation, self-perpetuating, happy in its self-sufficiency, and not at all dynamic. The late Henry B. Pflager had become president in 1945, succeeding Daniel Catlin, and he reigned until his death in April 1972. Henry was a likable, affable man, who had great affection for his city and its Museum; but in common with most of his board, he was apprehensive of the winds of change--and of politicians. The Museum, like the Zoo, was the property of the city and was supported by its tax revenues, and had, therefore, been obliged to list as its ex officio board members the Mayor, the Comptroller and the Park Commissioner. But by 1967, Pflager had managed to shed them and, as they never appeared at meetings anyway, there was no squawk about that. Open meetings were also not to be thought of, and so far as I know, the press was not informed of board meetings. So it may be said that any idea of a rotating board, of letting the public in on the operating process, of discussing problems with a politician, or of disturbing the status quo in the slightest, was unthinkable. However, about 1964, Pflager, slightly uneasy as to the Museum's future, paid some $35,000 to Booz, Allen and Hamilton, the well-known business engineering firm, for a general survey of the institution's future and never made it public at all! In fact, about six months elapsed before Henry could bring himself to show it to his own board.

In addition to just plain secrecy, obfuscation by the small controlling group has been the order of the day. As specified under the law which established the Zoo-Museum District, the governing body consists of five commissioners from the city and five from the county, and is, as has been described, self-perpetuating. But there also is a body of trustees of the Museum, this having been established in 1972. "Trustee" is an honorable and dignified word and, no doubt, is intended to give to those so honored the feeling of belonging to a policy-making, governing body. And this body is not self-perpetuating. Its membership rotates.

Do not, however, question any of the trustees as to: (a) who decided on building plans; (b) how much money was raised in its building drive; (c) why their director retired. A trustee will tell you that he or she is not privy to these facts--but he is a trustee nevertheless, and his name is duly listed.

No matter the stuffiness; in 1969, anyhow, it was a pretty good Museum, boasting a collection of about 15,000 works of art spanning 5,000 years and representing such prominent artists as Holbein, Titian, Hals, Rembrandt, Monet, Rodin, Picasso, and Van Gogh. And new pieces were coming in--some by purchase from the modest funds available, but most by gift and bequest. Moreover, there was one department which towered in strength over the board itself and was without equal to any other St. Louis institution--the Friends. This auxiliary comprised of some 6,000 dues-paying members, led by the superb secretary, Martha O'Neal, was the product of energy, expert volunteers, work and considerable money. Through the years, the enthusiasm, dedication and spirit of the leaders of the auxiliary have exemplified the best, the highest quality of volunteer services. Within its organization there are divisions, a Decorative Arts Society, a Contemporary Arts Society, volunteers for the operation of the Museum shop and the Docents. This last group of 45 amateur volunteer guide-teachers is remarkable. In order to qualify as a Docent member, stringent standards have to be met and examinations successfully passed under the requirements of the Museum's Department of Education. It is not unknown for volunteers

228

in some auxiliarys to be unreliable as to **scheduled** commitments, but not in the case of the St. Louis Museum Docents. Those who are scheduled to guide visitors or to attend classes and do not appear are quickly dropped. They run, in short, a model organization--serious, at least semi-professional, dedicated and valuable.

In 1969, I had written the report which finally culminated in the campaign for the Zoo-Museum District, but in the beginning I had thought only of the Zoo. As the concept developed, the idea of incorporating the Art Museum and the Museum of Science in Clayton began to emerge. It was easy to include the Museum of Science as we thought it would be good politics; we would be asking the county not only to support a city institution, but also their own, while offering city support for the county's museum as well.

It was not so easy to be enthusiastic about the inclusion of the Museum. Their board had never shown any assertiveness, the Museum had ridden on the Zoo's coattails in the 1962 tax election, would not be a vote getter and, in general, would be a drag on an effort by the Zoo to improve its position.

On the other hand, the Museum was closely situated to the Zoo in Forest Park, and was not without those in the Zoo world who appreciated its worth. Further, some of us who were going to undertake the campaign would have (as in my case, emphatically!) suffered serious domestic difficulties had we not taken the Museum along for the ride. So, as Mr. Goldwyn would have said, we included them not out but in.

Not that it was all that easy, for they had all the characteristics of a reluctant bride. To begin with, they did not like the original legislative bill we had drawn, principally because they were afraid they would not be able to maintain a self-perpetuating board. The snug little empire could not help displaying its *unter hosen*. We had the feeling they would rather have been left out, given up an extra million a year,

229

than lose control. And the argument for all this was a beaut--that certain bequests had been made to them upon the condition that the board be self-perpetuating, lest the ignorant politicians take hold. What the danger from those politicians was purported to have been we never knew--presumably the uglies might have burned the pictures and the library books and substituted *Playboy* calendars.

There was no denying, however, that the Museum roof was in danger, that the wiring was antiquated, inadequate and dangerous, that there was no climate control, that the collection was inadequately housed and, finally, that the budget was thin. Little remained after operating expenses to spend for acquiring new works of art, and the Museum had to depend on funds raised by the Friends for this purpose. And, of course, it is true that a good museum must have a reasonable amount available for purchases. There are constantly evolving new trends in the visual arts, and dependence solely on gifts would be both haphazard and inadequate. The Museum's argument was valid that the funds raised by the Friends for acquisitions could not be used for routine operations. Few donors want their money to evaporate in expenditures for day-to-day operations; rather, they like to feel that something definite and permanent results from such giving.

By 1969, actual operating costs were in excess of income; the future was indeed bleak. As is recorded elsewhere, the relief came just in time. Although the 1962 tax increase had raised income by 1969 to just over $700,000, it wasn't until 1973, the first full year under the new Zoo-Museum District, that income soared to a whopping $1,763,000, an increase of more than a million; and in 1976 it reached $2,100,000.

As soon as the campaign was over and the new tax rate assured, the Zoo set in action its program of rehabilitation, i.e., the repairs and renovation which it had described to the voters as urgently necessary. The Museum's course of action was otherwise. Rather than embark at once on such repairs, it decided to plan greatly--to dream what proved to be an impossible dream. Pflager had died in 1972, and his successor, George Rosborough, and his director Charles Buckley, envisioned a new day. About this they were quite frank, writing in the 1972 annual report that, "Rather than do a piecemeal job (of renovation) the conception of the long-range architectural plan has proceeded gradually through the year....." For the making of the plan Buckley had selected in 1971 the firm of Hardy, Holzman, Pfeiffer Associates, a New York firm of young men whom he evidently thought especially qualified. So far as I know, no consideration was given to St. Louis architects, but there is certainly no reason to question his motives.

Throughout the next year or two, various architectural models appeared and the Museum gave a series of dinners at which the architects explained the displayed models to those whom Rosborough and Buckley hoped would be donors to the building fund. And the price tag steadily increased, until it was reputed to be as much as $23 million--an absolutely staggering figure. Nothing of the sort had even been attempted in St. Louis. Well, yes, Hickok and Estep had collected equity money of nearly $20 million for the Stadium complex; but that began with subscriptions of $5 million and $2.5 million; and, besides, that was for downtown St. Louis, for professional sports, for the hotel and restaurant industry, all of which had great financial import for the entire region. The Museum had a limited audience, clientele, or following, however one might classify its patrons; and its proposed betterment would have no great meaning for the corporate structure of the town. It had angels--Pulitzer was reputed to have pledged a million, as was Buster May or his Beaumont Fund; but just about there, the big money ended.

In retrospect it is not too hard to see that such a large sum would seem possible to Buckley, who was not a businessman and had not participated in such major fund-raising efforts. But that a commission, including such experienced fund-raisers and capable businessmen as Ben Wells, George Conant, Maurice Chambers and Rosborough himself, could envision that kind of money was, to say the least, astonishing. They ought to have known it was not possible and should have insisted on that to Buckley, preventing his headlong rush to failure.

The Museum, true enough, had been accumulating some money. Beginning in 1972, its tax revenues were more than doubled and its 1975 annual report, published in the late spring of 1976, indicated that it was "able to project a total of over $8,000,000 available from gifts, pledges and tax funds," for building purposes. Information as to the amount produced in the campaign was hard to come by, but assuming that the normal operations were producing a surplus of a million a year, it would seem reasonable that of the eight million available for the renovation project not more than $5 million, and probably less, had been raised by subscription.

It was clear that the nearly a million spent with architects, if not wasted, at least had been spent for a project much of which would be put aside into the indefinite future. In short, it was no go. And Buckley, the director of 11 years, the dreamer of the big plan, resigned.

In the small but buzzing St. Louis art world, the event struck like a thunderbolt. No one believed the succinct statements given to the press and the public, that he had for some time been contemplating retirement, that 10 years was enough for any director, and that the time to quit had arrived. It was inconceivable that anyone could be so deeply involved in the largest project of his career, one which was to a considerable extent his own concept, and suddenly announce his departure from the scene when its initiation was about to take place. It was inevitable that questions would be asked, but no answers from Buckley, Rosborough, or other commissioners were forthcoming. Once again the Museum's secrecy prevailed.

On the whole, Buckley had been a good man for the Museum. Possessing neither the personal charm of Perry Rathbone, who was its director from 1940 to 1955, nor his influence on the building of important private collections, an endeavor at which Perry had been very effective, Buckley was nevertheless cultivated, well educated and particularly qualified in the area of decorative arts. That he was a bachelor and tended to be shy and withdrawn rather than outgoing and gregarious probably made his job less easy. Then, too, it is likely that he thought that raising the enormous sum of money he had in mind would be possible, and when he found that his miscalculations had been catastrophic, the burden was too much. The dream had collapsed. It would appear that he no longer wanted to work in a situation at which he deemed he had suffered failure. And it can well be assumed that the catastrophe created a normal amount of less than good feeling between him and his chairman.

And then what? There was no question that action had to be taken. Three years passed and no renovation worthy of the name had been accomplished. The Board of Commissioners of the Zoo-Museum District had been generous and granted the full 4-cent tax rate, allowing the Museum, in effect, to accumulate the excess against a future project. With the advice of the St. Louis architect Hari Van Hoefen, a partial approach, including some of the elements of the original plan, was adopted. Renovations were priced at $16 million instead of $23 million; and as some $9 million is presently available, there remains $7 million to be raised. Perhaps it can be speedily collected, but as the most interested prospects have already been tapped, it would appear the task is at best formidable. The original will have to be considered a master plan--one which may be broken up in order that it may be built in stages as the money becomes available. *

Well, art is long and time is fleeting, according to Mr. Longfellow; and the pictures, the sculpture and the tapestries can wait for the buildings to catch up with them. And it is heartening that the Museum's board, having suffered the partial debacle of their first architectural expenditure of $1 million for plans can with equanimity express confidence in their ability to find the needed remainder for renovations. In a way, though, one is reminded of Sam Johnson's comment upon hearing of the early remarriage of a man who had been unhappily wedded, "that it was the triumph of hope over experience."

*****

Already in this record there are listings of some of the fine assets of St. Louis, but there is reason for some recapping here. Higher education ranks well, and is very nearly of New England quality; medicine is first-rate and perhaps as good as the very best; the Museum is good, in fact very good for a city of this size; ditto the Zoo and the Symphony--but only in one institution is St. Louis unparalleled and unequaled, at least in the Western Hemisphere; and, oddly enough, this asset is not generally thought of as particularly important.

Most citizens would, if asked, name the Arch, the sports teams, education, the Muny, the Zoo, or the hospitals, as the town's mark of highest quality, forgetting that on Tower Grove Avenue, next to the park of the same name, there sits a

---

* Word now comes that the museum's latest fund drive has been quite successful.

72-acre garden embodying beauty, research, education--all superb--and rapidly increasing in all its values.

None of us living knew Henry Shaw, but he was obviously of such farseeing intelligence that if not a genius, he came close. An immigrant from England in 1819, he started a hardware company, and by the age of 40 was rich enough to retire to the pursuit of other than business interests. Public spirited and of philanthropic mind, he had intended to leave his estate, now the Garden, to his city as a park; but one of his important and highly intelligent friends persuaded him of the need for a true botanic garden. This friend was the great physician and more than amateur botanist, George Engleman, of St. Louis, a man who corresponded with Asa Gray of Harvard. This garden, Engleman said, ought to be more than a handsome, pleasurable display of flowers, shrubs and trees and should include facilities for scientific study, research and education. Quickly Shaw took fire, traveled, consulted the best authorities, including the people at Kew, purchased books, herbaria, and built the firm beginning of the institution. Moreover, when he died in 1889, he did not simply unload his child on the community, but left an endowment of income-producing real estate to maintain it.

His will, under the terms of which the Garden is still governed and operated, was a masterpiece. He specified that the director must also be a professor of botany at Washington University, thus insuring that the director's qualifications could not be below the University's requirements; and he included, as ex officio trustees, the Episcopal Bishop, the Chancellor of the University, the president of the public school system (now interpreted as the president of the Board of Education), the Mayor and the President of the Academy of Science. In addition, he specified a self-perpetuating board of 12 trustees to govern, to hold title and to run the activity.

As one might expect of an enterprising English-American of

the early and mid-19th century, Henry Shaw was a WASP. But, though his friends were pretty much Episcopalians of English descent, and his first trustees included no Catholics, Jews, women or blacks, still there is no evidence of bigotry on Shaw's part. He knew he had hold of something greatly valuable--something to which he could devote his energies for the remainder of his life. He actually founded the garden in 1859, wrote the will, or anyhow its last version, in 1885, and died in 1889, so he had the pleasure of working on his creation for more than 30 years.

There can be no question that he would be happy to see it now with its new Lehmann Library, its Climatron, its recently completed Japanese garden and soon-to-be boxwood gardens, its new English woodland garden, its society of 10,000 members, its research and educational departments. There was, however, a long period, pretty much from the 1920's until the early 1950's, when nothing happened. The trustees were satisfied to let the creature rest in peace, and it slumbered on. George Moore was director from 1912 until 1953, some 41 years, and for 25 years of that period he was also a trustee. Just as the Zoo in those days was the personal property of Vierheller, so too did the Garden belong to Moore. The research continued; the graduate work in botany at the University was at the Garden; the orchid displays were admired; but the trustees dozed peacefully--and while they did so, their income properties, their inheritance on which the Garden lived, declined.

But early in the 1950's, beginning with the energetic leadership of Robert Brookings Smith, the Garden was shaken from its lethargy. Smith brought the scientist Fritz Went in as director in 1958, and from Went's ideas came the Climatron. After Smith, Henry Hitchcock was president, and Went was followed by David Gates, who was equally qualified and energetic, and from him came the idea for the new Lehmann

Library, not only a beautiful structure by the architect Obata, but the safe repository of the famous herbarium, one of the most valuable research tools in the botanical world. Gates, however, found university life more agreeable, and his retirement to the University of Michigan led to the coming of Peter Raven in 1971. I am by no means alone in my judgment that his coming was the best thing that has happened to the institution since Henry Shaw himself.

Moreover, the trustees--while still self-perpetuating, as they must be under Shaw's will--have come to life. There is movement; of late, presidents serve but for three years; trustees are encouraged to remove themselves to emeritus status in old age; and the small ingrown group of management has been opened up--witness the trusteeship of the author! The Garden under Raven has become a living organism in the region, a part of the lives of those dwelling in St. Louis. It maintains decorative floral areas in public buildings, in hospitals and open-air beds at the Zoo, it educates children in beginning and adults in advanced garden work. Its lectures are heavily attended, its radio programs useful, and soon it is to offer demonstration home gardens.

The government agencies--engineering, scientific, artistic-- have flooded Raven's staff with projects, and today's interest in ecology has brought a degree of general interest from the public far greater than ever before in the Garden's history. We should expect that, for during the last decade there has been a bombardment of information, both pseudo and real, in the areas of pollution, energy shortages, ecological waste and damage, and the resulting confusions, fears and interests have thrown heretofore unthought-of responsibilities on the Garden.

For all life depends on plant life. Without it, there are no animals and no mankind. We are greatly fortunate, then, to have in our midst one of the world's great authorities as to man's environment; and through the present staff, skilled, energetic, in touch with their colleagues throughout the world, the Garden's mission has become important to a degree Shaw would not have imagined. As Emerson said, he builded better than he knew. How could Shaw have guessed that less than a century after his passing the world's population would be doubling every 36 years; that in so doing, hundreds of millions would be facing starvation; that the great rain forests of the world would be endangered, that man's industry would endanger the rivers, the air and even the seven seas?

No, he did not fear what he could not envision, but were he here today, without doubt he would courageously charge full tilt at the evils, believing that as men have created problems so they can solve them.

Although I have said that the Garden is not an intimate part of the life of the general public, its followers and friends are increasing and devoted. It seems characteristic of the race of man that in upper years he turns to the gardens of the earth, and loves growing things. The Romans, tired and disillusioned with what we should call the rat race, retired to country retreats, and so it has been ever since.

The bequests which the Garden receives not from wealthy ex-trustees or tycoons--although there are plenty of those too--but from modest unassuming people, people often unknown to anyone at the Garden, are both touching and indicative of what it does for the spirit of man.

Long may it prosper and grow!

*****

In ending this discussion of some of the cultural aspects of St. Louis, I readily confess to having made sharp criticism of some organizations and to have delivered only paeans of praise to others--those with which I have been intimately connected!

This of itself, of course, constitutes a kind of arrogance. Admitted. The Zoo and the Garden have not been without fault, grievous error and failure, perhaps as often and in as much degree as the Museum, Symphony, Arts Council and the rest. But I have written of them all as I have seen them and as best I could........SELAH!

CHAPTER X

"Listen! There never was an
artistic period. There never was
an art loviny nation."
                    James A. McNeill Whistler

All passes. Art alone
    Enduring stays to us;
The bust outlasts the throne,
    The coin Tiberius.

                            Dobson

In the realm of fine arts I have discovered that men are not necessarily born with inherent good taste, a love of beauty or discerning eyes; but all this may be worked for or stumbled upon. I give you two examples as introductions to some notes on the fine arts in St. Louis.

On a miserable, damp, dark afternoon in February 1924, there wandered into our rooms at Princeton one tall, red-haired, handsome, muscular and bored youth of 20 whose name was William Christopher Hayes, y-clept Ruddy. This "suite" was the residence of my roommate Lloyd-Smith and myself; one of the three rooms, designed for a small bedroom, we had made into a library. In a word, we were literary with a big L, and since we were both editors of the Nassau Lit and amateur dramatists holding forth at the college Little Theatre, we had definite (if extremely local) reputations.

Ruddy was our friend, but his interests were elsewhere. So far as we could tell, they were pretty well limited to rowing, alcohol, women and weekends. A bookworm he definitely was not, although at prep school his innate brilliance had won for him the medal for advanced Greek, an accomplishment which he had successfully concealed from us.

He indicated that his boredom was monumental, his finances so pitiful he could not venture even to Trenton for the weekend and that, since we were always reading, we must have something to interest him. In other words, he was so desperate that he wanted a book. The problem of what to give Ruddy was quickly solved as on the table someone had left a thick historical novel, a book of perhaps 350 pages, about the cruelly depraved emperor Caligula.

"This will do you, Ruddy. Lots of gore, fighting, intrigue, the whole works."

In a week he was back.

"This was the berries." (I believe that was a common expression in those days.) "I am going to be an archeologist."

We were aghast. "Ruddy, archeologists are scholars and, my God, you don't know anything!"

"You think so? I'm going to be an archeologist."

Well, I lost touch with him, although a decade after graduation I heard that he had talked himself into a Metropolitan Museum expedition to the North African Carthage territory, and that the leaders, coming upon a completely different set of findings than anticipated, were at a loss when Ruddy stepped into the breech brilliantly. He died in 1963, and the memorial articles about him at the Metropolitan and the American Research Center in Egypt were impressive; I suppose he would have gotten there anyhow, but I can still see the red cloth cover of Caligula when I picked it up and tossed it at him. Such are the happy accidents of youth, and how good to have been in at the conception!

As for me, I have written elsewhere of Lloyd-Smith's influence on my consciousness of beauty in the world, but he thought largely in terms of literature and nature. He wrote well, understood poetry and the drama and obviously would have had a brilliant career had he not died so young.

At the age of 27 he was managing editor of *Fortune*. Anyhow, despite all of the heady stimulation I had from him, my interest in and respect for the visual arts come from elsewhere.

During my junior year Professor Chandler Post was loaned to Princeton by Harvard University. His course labeled "Italian Art and Culture" was an elective, and I suppose, at that, it was Lloyd-Smith's influence that got me into it. Post would have been a sad sack indeed if he could not hold an audience in the palm of his hand with such a subject to enfold. But Post was more than a teacher, he was a distinguished professor. From Giotto to Bernini he presented his cast of characters superbly. What luck to enjoy that kind of introduction to the art world; to realize that aesthetics was not a word only for women and sissy males.

The entire Ivy League art world was pretty stuffy in those years. The famous Armory show at which Picasso, Braque, Cezanne, Brancusi and DuChamp were introduced to America had been held in New York in 1913, but there was never a word of these artists except in derision. Even Scott Fitzgerald, who had left Princeton only six years earlier and was already a success, was anathema to the members of the English department, who were only grudgingly accepting Sandburg, Sherwood Anderson and Sinclair Lewis and were by no means sure of T. S. Eliot.

So this was my introduction to the arts, but my interest in them lay dormant until about 1934, when Edith Aloe, my mother-in-law, began her great effort which culminated successfully in the building of the Milles Fountain on Aloe Plaza.

The years 1932 and 1933 marked the nadir of the Great Depression. St. Louis was beginning to stir only feebly in 1934 when Edith Aloe conceived this public monument; there could hardly have been a more difficult time. The Art Museum had been castigated for buying the Egyptian cat at a cost of $14,400 in 1931, when people were hungry, and here was a much larger project when so many still were out of work. But she wanted an appropriate memorial to Louis Aloe, her husband and my father-in-law, who had died in 1929, and while he certainly had been no David Francis, Henry Shaw or Robert Brookings, he had been an engaging politician and a constructive, public-spirited citizen.

He had been first an alderman and later president of the aldermanic board, but unlike most aldermen, he was only a semipro. Primarily he was a businessman, the Aloe Company having some small local reputation, and his political career was civic rather than professional. Nevertheless, he was good at politics--he had no higher education but was an impressive speaker--and he had spent many years in the grass-roots territory of ward affairs. He had spearheaded the $87 million improvement bond issue of 1924 and he looked confidently forward to the Republican nomination for mayor in 1925, hoping and believing it necessary to be the administrative officer to oversee the spending of it. In that he was disappointed, and bitterly so.

St. Louis then was Republican about as overwhelmingly as it is now Democratic, and nomination was tantamount to election. He thought his nomination had been decided upon, and, in fact, promised to him. His opponent was the ridiculous and actually paretic Victor Miller; thus, his competition was expected to be no problem. But Henry Kiel, the ex-mayor and powerful South Side German, had other thoughts and, at the eleventh hour, introduced a third candidate who drew just enough support away from Aloe to nominate Miller. A half-century later I have no idea what was in Kiel's mind, but the double-cross is no stranger to politics and it may or may not have been as some said--and Aloe believed--that Kiel was not ready for a Jewish mayor. In any case, the Aloe monument is, in the minds of St. Louisans, far superior to the Kiel Auditorium, if there is any comfort in such things.

The director of the Art Museum at that time was Meyric Rogers. In 1931, with the help of the League of Women Voters, he brought to the Museum an exhibition of the sculpture of Carl Milles, the Swede, who was a pupil of Rodin and a hero in Sweden--and, according to Rogers, was perhaps the best sculptor to handle water since the 16th century. That was high praise. Viola, the dynamic and decorator-trained daughter of Edith Aloe, called her mother's attention to the exhibition and suggested that she think about Milles. Edith Aloe looked at his work, fell in love with it--after all, she had been educated in Europe, and Milles' art had a Scandinavian-Germanic quality--and determined to have it. Moreover, she met the slow-speaking, charming Milles himself and they were quickly friends. But what to do and how?

Well, the $87 million bond issue was being spent, and one of its targets was the elimination of the skid row district, which is now the Market Street Mall from 20th to 12th Street. In common with nearly everyone, she believed the railroad station was to be as permanent as the Pyramids, and she wanted the site opposite the station as a location for a fountain. She was by no means wealthy. A widow with four married daughters, two of whom she had to help in those lean years, with a modest income, she was scarcely in a position to be a major philanthropist. She could not buy the monument; she had to persuade it to life. She was alone. I was the only son-in-law in St. Louis and but 32 years old. I had lived here only a short time, knew no one and was politically and civically not dry behind the ears. In a word, I was useless.

So she turned to that indefatigable hero, Luther Ely Smith, without whom she could never have brought it off. Smith was not the towering corporation lawyer of his day and never was particularly successful financially nor powerful politically, but he was nevertheless a dedicated St. Louisan, and persistence was his virtue. It occurs to me now, more than 40 years later, that his Milles Fountain efforts were a rehearsal, a warm-up for his campaign for the Jefferson Memorial on the river front.

His name, in very small letters, is on the green sward just east of the Old Court House and in front of the Arch, but his paean has never been properly sung. What one man can do, Luther Ely Smith did.

Strangely enough, Barney Dickman--by that time mayor, having been swept in during the Roosevelt-Democratic landslide--was sympathetic to the idea of a memorial, even to a Republican. I remember more than one dinner party at Edith Aloe's apartment at which she entertained the late Mayor Dickman, Baxter Brown, then president of Public Service, Smith and William C. E. Becker, the city's chief engineer, as well as Harland Bartholomew, city planner and engineer for the City Plan Commission. As to the actual machinations, the inevitable infighting that always accompanies that sort of thing, I knew but little and even that has escaped me. I know only that Smith was always at her right hand, would not let her despair, and the contract with Milles was written in 1937 at a price of $60,000. The clearing of the two blocks bounded by 19th, 20th, Market and Chestnut streets began. The figures, of which there were to be 19, were to be created at Cranbrook Academy of Art in Bloomfield Hills, Michigan, where Milles was then in residence.

Seen from this distance everything in those days was inexpensive, but it seems in retrospect that the artist made a far greater financial contribution than either Edith Aloe or the city. He had, of course, to pay for the casting of the bronze figures which must have cost half his fee and today would not cost less than $100,000. Moreover, the city counselors took

245

advantage of his innocence in insisting that even the plaster models from which the bronze figures were cast should belong to the city. This kind of obligation on the part of the artist is almost unheard of, since the creator is always recognized as the owner of his idea. In any event, when Milles wrote me some 25 years later and asked for his plaster models which were then uselessly deteriorating in the old Forest Park mounted police warehouse, I went to Virginia Brungard, the park commissioner, and argued that his request was fair. She was a fine woman, eminently reasonable, but quite properly said that this was outside her province and referred me to the city law department, whose head was then Samuel Liberman, a respected lawyer and well known to us.

Sam had not written the contract and had never seen it, but when he read it, he flatly denied the request. Probably it was no great matter, for Milles was old, was shortly to die, and worse, his vogue was passing. In today's art marts, a Milles appearing on the market would cause hardly the flicker of an eye. He was a creator of public monuments rather than objets d'art. This Aloe fountain, like his others in Falls Church, Gotteberg and Stockholm, is greater than the sum of its parts, especially as the moving water unites and vivifies it.

But I see now that I accepted "no" too quickly; the city should have been persuaded to relent. The rather sad sequel was that only three years later, when the mounted police building was about to be razed in preparation for the Planetarium, Mrs. Brungard asked me what to do with the figures. Our best local authority then being William Eisendrath of the Museum, we asked him to examine the material, which he did. He recommended their destruction. Each figure in the fountain, then, is unique--there are no other casts.

The creation of the sculpture and the construction of the underlying pool were not without minor frictions and comedy.

246

The city then had an art committee somewhat analogous to the present-day beautification committee, or perhaps it would be more properly comparable to the group known as the Landmark and Urban Design Commission. Its members were worse than stuffy. Though the 1930's were decades before the sex freedom which culminated in the 1960's with the complete disintegration of good taste, even the Victorians had understood that male humans were equipped with genitalia, and they knew that the Greeks, Romans, French and Italians now and then supplied their sculpture with them.

This distinguished art committee headed by one Francis D. Healy, an "art" dealer, reacted as do all political committees when given a chance to observe the progress of the work. Healy and the committee's aldermanic member, Hubert Hoflinger, were horrified to find that Milles did not intend to use fig leaves. In my memory, the public debate they started was the most trivial dispute ever argued in St. Louis. It is evidence of the comparative innocence of the times that this nonsense engendered editorials, cartoons and letters to the press. The *Post-Dispatch* and the *Star Times* leapt to the defense of the artist, and the *Globe-Democrat* of the Lansing Ray era grudgingly followed. And not all committee members were horrified. Museum Director Rogers, sculptor Victor Berlendis, city forester Ludwig Bauman and Baxter Brown kept the matter sane.

On May 11, 1940, the fountain was dedicated and was, with some minor exceptions, an instantaneous success. The city at once took it to its heart, adopted it in great pride. Soon it was reproduced in great profusion on post cards, photographs, in corporate advertising and was the subject of much amateur art.

Its deficiencies were two: The fountain was useful only in daylight, as there was no lighting system, and the water was too elaborate for the size of its pool. As has been said, Milles'

247

great talent was in the use of water; his adjustment of his jets was superb, some of the jets rising 40 feet over the basin. The problem was that when the breeze was above eight miles an hour, the water tended to drift over Market Street, and motorists immediately complained of their wet windshields. And since the automobile is the golden calf, the true religion of all Americans, this defect was quickly corrected by changing the pumps to some of lesser capacity. The present water flow is by no means as gloriously impressive as the original but certainly serves pretty well.

In the year 1954, when Edith Aloe was to become 75 and when, by coincidence, Edison's electric lamp obtained the same age, our family and the Aloe Company made a gift to the city of $7,500 as her birthday present so that the right lighting could be added. The engineering, as well as a fine celebration party, were contributed by Union Electric Company. Our friend Wesley McAfee, its chairman, presided at the occasion. The electric company was celebrating the Edison anniversary and for the event lit the Plaza with a 75,000-watt bulb.

Until the coming of the Arch, it was the city's proudest ornament and to many it still is. But the trains no longer run, and the throngs who crossed the street to be refreshed, as they changed from the Pennsylvania to the MoPac, have long gone. The city's maintenance of Aloe Plaza was deplorable. For a long time, the Park Department contented itself with turning on the water each spring and removing the electric fixtures in the fall to save them from vandalism. The decades passed, and the granite coping around the pool moved with the winter's ice; the concrete cracked, while the magnificent bronzes were blackened and encrusted with the pollutant fallouts of succeeding decades. As I thought of Edith Aloe, it seemed intolerable that her life's greatest effort should sink into decay.

Once I remember driving up to the office of Louis

Buckowitz, the Park Commissioner in 1970, and saying to him: "Louie, get in my car!"

"Where are we going?"

"Never mind, just get in the car."

Down to 20th Street we went and I showed him the heaved pavement, the fractured granite, the empty spaces from which the bronze plaques had been stolen.

"Louis, you've got to fix this damn thing. It's a disgrace."

"How much will it cost?"

"I don't know--$100,000 maybe."

"I haven't got a dime."

And he was telling the truth, for every park commissioner knew that as the city's expenses increased and as its tax base contracted, the first budget to be cut was always parks. But again our family had some help.

Robert Orchard, who from time to time was helping Mayor Cervantes raise a little money for the care and preservation of public monuments, was of assistance both in obtaining two corporate gifts and in guiding me to Mel Beauchamp, whose Beautification Committee had some access to federal matching funds. Our family contributed about $30,000, and rehabilitation was assured. It is perhaps interesting to note that the entire fountain in the 1930's cost about $156,000; its repair in 1974 cost $175,000, and even this latter amount would have been larger had it not been for the contribution and really expert service of Phoebe Dent Weil, the art conservator who, with Washington University art students volunteering as her apprentices, cleaned and resurfaced the bronze figures. Her work was largely a labor of love, although I believe she considered that the new methods she improvised were useful additions to the art. Her several papers on the care of bronze works of art are now classics in the museum world.

Those notes on the fountain are too lengthy, but somehow the point has to be made that if the cities will not take care of public art, there will be little incentive to donors to provide it. Nor does it suffice to say that art museums are the proper and safe repositories. They are indeed, but sculpture of any size needs to be out-of-doors. Europe has shown in Florence, Rome, Stockholm, Paris, London and scores of other cities that public, intimate, daily display of such ornamentation is good for the spirit and is loved by the people. In addition to neglect, we live now in an era of lawless vandalism, which adds to the problems, but, I suppose, we can only say this too will pass and that, therefore, the times must be endured.

So much then for the Milles Fountain, but there is one small footnote as supplement.

In 1961, some 30 years after Edith Aloe's very successful effort, Isabel and I, having become somewhat more prosperous, thought of doing for the airport what our mother had done for the station. We thought of sculpture to be placed in front of the new Yamasaki airport buildings. Mayor Tucker readily accepted our offer and appointed a selection and purchase committee consisting of Gyo Obata, the architect, Richard Weil, a knowledgeable collector and our friend, and William Eisendrath, of the City Art Museum.

The result was the two large Henry Moores which Eisendrath recommended and negotiated for after a rather extensive search both in this country and in Europe. The selection was made after he had considered and rejected pieces from such major artists as Lipschitz, Naum Gabo, Max Bill and Arp.

At this writing, only a little more than a decade later, it would seem that the sculpture is good, and Moore's reputation has grown--many critics would name him today's greatest sculptor. But it is certain that our idea was mistaken for many reasons.

The airport was simply no place for sculpture, certainly not at its front door. Whereas the form of the railway station was

250

fixed, not to be changed and, in a way, the atmosphere was calm and unhurried, the reverse was true at Lambert. Construction and confusion never stopped. The air traveler moves fast, is in a hurry, has no time for the contemplation necessary to receive any sort of impression from the serenity which Henry Moore had put into his art. The sculptures simply did not work in that location, were almost ill at ease.

We could not, of course, ask for them back, but I thought I *could* ask that they be transferred from one city department (the airport) to another (the Art Museum). And Charles Buckley, then the Museum's director, and Henry Pflager, its president, were naturally eager to have them. But the Museum had no sculpture garden, no out-of-door location which the works cried out for, so we suggested that the Museum accept them but at once loan them to Shaw's Garden until such time as the Museum had a proper setting.

This was agreed to. An ordinance was necessary, and never was one passed more easily--the aldermen could not have cared less.

The Moores were moved in 1970 and do so well at the Garden that it will likely be a sad day on Tower Grove Avenue when the Museum claims its property, but then perhaps it never will.

CHAPTER XI

"The optimist proclaims that we live in the best of all possible worlds; and the pessimist fears this is true."

James Branch Cabell

When the city of St. Louis made the decision--which in retrospect appears disastrous--to secede from the county, the reasons were both economic and political. There was contempt for the vast area stretching from the city boundary to the Missouri River on the west, and to the Mississippi on the north. It was generally believed that the ignorant, poor farmers had nothing of value to render to the bustling city, and that there was no valid reason to carry their burdens. This action was roughly equivalent in economic consequence to England's giving up the 13 colonies, only the city did it from choice, whereas Great Britain at least had the good sense to struggle, if but halfheartedly, against the separation.

One of the most common quotations about the error of government is the worn-out one: "Those who will not read history are condemned to repeat its mistakes." For all its solemn and seemingly wise warning, when you get right down to it what does it mean? I rather think the great German philospher Hegel was closer to the mark when he wrote, "What experience and history teach us is this--that people and government have never learned anything from history, or acted on principles deduced from it."

Why is this? Well, I should think largely because of what Sir

John Seeley, an Englishman, wrote: "History is past politics and politics present history." In the case of the city-county separation indeed it was.

In common with most of my fellow St. Louisans, I have always known that about 100 years ago the city left the county and became a free and independent entity, but I did not know why or what the details were. The story is both simple and complex and those who want all of it are referred to the excelent discussion by William Cassella, Jr., a political scientist and former member of the Missouri University faculty. The article, published in January 1959 by the Missouri Historical Society, is readily available. Some of what happened then is so relevant now that the essential elements at least can be briefly listed here.

In 1870 the area of the city of St. Louis was but 18 square miles, its western boundary being Grand Avenue, but its burgeoning population was 310,000, while but 27,000 lived outside the city in the remainder of the county. Although the taxable assets of the city were rated at $150 million, and the county at only $14 million, the county court, which governed the entire county, exercised considerable control over city affairs. It could and did assess, tax and spend to a degree which had been causing irritation in the city as early as 1847.

Further, as in the legislature a century later, the county court was rurally dominated, and the city was regularly outvoted on the bench of the court. Special taxes to improve the county fell largely on city residents, and corruption in the county government was deemed rife by city fathers.

By the year 1875, a Constitutional Convention had been called, and St. Louis saw this as an opportunity for relief, as the mechanics for secession might be provided for, as in fact they were. A provision was included for a referendum which would produce both secession and home rule.

Just before the convention, the county had refused to

support an extensive park plan which the city had devised and wanted badly. It proposed Forest Park for the west, O'Fallon north, and Carondelet on the south. It was a reasonable, well-thought-out plan, and its defeat added fuel to the controversy. Opinions about so drastic a remedy as secession for the real and supposed wrongs were not unanimous, however, and the "regular" political organizations, which had something to lose, fought bitterly against the move. But, though the vote was close, regarded by historians to have been crooked, and was appealed, it was finally settled that the charter and the separation had both carried.

It seemed a great victory, and but one member of the St. Louis delegation to the Constitutional Convention had been fearful of it. One Nicholas Martell had opposed separation saying, "I am in favor of total consolidation, but I am not in favor of dividing it (the county) splitting and hacking it in this manner. I vote No." And his was a lone voice--the pack was in full cry.

The city's area was increased from 18 square miles to 61.37, the area provided for in the new scheme. Most of the newly annexed area was sparsely populated and was deemed ample for the city's future growth. The immediate general reaction of the city was one of jubilation; the city had been emancipated. And while it is easy now to fault those who caused the action, we ought not to forget that a century ago the addition of 43 square miles to the city's area seemed adequate indeed.

There is, however, no question that the separation was a horrible error, totally unnecessary, even admitting the huge corruption in the county government of that time. As Cassella says:

"Entirely too much emphasis had been placed on the assertion that the county court was imposing its control upon the city.....The voting population of the city so far outnumbered that of the other sections of the county that officials......generally reflected the preference of the city voters. If the energy generated in opposition to the county court.....had been exerted in securing a reform administration, the long-run results might have been far more satisfactory. St. Louis might have achieved the advantages of home rule without resorting to the drastic surgery of separation."

The euphoria did not last long. By 1900 the city and county were quickly becoming a single urban area, and the existence of the two governments began to irritate and to accentuate all mutual problems. Increasingly the separation was seen to be an error, and four attempts in this century to put Humpty Dumpty together again have failed. There have been small successes in the establishment of both the Metropolitan Sewer District (1954) and the Zoo-Museum District (1970) but the basic problems remain.

So it is that a century later the situation is partly reversed with the inner, parent city steadily losing its more affluent residents to the county, its total population declining and its tax base eroding. In addition, its welfare burdens are increasing as its population mix has become increasingly black; its school system is suffering; its crime is both expensive and frightening (though, in all fairness, perhaps no worse than in all major American cities), and its citizens are somewhat unhappy with a general feeling of malaise.

These conditions, so evident to all, suggest that answers ought to be sought to the questions so often asked--how can the city and county get together, and can the city itself be saved?

Now it is the American way to believe that all problems can be solved and all questions answered if only enough sweat, imagination and money are brought to bear. But faith in our ability to find solutions has been shaken by the results of the spending, research and statesmanship of the last 30 years. There is little to show for them but corruption, bribery, unsuccessful housing, rising crime, disbelief in our corporations and our elected rulers, and our low standing in the regard of most nations. As a nation, we waver in our purposes and, worse, we do not seem to know what they are or ought to be. Nevertheless, hope remains that a solution to the city-county problem can be found.

The two, by now ancient, questions as to the city and county are hard nuts to crack, and, as noted, what has been accomplished to date is almost nil. It would seem that in order to examine the matter, we ought first to decide from what base we begin. I mean, of course, that we must ask ourselves what is our present condition and then try to perceive our options for the future.

To begin, then, let us not fall into the error of thinking that the old city is without great strengths, for in it are most of the good qualities of the entire metropolis. These qualities are surprisingly many and listing some of them may be useful. Consider:

> St. Louis University
> Washington University's famous Medical School (which is within the city limits, as is the eastern edge of the mother university).
> A fine Junior College
> The garden of Henry Shaw
> The Zoo
> The Planetarium
> The Art Museum
> The Symphony
> The Missouri Historical Society
> The Municipal Opera

There is, nevertheless, no denying that with the area's expansion, the old inner city has surrendered some of its excellence to the surrounding county. Two junior colleges, and the splendid Webster, Maryville and Lindenwood Colleges are county domiciled, as is the huge branch of the state university, UMSL. And hospitals and physicians move in increasing numbers to the county, but the Medical School anchors remain firm in the city and seem fixed in their purpose to stay.

The garden of Henry Shaw on Tower Grove Avenue is one of five or ten important botanical gardens of the entire world, and under its current management it has the promise and potential of rising to the summit. It offers not only great beauty, but its research also looms large in today's world which is nearly on the verge of widespread famine. It attracts, moreover, continually increasing financial support and public interest.

The St. Louis Zoo is a good one, and very much on the ascendancy since the establishment of the District Plan. While not on the plane of San Diego, New York, or the Smithsonian at Washington; still, its strengths are considerable, and it is generally well liked. It, too, is well supported and grows in stature.

I have difficulty in assessing the strengths of the St. Louis Art Museum. That it has a great deal of value, including a constantly growing collection, some of which is superb by the most rigid standards, is unquestioned; but it is at least somewhat below the institutions in Washington, Cleveland, Chicago, Philadelphia and Los Angeles; and, of course, is not to be compared with the great museums of New York. But then St. Louis is a regional city, and I have heard my knowledgeable friends, such as Richard Weil, say that this museum is about what we ought to have. It also has greatly improved potential since the inception of the Zoo-Museum District with the accompanying growth in tax income.

In my time, it has employed at least one distinguished director in the person of Perry Rathbone, who, in addition to his primary job, aided and encouraged private collections. Of this there is more elsewhere, but in the context of this

257

argument it must be regarded as a good museum which serves the needs of St. Louis in the educational and visual arts pretty well. Then, too, it now has a young director, James N. Wood, who gives great promise.

Currently the Symphony, if expenditures mean anything, is first rate; but again not on the level of New York, Boston, Philadelphia, Chicago or Cleveland. It is presently housed at Powell Hall in the inner city, but it is hard to see the Hall as a long range home; and in any event its audience is small. Like the Art Museum, there is more to be said of the Symphony in another chapter, but that it is a strong asset is certain.

Then, too, the city is the home of KMOX-Radio, a Columbia Broadcasting Company station. But this is no ordinary radio facility. Reputed to be the most successful one in the nation, headed by the energetic, civic-minded, and indefatigable Robert Hyland, it brings entertainment, sports, news and public affairs to the St. Louis area in high degree. Hyland's stable of performers, headed by the natural wit, Jack Carney, and the attractive sports figure, Jack Buck, probably involves a payroll topping any station in America.

(High marks must also be awarded Channel Nine, the public television station supported by the Arts and Education Council and by other subsidies; but it cannot be considered an inner-city project, for like most of Washington University, it is just over the city line.)

I draw a curtain over commercial television which is what it is everywhere--no more, no less.

Although my experience with the St. Louis Municipal Opera--the affectionately named Muny--has been substantial, having served as a trustee for 30 years and as its president and chairman, there is not much to add to what every St. Louisan knows about it. It is easy to evaluate--it is a civic, economic and recreational asset of great value, but it is somewhat more difficult to praise it without stint for the quality of its

258

productions. During the first half of its highly successful existence it was a repertory company presenting operettas of which there are dozens, and later the wonderful musicals of Kern, Rodgers, Porter, Hammerstein, Berlin, etc. As the "Robin Hood," "Red Mill" and "Student Prince" type of productions began to lose appeal, they were succeeded by "My Fair Lady," "Oklahoma!" and "Kiss Me Kate." But the great composers are old or are long gone, and it may be that the golden age of popular music will not soon return. As we write this, Hammerstein, Romberg, Porter and Coward are no longer with us, and Berlin, Rodgers, Lerner and Loewe are growing old.

Added to the lack of talent is the fact that Broadway no longer spawns musicals by the score. How can it, when it costs over half a million to produce a musical, which can close in two weeks, and even if moderately successful, will hardly return its investment?

Slowly and ponderously, the Muny has moved from its many decades of schmaltz into a certain amount of quality--The Royal, Dutch and Stuttgart ballet companies, Moiseyev Dancers, Broadway productions, etc.--and to the one-man, one-night stands apparently so much in demand. In any case, one thing is certain: The Muny is a pillar of the town and as much a part of its logo as Budweiser, the baseball Cardinals and the fabled shoe industry.

And if it is an opulent example of superb mediocrity, it has, nevertheless, during its nearly 60 years, built and maintained the only non-profit, recreational, cultural (well, OK, *semi*-cultural) organization which, without tax or philanthropic aid, has supported itself and built a $5 million theatre from its own earnings. Some 20 million tickets have been sold during these 60 years, many of these millions to visitors who have contributed collaterally to the city's economy.

Then there is the gigantic professional athletic system, both the baseball and football Cardinal teams and the hockey Blues--all three of which are civic powerhouses involving huge payrolls and substantial capital investment, and drawing scores of thousands of visitors and millions of dollars to St. Louis.

All of the above are perhaps the major assets, but there are dozens of lesser values, a Planetarium, the Historical Society, secondary schools, restored houses of museum quality and last, and perhaps most important of all, the heart of the finance and banking community.

There are three major bank holding companies in St. Louis: Mercantile, First Union and Boatmen's. Formerly known as the "downtown banks," their officers tend to have a community viewpoint a little broader than those of the industrial corporate leaders. In fact, they must.

The leaders of Monsanto, Busch, McDonnell-Douglas, Interco and all the rest may or may not be intensely concerned for the welfare of the region--indeed some like Gussie Busch, Jim McDonnell and Buster May, have been superb. But their primary cares will be for their own organizations. And in these days of conglomerate corporations, inevitably they would locate a plant elsewhere if necessary--just as they would discard a sickly subsidiary.

The banks and the utilities have no such options, for their business is in and of St. Louis, and they must try to save and build it. Thus there is the record of Jim Hickok of First National, and the Stadium construction; Lasater of Mercantile, and the Mercantile Center; Brandin of the Boatmen's, and their tower; and Stalnaker of General American Life, and his imaginative office building by the brilliant Philip Johnson. Without them and their influence, the Convention Center and its accompanying new hotels could not have come into existence. All of which is to say that there is solid determination that downtown shall not disappear.

All right then, enough of the euphoric good stuff--the sweetness and light is clear, but it does not spread very far. The other side of the coin is dark indeed. There are dozens--no scores, well, maybe even hundreds--of blocks north of Olive and Lindell and west of 12th that are full of windowless houses, ransacked apartments, littered streets; if not quite so abandoned as these whole neighborhoods, there are areas farther west and north which are not far from blight. Motorists will do well to avoid some of this area even in daylight, and blight and decay seem perilously close to the best of streets, even unto Portland, Pershing, Kingsbury and Lindell.

That there are strong locations, almost like medieval, baronial, castle strongholds in the midst of lawless savagery, is cause for hope. And some of the experimentation has been good; e.g., Laclede Town works well, and so does Plaza Square, as, I suppose, does the Teamsters' apartment complex on Grand Avenue. There is the fine conception of new living space sponsored by the hospitals and medical schools in the inner-city Forest Park-Kingshighway area, and there are the Ralston Purina efforts on the near South Side. One can only hope for their unqualified success.

But the problem diminishes hardly a whit because of these accomplishments; the blighted area is too large, too widespread, and too poverty-ridden to be aided by them. The questions of city survival and the city-county relationship, it seems to me, are essentially one, not two.

To tell it like it is--well, the root of the problem is the race situation. All over America, not just in St. Louis, there lies a kind of euphemistic haze which prevents open discussion or acknowledgment of this basic problem. As a result there is no attempt to solve it via a frontal attack.

Oh, it's talked about constantly, but clandestinely, furtively, in about the same way as venereal disease and cancer once were; but openly and courageously--hardly ever. I have no doubt that if there were no blacks in the inner city, the political combination of city and county, in one form or another, would now be in the making, if not already accomplished. But I have seen the obstacles clearly.

In 1970, when we were politically engaged in the effort to bring about the Zoo-Museum District, I made a number of appearances at various town hearings and meetings in the county. Many of these were attended by interested citizens who were decent enough and were there because of something that would affect or infringe upon their homes and families. It was shocking and sometimes almost frightening to see the utter hatred which flashed when the matter of a city-county merger was raised.

It was all too apparent that they feared the blacks as harmful to their physical safety, to their property values and to their children's schools. Many of them have, with no little effort, moved to the county from the city, believing that they were insuring their families better education, more stable housing, less chance of being victimized or vandalized. And which of us would say there is no understanding of their concerns?

Do not, however, ask a countian, no matter how intelligent or well favored (or liberal), especially if he is a politician, why he does not favor a coupling with the city. If you do, you will get a dozen reasons why it is inadvisable. But never the real one. It simply is not to be publicly mentioned.

Well, then, what is going to happen? What is the future of the St. Louis area--always assuming that it has one, and *that* we must assume, if only because in all history the future has always rolled around. Even Rome when Alaric was storming its walls had a future, and 1500 years later is a highly regarded city. True enough, Sparta, Troy, Corinth have vanished as have Carthage, Ephesus and perhaps 10,000 others, but this alternative we discard; otherwise, there's no point in this exercise. The future, then, with the solutions to the St. Louis problems, can come in at least two ways, or with a combination of both. Either the consolidation of city and county can be forced upon us by central authority, or we can make a bold effort to meet and conquer the dragon head-on. It seems to me, however, that we are unlikely to take the latter, voluntary course and that, therefore, the former is the more probable.

I am one who 15 years ago was converted by Riencourt, in his book "The Coming Caesars," to the certainty that this democracy, like all others, will give way to a dictatorship in some form; and I find that a good many who then accused me of being batty on the subject have come to agreement. Whether or not you have thought about the possibility, you will certainly allow that central authority will continue to increase and encroach if for no other than purse-string reasons. The hand that writes the checks will, and does, make the rules.

Witness how for months and even years we waited, with bated breath, for decision on location of our regional airport, on federal grants for hospitals, universities and the arts, and on revenue-sharing for the balancing of municipal budgets. Those same people who, 20 years ago, correctly prophesied that acceptance of governmental help would lead to federal interference with the recipient's operation are now the loudest wailers and protestors if the funds do not keep coming.

On the surface, some of it looks good and very necessary, for how else could clean-air policies be enforced, or the rivers and lakes be kept clean, except by the threat of withholding funds? I have no quarrel with that; it is perhaps a few degrees better than the outright dictator, and if there is small chance of composition of city and county by agreement, perhaps it is the best--maybe the only--prospect.

But before exploring the chances of an improved regional political structure, I should like to try to come to grips with the black problem, at the same time recognizing the inadequacy of my experience and the far greater qualifications of the experts.

I begin by quoting from Carl Holman, the distinguished president of the Urban Coalition, a friend of and advisor to black leaders, and one of those most trusted by blacks who are not leaders. According to the *New Yorker* (May 24, 1976) from which this material was obtained, Holman, a recipient of a Whitney Fellowship at Yale, editor, teacher, civil rights worker, has devoted his life to improving the condition of blacks and the relations between blacks and whites.

The interviewer and author who has known Holman for some years says: "I was surprised by the intensity and despair of his remarks." The following remarks are direct *partial* quotations, and I have taken great pains in making sure that they are not out of context.

"Cities are out. They're out of style--despite all the noise about New York. Some urban experts suggest that the blacks who were salvageable were swept up and out into the suburbs--into decent jobs and all that. And they were acceptable because they do not frighten people with their difference. So the ones who are left behind are locked in a life style that the rest of America finds repugnant and they are considered unsalvageable, you see, and it is considered a waste to spend time and money on them.

"People have been going over these great land workers for the blacks, and nobody's looking at the rifts that began to appear. Busing is a trap for blacks. There is so much hostility and tension. There are three options: busing, compensatory education, career education. We are losing all three options and ending up with zilch. The truth is people are not happy with the status quo. There is a great move to the status quo ante. I think it is a mistake, if one looks at race in this country, to look at legislation or the so-called big issues because most blacks are not involved in these. Now blacks see their leaders ignored by the executive branch of the government, ignored by the legislature, ignored by the media and they bring no victories. You talk about black mayors and they say, 'Yea, what can they do?' What's happening now is a great cynicism not only among black leaders but among young blacks as regards their leaders. You see a kind of dangerous cynicism among young blacks, the kind of despair where you don't care whether you live or you die. What can we say? We can't keep going back and saying, 'Look at our civil rights victories.'

"Even white people think politicians don't care about them. Then what the hell do you think blacks think? There's a great feeling of being out of it--outsiders in your own country--which was a feeling they began to lose in the 60's and it's coming back double-barreled now. It's beyond such things as the percentage of blacks that are unemployed. It's the basic non-caring for those who don't make it. Too bad about them, I've got mine, Jack.

"Bernard Anderson, a young black economist at the Wharton School has been saying that we are coming up with a generation of young blacks who have never had any job experience. They have been jobless and they are going to stay jobless and can't even collect unemployment benefits. The President knows what it means when he says we have to wait three or four years to reduce unemployment by any significant amount. And he knows another thing--he knows he is not going to be contested by liberal whites, as he might have been before, because it is less and less popular to defend blacks, and because blacks in the know have become more and more disaffected and vote less and less."

At this point the *New Yorker* reporter asked Holman what might happen, and this is how he answered and ended the interview:

"In terms of young blacks and blacks who are out of work,

they don't feel any of the old allegiances--to liberals, to labor. I see a kind of opacity--you can't get through. The kind of subterranean and sporadic violence we're getting now is worse than before. My son said that he knows a lot of young black folks who say, 'What's the use of living? We might as well be back in slavery because then we'd get a meal.' It was so different from the kind of militant statement you'd get a few years ago. Young people feeling defeated is unusual. You get to the point of asking what the options in this country are if you want to get up and out. The options for blacks are shrinking. They'll show you a black who has a fancy job in a computer firm, but the cold hard fact is that the income gap between blacks and whites in the last 15, 20 years has not altered to any significant degree. What has altered is that there is a thin layer of blacks who are getting ahead. And that's a grim, grim reality. Nobody knows what the final straw will be."

And there you have it from one thoughtful, distinguished, crusading, fine black. He has no answers, cannot see the future; or, if he can, it looks dismal and he has no solution. I put into three categories the blacks of which he talks: the thin layer of those getting ahead--doing well; the young with any education and thoughtfulness who are discouraged; and the great mass of the oncoming generation whose education is hardly worth the name, who are, and will remain, jobless.

A little while ago, when I began this chapter, it was about city and county, and the need for somehow putting them together. We have wandered far afield on the race question, but again I am convinced the two are intertwined to the point of being inseparable; so, painful as it is, it seems to me of great import to keep exploring the future possibility of--well, of what? Do we think the solution as integration, as equality before the law and in education, socially in terms of a fused race? We do know that in Brazil, which has, for a couple of hundred years, been fusing native Indians, Africans and white Europeans, there has been much boasting of no racism; and it sounds good, except that now there appears a rash of books indicating that, far from being all sweetness and light, there too the black is at the bottom of the ladder.

It is necessary for me to talk to those who know more about the problem than I--blacks, sociologists, politicians. As in the quotations from the Holman interview, it is difficult to find much optimism. One of my especially close friends is Circuit Judge Thomas McGuire, who succeeded me as president of the Zoo. Tom is a fine citizen, had a remarkable record as City Counselor, has served in civil, criminal and juvenile court procedures--in short, knows the score.

He has said to me, "What can you do? A black girl comes before you pregnant at the age of 12; by the time she is 15 she may have three children. The welfare thing takes over. And how is education possible? What does it mean?"

So you say, "OK, Tom, what then do you see in the future?"

His reply: "I don't know."

Who does know? Who has an answer? The liberals--not all, but it seems most--cling to the worn-out, already discredited answers. By that, I mean their earlier ideas that good housing, equal opportunity and, above all, education would solve the integration problems. There is good will and a modicum of good sense, or rather sweet reasonableness, in these concepts--but experience thus far has indicated failure.

All too familiar are our St. Louis examples: Pruitt-Igoe, typical of housing failure; child welfare and food stamps-- excellent in purpose but counterproductive of massive ripoff and corruption, and of generations finding work unnecessary; the St. Louis public school system administered by magnificent public servants, but deteriorating into educational mockery, producing illiterate "graduates."

You and I--not only the ultraliberals--have said the blacks

267

must be educated, that it is the only solution, that it will take many years, even many scores of years, but that eventually it will provide the answer. All of us who gave a damn believed it. And billions were spent, but somehow something has gone terribly wrong. I am almost persuaded that education does not come to those who do not really want it and strive for it.

What? You say no schoolboy wants it, and yet the millions of reluctants have been more or less well educated. Yes, the boy *was* reluctant, but his parents, his family, his priest, vicar, rabbi--they counted on it, insisted, and the boy had to accept his sorry lot and realize there was no way to learn the algebra, geography, history and the language except by strain, sweat and suffering.

But at this point I see that I really don't know what is happening to the school system, to the black pupils in it; nor do I know too much about the blacks in St. Louis generally. Two people who do know come to mind: George Wendell, Professor of Urban Affairs at Saint Louis University, and Daniel Schlafly of the school board.

First I talk to George Wendell, a bright, concerned, optimistic man, and one who knows the St. Louis community well. For him I have three questions:

Can city and county be somehow put back together? What is happening to the blacks, and what is their future? What of the city itself?

Wendell is by nature optimistic--sees the glass as half-full rather than half-empty. And he says:

"About 8,000 blacks per year have been leaving the North Side of the inner city and moving mostly to North County. And they have been moving up to middle class. But I make a distinction; there are two kinds, as it were, of middle class. The true middle class have both middle-class income and desire as to style of living and education for their kids. The second group have middle-class income mostly because both man and wife work. But intellectually they are still slum dwellers, children are neglected, no thought for education and all that."

"But, Dr. Wendell," I ask, "what of those left in the inner city? Are those the unsalvageable last remainder of which Carl Holman talks?"

He shrugs his shoulders. "I guess so."

"Then how can you be so optimistic?"

"Well, look at those who are making it--doing well."

"But Holman calls them a thin layer."

"Yes, now, but there will be more. Here's Jackson, a marvelous black, in Chicago, respected by them, preaching the Protestant ethic--they've got to do it on their own, as did the other minorities. That's encouraging. I tell you I'm not the only optimist. Bancroft sees it this way; as was the case of the Irish, Poles, Jews, Italians--you write off the first generation and work with the next generation. Your reward comes with them."

"I see that, doctor, but what are we to make of the stories that the oncoming generation has no discipline in the schools, often beats hell out of the teacher, has no concept of study or learning. Is it true that many of them 'graduate' and are illiterate?"

"Yes, they are often just passed on." (Note to myself--check this with Dan Schlafly; is it really so bad as gossip has it?)

"But anyhow, you believe that eventually the education has to work?"

"Well, it has to, doesn't it?" I don't consider this an answer and go on.

"Doctor, can we now talk city and county?"

"Oh, yes, there I think we are much better off. When Tucker was mayor, there was little rapport with the original McNary, the county supervisor. Then Cervantes and Larry Roos, evidently, cordially hated each other. Now John Poelker is mayor, Gene McNary supervisor--they meet, respect each other, are working on many items of cooperation. And you might know that Victor Brannon of Governmental Research is working on a study as to the possibility of reentry of the city into the county."

"We have, of course, made a few passes at that, or a merger, or a borough plan before, without a glimmer of success."

"Yes, but we made horrible mistakes, perhaps we will do it better and succeed."

"And now, doctor, the third question; What of the city itself? We can see the downtown progress, but the whole town--do we keep on losing?"

"I don't think so. There is great energy, the hospital plans, the Ralston rehabilitation effort, the group in the West End. We don't need any more failures like Pruitt-Igoe, but the repairing of neighborhoods is not unthinkable. The town will live."

I confess to disappointment and came away with a liking and admiration for him, but with a sense that I got no answers. He had spoken of the latest Governmental Research study for city reentry into the county, and only two days before, I heard its director Victor Brannon's preliminary report to the members of Civic Progress on the matter--then confidential. And I thought what Brannon said was naive.

What he had said was this: were the city to reenter the county immediately, or anyhow soon, there would be a saving of $5 million in employee efficiency alone. The so-called "county" offices of the city would be turned back to the county where they belonged, but the efficiency of county offices (recorder of deeds, tax collector, etc.) was such that this saving would result. However the county would have to resign itself to the fact that the city, to some extent, (several millions?) still would be short of income and of necessity would increase the county's cost--i.e., taxes.

But it is difficult for me to see that their so-called advantageous savings and increase in efficiency are anything but political liabilities. Elsewhere I have mentioned an alderman, Ray Leisure, whose main interest in city government is the jobs he can obtain and control. "Well," said Brannon, "you must fire 900 of the city employees."

I don't think he was serious, but if he was, my answer would be, "You want to bet?" Certainly the city has too many employees--but they are the strength of many of the politicians, the guts of the machine.

Efficiency, thy name is anathema!

Consider the county with its 93 municipalities, its 26 fire departments, its 54 police departments, its (believe it or not!) 106 taxing authorities and its inability to refine and consolidate these. If Ladue cannot marry Frontenac, and Clayton cannot marry Richmond Heights, then try to imagine how much love they would have for St. Louis.

Again, the fundamental matter of education must be considered--it was time to talk to Schlafly. Before recounting what he said I want to record what this man is. I am not his close friend, he is 15 or 20 years younger than I, but I have known him a long time and do not know a more superb human being. I put him in a class with the late Ethan Shepley, and I have no higher praise. A Catholic, and I suppose a devoted one, Dan has almost single-handedly carried on his slender shoulders the burden of keeping quality in the public schools of St. Louis--an anomaly for a man who might be expected to be interested only in parochialism. He has fought the greed of the self-seekers who were accustomed to using the school system and its finances to their own ends, and time after time he has won. Like Henley's man "his head is bloody but unbowed;" bloody because it is inevitable that he loses too. The bastards are all around him.

Nevertheless, he answers the bell and holds his position

271

against bigots, crooks, teachers' unions, petty politicians and professional blacks, because he is a natural-born fighter, and because his concerns for education and for the blacks seem unending. Born a couple of thousand years ago, he would likely have been burned, stoned or crucified.

Not that he looks the part; he snarls, uses the four-letter words, talks of himself as a realist, and strives--but not very well--to conceal his basic, warm decency. Nor can he help being an optimist; why else would he keep on fighting? So it was that I asked him:

"Dan, what of the future of the blacks in St. Louis? What happens to them and to the city?"

"Well, to begin with, they move out of the inner city. Those who can are leaving the North Side--the inner part. And new ones are not coming in--their population has declined just as has the general population."

"Yes, Wendell says we have lost about 8,000 a year to the county--especially to the North County. You would agree?"

"Yes, and the school population goes down too."

"And the school population is two-thirds black now. Is the school system continually deteriorating?"

Dan chewed on this one for awhile before answering. You could see it hurt him--then:

"Yes and no. Many teachers are bad, inadequate, and here's why. Twenty years ago the postwar baby boom was hitting us, we had not enough teachers, not enough school rooms. Classes went to 40 in size, and teachers, well, we took bodies, what we could get. We've still got those inadequate people, with tenure, now built into the system.

"We did have Kottmeyer, first under superintendent Phil Hickey, then after Hickey's death, as superintendent himself. He was great. But in recent years there have been promotions only from within, from the administrative and teaching ranks of that same inadequate personnel. That's why we had to go

272

outside for new blood when we took Wentz, the new white superintendent. He's great, the very best. But we won't hold him without complete board support. Anyhow, classes are smaller--things look better."

"But we read you 'graduate' illiterates; is that better?"

"No, of course not. And we do, but it's not hopeless. Look, the number of concerned black parents is growing. I've been to night meetings at all or nearly all of our schools; they are there; they want education for their kids."

"Oh, come on, come off it! Wendell writes that 44 per cent of all births in St. Louis are illegitimate; Judge McGuire tells me of mere girls with three children; Andrew Brimmer, black economist and former Federal Reserve Board governor says those with few skills and less education are falling behind and that nearly three million or 28 per cent of all black children are fatherless. How do you find concerned parents among these?"

"There's that, I admit. But the worst is here now. You can't compare these children with those of the immigrant waves of the last century, the Irish, Germans, Jews, Poles, Italians. Or maybe you can--this way. Those people were motivated. Their children, or anyhow their grandchildren, became lawyers, doctors, engineers, teachers. For 75 per cent, the mobility was upward. All right, that won't happen with the blacks in those numbers. Not 75 per cent, I grant that, but, yes, I think 51 per cent. And many are already doing it.

"I'll tell you this, though, about black politics in St. Louis. They don't have the clout they are generally believed to have. A few years ago they said we'll have a black mayor by 1975. Well, 1975 has come and gone and no black mayor, and you won't have one by 1980. Why? Because half of them don't register and of those that do, 80 per cent don't vote. So the whites in South St. Louis and the rest of the town can always elect if they really want to."

There it is--you may doubt his optimism but he does care,

and he fights skillfully. He is right and so is Wendell about those who are making it. Many do work hard and effectively, and it is gratifying and encouraging to see the quality of Ted McNeal, the erstwhile state senator and police board president; Judge Theodore McMillian and scores--hundreds--of others perhaps not so prominent but capable and earnest in their work. The heartaches these men must have, because of the general educational picture and the crime scene, can only be guessed at. The non-black must surely believe that if he is concerned, then what must be the quagmire of discouragement in which the black himself struggles?

Hope is not lost. There is greater opportunity, and the invasion or rather opening of the teaching, medical, banking and legal professions has been progressive--even spectacular--and we are beginning to see the near domination of professional athletics by the blacks. The chief obstacle as I see it is the *difference*. The black is black and I obviously do not mean this as a racist statement. But nevertheless, you dare not say it.

I have no patience with the arguments between anthropologists that brain characteristics are the same or inferior or superior, or that environment is all and heredity nothing, etc., etc. Argue it forever, they are different; the color is not the same.

The human race, this ignorant, spiteful species to which we belong, does not like differences. And it's no good saying, as Hammerstein did, that we have to be taught to hate. Baloney! Hate comes easy. Here's a modern score card, the lineup for today's gladiatorial contest:

North Protestant Ireland versus South,
Bangladesh versus India,
India versus Pakistan,
Arabs versus Israel,
Moslem Lebanon versus Christian Lebanon,

Greece versus Turkey,
Cambodia versus Vietnam,
Ethiopia versus Somaliland.

And you may have noticed that they play with real bullets. How many were obliterated in World War II? Twenty million? But all of the above listed for today's games are the same color. Their differences are what? Well, religion and cultural background--differences which would seem to a philosopher so trivial as to make killing unthinkable. And yet they kill. What then of the color differences? No matter, perhaps the American dream which has worked so well for others can also handle the color and social differences--but it doesn't yet know how. Yes, there is optimism here in St. Louis, but as yet no method, no clear, evident fathering to success.

There is for me, then, no answer to the problem of the blacks in St. Louis; but one thing is clear, that the problem is another hindrance to a rejoining of city and county--one more hurdle which did not exist during the previous four attempts.

*****

The separation as an instance of the region's bad luck is obvious to all, but it would be in error to think of it as the only one. I suppose all cities can count their past mistakes, but it seems to me that this town has often chosen its own misfortune. Here, there were no devastating earthquakes, floods, plagues, drouths, wars or famines; but there were dynamic decisions on the part of city fathers leading to disaster, and there were non-decisons, lassitude or plain fatuousness which served equally well. Of all, losing the early railroads was the worst.

A hundred and fifty years ago, the town's pride was very great. Why there was even conversation to the effect that the capitol would soon have to be moved here from Washington. A hundred and more steamboats were tied up daily at the river front; the West had to be opened up and this was the juncture of the two great rivers; the flow of goods on the Mississippi must change from steamboat to flatboat here because of the shallow channel above us; and we were already rich and mighty comfortable.

It was about this time that some damfool bankers in the effete East were playing with a new steam toy called a railroad, and so bumptious were they that they schemed to project its rusty iron rails and rickety wooden trestles over the mountains and as far west as St. Louis. Actually they had already had a little success, having gotten from Baltimore all the way to Ohio (the B & O), and they proposed to the St. Louis bankers an extension to the Mississippi.

The turndown was emphatic and prompt. Any one with a grain of common sense could see that the railroad was an unnatural toy, a fad soon to fade away, and that nature had provided the mighty rivers for man's use. Anyone could see that St. Louis, situated as it was, occupied the catbird seat and was blessed by the Almighty as the exchange point for the "exotic products of the South" (New Orleans, Central America and the Carribean) and the great natural forest and mineral products of the North (Minnesota, Wisconsin, etc.).

Moreover, the West was about to be opened and who but St. Louis had a monopoly on the wide Missouri on which flowed the great fur trade?

What followed hardly needs repeating. The eastern bankers and railroad people scratched their heads and searched out a village of some 2500 souls at the bottom of Lake Michigan. Within two score years the small town of Chicago became the rail center of the continent, hog butcher to the world, manufacturing rival to the East and, not long after, the nation's second city. When the railroads bypassed St. Louis by building the Illinois Central from Chicago to New Orleans and created a shortcut to Kansas City and the West via the Rock Island bridge which crossed the Mississippi to the north of us, there was an abrupt collapse of the river monopoly of which the town had been so proud.

The innate vitality of St. Louis was hardly impaired, however, and both spirits and prosperity remained high. Indeed when David B. Francis held his World's Fair and Olympic games here in 1904, the city rode the crest--and many hold the fair to be the high point in the region's history, believing that we have been sliding downhill ever since. The elan of the town was such that its denizens were pleased rather than upset by the slogan "First in shoes, first in booze, and last in the American League."

As late as 1927, when I arrived on the local scene, a half-century after the divorce of city and county, the more thoughtful knew the separation had been a mistake, but the matter was of no general concern. True, the county seemed considerably closer to the city than in 1876, when distances had been formidable. Then, there had been local steam trains but there were neither automobiles nor the electric trolley system which for some four decades was to carry most urban and suburban traffic.

There is a word to say here about that trolley which today is unknown to all but the oldsters. It was such a successful vehicle, so efficient and relatively simple that in our inimitable American fashion we abandoned it in favor of the bus and the private auto. But if not to the trolley, we will return to some form of public transportation. A prophet is usually a fool, but I'd like, nevertheless, to guess that perhaps nine decades will suffice from the Henry Ford explosion about 1910 to the collapse of General Motors. Which is to say that the oil shortage, the pollutant factors, the necessities brought on by the general lowering of living standards will all come together about then.

Nor is all this a cause for panic--plenty of money was lost on streetcar stocks and the country survived. Don't sell your GM stock either, because (a) I may be wrong and (b) even if I am right, the company will likely roll with the punches and head in other directions, even more profitably.

*****

Is it then so devastatingly bad that city and county are separated? New York is not fragmented yet it lies almost hopeless in squalor; the mayors of all big cities, whether consolidated or not, cry bankruptcy and despair. Is the city any worse off than it would be if it were a member of the county which enfolds it and were but a sister city of the 93 municipalities and the 105 taxing authorities which constitute the county?

Why not first try the simple things? Why not consolidate within the county? After subtracting the city's 62 square miles in 1876, the county still had 510 square miles within its boundaries. In this area are a collection of 93 towns and villages, and the aforementioned 54 police forces, 26 fire districts and departments, a half-dozen independent sewer companies in addition to the Metropolitan District which services the East County, school districts and much open land outside the limits of any municipality. The county is united in only one way, and that is in its steely determination not to take in the city.

I would be in error to ascribe this attitude entirely to the fear of the black. The political and petty bureaucratic officeholders, and those who would like to be in their shoes, have great interests in the status quo. Mergers, reorganizations, elimination of overlapping services could certainly give a better break to the taxpayers, but they would also eliminate jobs, lessen opportunities for patronage and business favoritism and take away petty empires. Who needs that! (Of course this applies to the city as well, particularly to the city blacks, who fear they will lose political clout if they become only a small part of a government of two million.)

The ultimate in local authority and irritating triviality is, I submit, evidenced by the seven changes in speed limits between Lindbergh and Schoettler Roads where there is no change in traffic pattern--and that's, of course, because different authorities control the various stretches. But, again, what to do?

Hope and idealism are in no way synonymous, and there is hope. There are three avenues which could lead to some form of consolidation, or at least three that occur to me. First, there is voluntary cooperation on a large scale, including city re-entry, borough plans, mergers, etc. Forget it! That kind of voluntary action looks good in a *Post* editorial or at a meeting of the League of Women Voters, but I don't see it getting much farther.

Second, there are degrees of cooperation to solve individual problems. The Zoo-Museum District and the Sewer District were voluntary efforts which succeeded because the public became convinced of the necessity and there was little political opposition. Perhaps this could be extended--perhaps to a Metropolitan Police District, or Fire District--and in so doing the tough problems (school, racial fears, etc.) could be bypassed. All right, so you would not have an ideal consolidation, but isn't a half loaf pretty good? However, districts are not easy to come by either, and I rather favor the third plan which involves enforcement from outside--from the Feds.

Now I am not in love with the process; it's just that I believe that's how it will come. Not everything the agencies do is bad; occasionally their enforcement powers or, anyhow their money, can be constructive. Let's for a moment think about our multifarious police forces, their lack of communication, their differences in quality, and realize that in all of England 40 million are served by the London Metropolitan police. Patently, 55 organizations make no sense, but, just as clearly, there will be no real voluntary consolidation so long as Ladue likes to see its uniformed boys whom it knows well, and Frontenac wants to control its own. Now the Congress under the so-called Safe Streets Act of 1967 has been pouring huge amounts of money into the states to aid in crime prevention and control. There's some question as to its results, if any, but anyhow Missouri's share has been in the area of $18 million a year. It's commonly known as L.E.A. (Law Enforcement Assistance) money, and I did some work for Jack Danforth for a couple of years in connection with it. Additionally St. Louis received direct grants and altogether received the lion's share of funds in the state. It now depends on it, as do all the other recipients of Uncle's largess.

Let us imagine a little farther--can we not visualize a Washingtonian, one fine day, calling in a colleague and saying:

"Joe, is it true that St. Louis County and the city have 55 different police forces?"

"Yes, I believe they do."

"But that's crazy! Why?"

"Well, I don't know; that's the way they seem to like it."

"Have they tried to do anything about it?"

"Not much I guess."

"How much federal money do they get?"

"Oh, I'd have to look. Maybe $6 million a year."

"Can't we do something there?"

"We could certainly try."

The more dependent we are on the money, the more willing we are to comply, and the more likely is a police district federally conceived and enforced. Can you not see it working with hospitals, fire departments? You have already seen the pressures on school districts. If you have a full-blown dictator, the genuine article, then you get the whole merger, perfect in all form--but assuming he does not appear, the central force is there, to command some betterment, and it will grow in power. Do we have, on the local scene, the people to make such actions possible--to guide such efforts intelligently and constructively? It is true that on the national scene we weep for our lack of heroes--the Bicentennial year provided no Adams, Lincoln, Jefferson or Franklin. But we have not been without giants in St. Louis, even in my day. These men loom large. Did not Jim McDonnell send men to the moon, knock from the sky the Russians' best fighter planes, and employ scores of thousands to the benefit of his town in so doing? Did not Edgar Queeny develop a small maker of aspirin and saccharin into the third or fourth largest chemical company of the world and, while he was doing it, bring Barnes Hospital back to its position as one of the great teaching hospitals of the Western World? Did not Jim Hickok almost single-handedly raise the spirits of the river city as he tramped the streets of downtown raising $20 million for the stadium complex?

Did not Jim Ford, a worn-out and dispirited banker, take new heart in the 30's, rejuvenate himself and make St. Louis clean of its disgraceful smoke? Did not Ethan Shepley and Tom Eliot raise a fairly stuffy "streetcar" university to a distinguished institution in their efforts at Washington University? Did not the extravagant, flamboyant, horse-riding playboy Gussie Busch emerge, upon the death of his cousin, as a dynamic businessman, a public benefactor, a citizen of high merit? There were some giants. Is the breed dead? Not likely--there must be the will, the energy, the creative imagination to do what ought to be--what can be--done to repair the city-county disaster of a century ago. The brains, talent, skills must be here though perhaps not in the public sector. I have no doubt of it. But they ought to get at it!

CHAPTER XII

"But good gracious, you've got to educate him first. You can't expect a boy to be vicious 'till he's been to a good school."

Saki

It is now 1978, the 202nd year of the Republic, the 76th year of my life spent in that Republic, and the 51st year of my residence in St. Louis. Nearly all the years have been happy ones, full of friends on all sides, an active if fairly mediocre business career and an increasing involvement in community affairs.

I know my limitations. I was and am not a particularly adept, shrewd, imaginative, analytical, charismatic, hard-working business type. I got by and I was lucky. Let's say I was as good as most, better than some and miles behind the real leaders both in St. Louis and in my own field, which was the health supply industry. I'm not sure that even now I understand what qualities make the giants what they are; I only know that I never had these qualities. But I got by with occasional flashes of capability and huge amounts of help from others.

And I had luck--lots of luck.

The first is that I lived at all past the age of 6. The year was 1908, and the scene was the frame house on Bradford Street in Charleston, West Virginia. I had been born there in June 1902, and was soon the elder of two boys as my brother Louis arrived just two years later. Our parents were David and Mayme Baer--a fine, middle-class, German-Jewish couple.

Louis had been saved at the age of 2, almost miraculously, from a vicious attack of spinal or cerebral meningitis only because the young, beautifully educated and later famous Dr. Friedenwald had but recently set up practice in the small town. Whether it was because he had few patients as yet, or whether he was influenced by the solid stature of the Baer couple, he did literally move into our house and did not leave it for 10 days. And he brought the infant through. Louis was left with only a slight speech defect which was afterwards cured. His physique was undamaged, and some years later Louis was active in football, wrestling and the like.

As for me, my illness was wrongfully diagnosed. I simply lost my appetite when I was 6, became listless and was obviously declining. The local doctor finally decided it was the ever-present (in those days) and dreadful tuberculosis called "consumption." He suggested Arizona, although he held out no real hope for that therapy.

"Well, perhaps," said my mother, Mayme, "but first we'll stop in Cincinnati."

This was the first big decision affecting my life; indeed it was the *sine qua non*, as without it I should have quickly died.

Cincinnati was not only our nearest big city and therefore would have good medicine, but also it had Baer relatives including Fanny Adler, a sister of one of our aunts and a trained nurse, who would know the medical score. Well, mother and I went to Cincinnati and through Fanny to a Dr. Christian E. Holmes. In about five minutes he found an atypical mastoiditis (I had never had an earache) which would require radical surgery. The operation, however, if it could be accomplished at all, must be delayed because the poisons which had invaded the entire system had affected my kidneys. It was chancy, the odds not good, but there was no choice. He had a private hospital on 8th Street, where I stayed for six to eight months, and here am I 69 years later.

Of course, Holmes was a great man--my first contact with the breed. Born in 1857 he "read" medicine, and in 1891 he married Bettie Fleischmann of the famous yeast family. Together they owned and ran the hospital. They were not only healers for me, but teachers and kindness itself. The child loved and was awed by them but naturally did not appreciate them.

I know I'm off the track in that this long-ago episode is far from St. Louis, but I can't leave it without saying that Holmes was not only among the best specialists of his age, he was the chief proponent and founder of the Cincinnati University Medical School. The Christian E. Holmes Hospital stands magnificent in his memory. He died, at last, shortly after World War I, from the infamous influenza, a direct result of his Army overwork at Camp Sherman, or so his biographer wrote.

The second piece of good luck for me also involved Holmes, who was by now a hero in our family, the first, incidentally, of a long list of physician heroes. About 1913, some five years after the first serious illness, I was threatened with another mastoid infection. This time it was in the other ear. Now there was an early diagnosis, however, and off we went to Cincinnati. I was in better shape, and treatment sufficed without surgery, but there were no antibiotics for quick resolutions of stubborn infections. Instead I had to undergo interminable irrigations, eardrum piercings for drainage, leech applications and general misery. Again a stay of several months was necessary, but there was a wonderful bonus--a fortunate throw-off from the sickness.

There and then I learned the pleasure of reading and experienced the excitement that books would hold for me. Nowadays an 11-year-old boy, in a hospital for months on end, would be busy with radio and television, both of which were yet to come in 1913. Then there were but books to pass the time and I acquired the grandest of all habits. I was not precocious and I read only the stuff that would appeal to an 11-year-old; but I did go through, or anyhow start, Alcott, Alger, Henty, Tom Swift and the Rover Boys. The pleasure was enormous.

Meccano was a new toy then, and construction could be undertaken on the hospital over-the-bed table. My father bought me a small set of the new building toy, and I used each painful dressing period or unpleasant trip to the treatment rooms as an excuse to extract additional parts, gear wheels and the like from mother, as bribe for undergoing pain. It wasn't easy, for money was scarce, but I did acquire quite an inventory of steel. My contraptions became increasingly elaborate.

Even though I was not destined for engineering, the recreation was great, the time passed, and there was definite education in the months spent there. So the illness had its compensations. I remember that when I came home to Charleston, even though I had missed a lot of school, I was promoted to the sixth grade in the fall, and my reading and spelling were well ahead of the class. In those days 11-year-olds in West Virginian public schools could read. One hears now of high school graduates who cannot, but there was none of that nonsense then.

In 1971 a small volume was published entitled *Baer-Lowenstein, A Family History*, and I was the author. It is, of course, a private book, as are all such family records, but I quote from it to establish my own background.

"The Baers came to America shortly after mid-19th century from Nagelsberg, Germany. Now Nagelsberg was and is a small, rather mean suburb of Kinzelsau, a town of about 8,000 to 10,000 in the province--then kingdom--of Wurttemberg. It is about 60 kilometers from the city of Stuttgart and lies above a pleasant valley, and, so far as I know, has no claim whatsoever to distinction. Therein was born and dwelt one Fiest Baer whose wife's name was Babette and these two were born respectively in 1817 and 1831. They were my paternal grandparents.

"They produced 12 assorted children, of whom the ninth was my father, David, born in the year 1865. Beginning in 1868 most of the 11 children who survived gradually emigrated to America settling in both Cincinnati, Ohio, and Charleston, West Virginia; but their mother Babette stayed at home until the death of her husband in late 1886. Then and only then, and accompanied by one son and one daughter, last remaining members of the family, did she consent to leave the Fatherland and to join her older, and by now pretty well-placed, children in America."

Why did my father, and several brothers and sisters, pick West Virginia? Actually I suspect he had little choice, since his older brother Ben was well established in the wholesale liquor trade and offered him a job. And a sixteen-year-old immigrant, ignorant of the language, and also of nearly everything else, wanted only to go to work and to study for his citizenship in America, the promised land. There were little or no welfare funds in those days, and it was work or go hungry.

As to my mother's side of the family, her Americanization was nearly a generation ahead, for she had been born in the same West Virginia town in 1876, the sixth child and third daughter of Salomon and Henrietta Loewenstein. The Loewenstein family was in Charleston because Salomon, my grandfather, had been in the Army of Western Virginia. He had served as cook and rifleman in a company whose captain was a nice young fellow named McKinley and whose regiment, the 23rd Ohio, was headed by an imposing Colonel, Rutherford B. Hayes.

Now it happened that the 23rd Ohio, for a considerable period late in the war, lay bivouacked in the pleasant hills about the Kanawha River which flows through the

286

spectacularly beautiful valley of Charleston. So it was that Loewenstein, having been a pedlar of some sort in Ohio before the Civil War, decided to stay where the prospect was pleasant. He was also a harness maker and was evidently experienced in leather making.

All of which is prelude to my appearance, as above noted, in 1902. Just as my first piece of good luck was the intelligent decision made by my mother to expose me to Cincinnati medicine, so my next good fortune resulted from another of her ideas, this one about education. She herself had had the usual small-town schooling which meant graduation from the local high school. There had been no thought of college, for after all, she was a girl, and besides, there was little money. Indeed but one of the brothers went to a university, and that was because he wanted to study law. They did manage the money, a pitifully small amount, for that effort, and it proved well spent as his career in law and banking was locally outstanding.

In any case, there were no such thoughts for Mayme, nor did she hold the slightest expectation and, so far as I know, desire for any further education. What she did have was an enormous respect for learning, as did her entire family. But I confess that now, 63 years later, I can only guess at her thinking in sending me off to an exclusive New England preparatory school.

Oh, I know how she found the name of Choate. She simply went to the fountainhead of all knowledge, Cincinnati, whereupon a distant cousin said that she knew of a school, a fine one in Connecticut. But why me? I can but guess that Mayme, having taught school for a year, having been told by a teacher that perhaps I had some possibilities, and feeling that the local schools weren't too much, decided to aim high. Moreover, it could have been that the brilliant young Rabbi Battan, who had seen me at Sunday School, urged her to send me away. I had actually started freshman year at high school, had been there one day when the following conversation ensued on my arrival home:

Mother: How was the first day at school?

Me: All right, I guess (OK was not then universal).

Mother: Well, you are not going back.

Me: Why not?

Mother: Because your father and I think the schools in Charleston are not very good and you should go away.

Me: (Suspiciously) Is this Dr. Battan's idea?

Mother: Never mind whose idea it is--you and I are going next week.

Me: Where--Exeter? (It was the single name I knew, a rich cousin having gone there.)

Mother: There is a fine school that Belle Stix in Cincinnati has told us about--the name is Choate.

Me: Well, all right, I guess.

It can be seen that I was docile, obedient and respectful. I did what I was told. It never would have occurred to me to rebel, or even question her decisions.

School had already started in late September, 1915, when the New Haven railroad deposited us in the strange (to me) but pleasant New England town of Wallingford about 11 miles north of New Haven. For the next five years it was my home, except for vacations. As the taxi drove us up to the Choate campus, and especially as we rounded the sweep of road up to Hill House, a feeling of awe arose. This was something beautiful and unimagined.

The school has grown in size now and encompasses many other buildings, a library, hospital-size infirmary, a gym, a winter exercise building, hockey rink, science buildings and more. The splendor must impress many new boys as they come in suspicioned innocence, but none I am sure, will be more dazzled than was the small West Virginia lad, fresh from Kanawha grade school. Into the headmaster's study we went, and there I met George St. John. I soon had no doubt that this was a great man and, in perspective, I still have small doubt.

I suppose he was then about 38, but, of course, I thought him a very mature, middle-aged man.

"Spell 'necessary'," he barked.

I did it.

"How much is 7 times 8--quickly!"

It was the proper amount.

"Who was the second President of the United States? Quickly now."

Again I had the answer.

I was in.

The Atwater House, where the boys of the lower school were lodged, no longer exists, having long since been abandoned, and I think razed, to be replaced by a group of red brick, white-columned Georgian buildings of the Choate pattern. Ah, but to me it was a very handsome building that first year, and even now in mists of nostalgia. Of course, I had no standards of comparison. I had no idea of what Kings College at Cambridge, Blair Hall at Princeton or even Andover Academy were like; indeed I had never heard of them, and this new little world seemed very fine to me. In point of fact, it was one of those agreeable, sprawling, white clapboard, New England frame houses, built about 1860, much used and worn by the Atwater family. It had sagging porches, soft-wood, wide-planked floors and a general air of middle-class solid, New England, no-nonsense respectability.

It was rather set off from the rest of the school, not so much physically, for it was at the edge of the main campus, but administratively. It was separate because the boys were all about 12 and 13 years old, too young for active high-school participation.

Our group constituted the first and second forms, Choate having been modeled on the English public-school tradition.

St. John's hero and idol was Thomas Arnold. For those unacquainted with the British private-school system (called by them "public schools"), the grade numbers are in reverse so that the sixth form is equal to senior year at high school, or 12th grade, and the numbers decrease down to form I, which is first year junior high or 7th grade. Since the quality of teaching was far higher and the work load expected to be carried far heavier than anything I had known, I was demoted to form II or the eighth grade.

There was a house matron, for we were little boys subject to German measles, pinkeye and homesickness, but mostly there was the resident housemaster, the energetic, dynamic, compact, athletic Ray Brown, whose domain, almost whose property, the Atwater House was.

There were other masters too, but mostly I remember Ray Brown in Latin and geography. I had no real idea of what study meant, but my eyes were soon opened. Brown was something of a martinet--he had the answers to everything and eyes like gimlets. Often we were a little, but not I think too much, humiliated. If he bawled us out before others, he made it stick, and I recall no psychoses; if the fault were intimately personal, he handled it privately. Once he stopped me and (not asking me but telling me) let me have it sharply for not brushing my teeth. Lord, they must have been bad for him to have noticed! But then he removed his partial denture, waved it at me, and said that this was what he had gotten from bad dental care and, by golly, I had better brush my teeth!

He had the problem of the general welfare of his charges, the morning shower that was mandatory (and cold as a miser's heart), of clean shirts, of scuffed shoes, of clean fingernails and of torn collars. Yes, this was the time of an attached soft collar in the daytime and detached, stiff, white Arrow or Van Heusen at dinner. And he was good at it--dedicated, single-purposed. He could snap from Point Barrow, to *ferro ferre tuli latus*, to the box-score abbreviation of Francisco Pizzoli (Ping Bodie in case you were interested), and he could do it fast. He inserted under the skins of 13-year-old animals some measure of alertness, of snap and polish, and a sense of pride. His breed, I suspect, is not legion, and there must be many educators who would not approve of his methods, but we learned. We also learned something of football, baseball and the rudiments of hockey. I think now that Ray Brown was for little boys, because he was no hero to the upper forms, and later, when I was older, I got away from him. But my memory of him shows him bright and clear, a spare, muscular little man, not handsome, with sandy or reddish hair, and a sort of underslung jaw--a good teacher, not of prominence in the arts or sciences, but just right for small boys on the threshold of adolescence.

Of course, there was more than his presence to the Atwater House. Sunday evenings were given over to readings by Clara St. John, the headmaster's wife, from the great romantic novels. And she was superb. A sister of Charles Seymour (who later became president of Yale), she had been magnificently educated in the humanities. Her readings, while not dramatic and humorous like those of her husband, were quiet, absorbing and altogether fitting for Sunday nights around a wood fire, snug against the roaring New England winter winds outside. If pressed, I might or might not be able to tell the story of "Quentin Durward," "The Black Arrow" or "The White Company," but the image is bright and clear with me of that intelligent, calm face and the magic romance of the tales. No radio, no television, no moving pictures, but rather superb evenings in the wondering awakening of late childhood.

Ah, but all this was nothing compared to the early and late fall afternoons in Connecticut. Here were the brilliant, and later somber, autumnal colors that decorate New England with heartbreaking beauty, the crisp turf and--most of all--the clear, bright air, the cool, sharp crackle of a bright fall day, the sharply etched hills and our own football field. Sheer delight! I had played in back lots, on cinder schoolyards, on cement pavements, and without anything resembling a uniform. But here we were a team, the Midgets, a squad proud of ourselves, and we had uniforms, real uniforms with shoulder and hip pads, and headguards, and shoes with cleats. And far above us on the varsity field, Mr. McOrmand was working with the school teams, the big boys. On a Saturday afternoon there would be a real game with Westminster or Taft or Loomis or Kent, and we would be right there cheering, a part of it.

In short, within weeks I was a very happy boy. All the remnants disappeared of childhood illnesses, the sniffles, the lassitude, the lack of the unmatched feeling of vibrant health. I didn't think about it in so many words, but the condition was good--I felt well, even keen. Young, all unknowing of real school values, and generally ignorant as I was, I could nevertheless feel, all around me, something much to be desired. The awe in which I held George St. John and his faculty, the stern discipline of the teaching, the spiritual atmosphere which the school tried hard to maintain (and I think with some measure of success), the Kiplingesque attitude towards games, the class consciousness of which, snobbish as it was, I now felt myself to be a part--all these and many more undefinable aspects were both stimulating and encouraging. Nor do I think I was the rare case, even having come from the small-town, middle-income, Jewish setting. My transition from Charleston to Choate was of greater contrast than that of most of the boys; but they felt the spirit too.

Most of the student body were from homes in the eastern United States, and of this majority the largest number were New Englanders. Generally there was money, and behind the money usually some generations of decent educational tradition. Even the two or three day students, from modest families in the town of Wallingford, somehow had a New

England flavor that raised them, in my estimation, higher, far higher, than anything I had seen at home.

That, then, was the first year of boarding school, the beginning of real education and the preliminary year to adolescence. It is not my purpose to describe at length American private secondary school life in the first quarter of this century--others have done that at length. I have only to set a background for my own growth. Besides, it now seems very long ago.

I know that I was lonesome at times, that I often felt left out and did not know that growing up is always painful; but, for the most part, there is an aura of truthfulness, good will, high standards and aims surrounding my memories of those years.

When we were 15 and 16--awkward, untidy, prurient minded, not (with few exceptions) attractive, nor likely to be for a year or two--a good boarding school was very much a place to be. As I have said, there is a dim veil over the entire Choate experience. Largely forgotten are the struggles, the boredom, the battles with textbooks, the petty triumphs and failures, the 1,250 days that five years in fact were.

It's all romantic now, and what shines through the distance of more than five decades are the pleasant things. And what were they? Well, listening to the first readings of "Lorna Doone" and "The Cloister and the Hearth"; standing in front of the cheerful common-room log fire; viewing the weekly grades posted on the Hill House bulletin board, particularly when A's and B's predominated; having a taste of philosophy, when Frank Wheeler would take off in the middle of his Cicero class to discourse on the human soul and its place among the stars. Oh yes, and the Saturday night community singing in the dining hall (Gaudeamus Igatur, Excelsior, Lord Jeffrey Amherst, etc.) and a Sunday sermon at school from the distinguished head of Andover.

There was more, much more--St. John's own reading from

293

"Nicholas Nickleby," high theatre as he did it; winter skating on the deep frozen pond and spring in New England ushering in baseball, track and rowing.

One year merges in memory with another, and suddenly I was 16 and a fifth-former, ambitious to be a person, to stand out. There were various ways to be a person at Choate--quite a few extracurricular activities, including, but not limited to, *The News*, which was the weekly student newspaper, the literary magazine, the yearbook, the dramatic club and, of course, a myriad of athletic activities.

And because I was energetic at 16, I tried everything. The first attempts were clumsy and unsuccessful, but little by little, small measures of achievement resulted.

In all these, we were encouraged by the faculty. St. John wanted the Greek ideal of the whole man, and he wanted him religious too. He was fond of saying that if he wanted a job well done, he could be sure of it if he gave it to a boy already too busy to take it on. Strangely convinced of the value of activities away from the curriculum, his influence on me in this respect worked, indeed it set a pattern for my entire future.

Unquestionably, for me it was the beginning of such values as I may have developed for leading a full life. There have to be platitudes in this book, and I may as well add this one--the world is a very wide place--much too wide for one lifetime. It is indeed so full of a number of things, as R. L. Stevenson knew so well, that to stay in one corner--mentally or physically--is a waste of the only irreplaceable thing, life itself. I feel a great lack in knowing almost nothing of botany, astronomy, physics, geology, sailing or Greek. The world does not have full dimension without them. And, oh, for even mediocre ability in French, Italian or the piano!

But not having these, how grateful I am for a little history, the poetry I have loved, a smattering of the drama, architecture, music and the visual arts.

How marvelous is the Acropolis when Solon, Themistocles, Pericles mean something to the traveler, or Chartres Cathedral if Henry Adams has been read! And do you know Ghiberti's Florentine doors—those which Michelangelo said ought to be the doors to paradise?

However, and clumsily, I am getting at something else. Life itself has been, for me anyhow, better, more savory, additionally zestful because business was not the only approach to it. I know full well that I would have been more successful financially, would have done a better job for my stockholders had I concentrated more on the Aloe Company.

When I came to St. Louis, participation in the community was urged upon me almost at once, however, particularly by Ben Loeb, who was quickly a hero to me, and by my classmate, Gale Johnston, of the Metropolitan Insurance Company, and later the Me antile Trust. Then, too, I married into the Aloe family whose members were strong community workers. My father-in-law, Louis P. Aloe, was already quite ill and his effective efforts were at an end, but he had run the Aloe Company with his left hand while his main energies were involved in city politics. Edith, his wife, thoroughly approved of community effort.

I should find it difficult not to accept the criticism that neglect of business, at times, in favor of civic effort was due not so much to an overwhelming zeal for public welfare as to a self-serving desire to escape from a difficult job to which I could not bring enough imagination. Besides, I was often lazy. I suspect that even my leave of absence for the Armed Forces in 1942 was in part, albeit subconsciously, an escape from the two-dimensional job in favor of the romance of what obviously was to be the great American effort against Hitler. Even in the medical department of the Army, I had extracurricular activities.

Each man has to create his own values, since there are no

absolutes; for me, starting with the Choate and later Princeton experiences, variety of interest has been paramount. The word "service" belongs in there somewhere because I realize I have been something of a "do-gooder." But I do not now and never have seen myself as a humanitarian. No, the service accomplishments were good like any other because of the satisfaction of getting something done. Another platitude, if you will: the one who does the work gets the most out of it.

As to values, then, it is clear that they must be different for each man. It's all very well to look at Schweitzer, Churchill or Albert Einstein, but such giants are not to be models for those of us who rate ourselves as average. They shine brilliantly in our civilization and in our lives. We have gloried in them because they gave us hope for mankind, but they are far above and not truly of us. In any case we do not see how we can imitate them or climb to anything like their levels. Such efforts would be absurd.

Well, then, for me attainment has to be more modest. It's good to realize one's own limitations--perhaps it's part of the beginning of wisdom, and I came to see early that I would not be first-rate at tennis, golf, music, languages, philosophy or mathematics. Expertise is, anyhow, not the universal necessity except to a pro. A smattering of a great many matters has provided enormous interests, a lively zest for the daily round, considerable satisfactions of curiosity--in short, has added dimensions to living, especially in the upper years. I like to put it this way: you don't have to be a Renaissance man to live well--you can make out nicely just being a Renaissance bum.

Or as the Earl of Lytton said a hundred years ago: "Genius does what it must and talent does what it can."

Of the making of all this then, Choate supplied the foundation. I am grateful to the school and for my luck in getting there.

CHAPTER XIII

"Of course he remains essentially American in believing all questions have answers."

Anthony Powell

I have journeyed, for the most part pleasantly, through more than seven decades and am not much given to looking backward; the road ahead has always seemed more inviting, but it begins now to look short. A cul-de-sac is inevitable and, as old men are given to dreams, so memories are more numerous than of yesterday. They come and go, in no sort of order, and as they disappear others take their places; now a glimpse of childhood in the West Virginia Kanawha Valley, a sharp impression of a small football triumph on a crisp fall afternoon in Connecticut, the first reading of Prospero's final speech in "The Tempest," the awe at the initial visit to Westminster Abbey, the golden glory of Fra Angelica at the Uffizi, Walter Hampden in "Cyrano," George Mylonas lecturing to us as we sat in the sacred theatre at Delphi with the golden eagles of Zeus circling overhead; and so on by the hundreds. Much has been missed--no one lifetime can experience it all--but there is nothing to regret and so much to be thankful for.

It is not easy to select those who have made the greatest impact on one's life. Chance is, of course, all important in the getting of friends, just as it plays so great a role in life itself. In the beginning, parents, close family members, and then teachers--Wheeler, Brown, St. John at Choate--Kennedy, Spaeth, Post at Princeton--and later, and always since, the joys

297

of a wonderful wife's influence and companionship.

The lucky ones, among whom I count myself, also find strength, stimulation and much more from a friend or two. When Ben Loeb died, I was as helpless as the strongest of us always is in the presence of death. In a sort of desperation, I wrote a newspaper column about his life, and I can now find nothing better to say about friends than what I said then.

It is by no means easy for everyone to make friends, and perhaps those who have them by the score cannot realize the heartaches of those who have.only a precious few, or none. Most of us, however, appreciate the rare relationship and we try to water that flower, and tend it carefully lest it wither. We depend upon those relationships, for they sustain us as no tangible support possibly can. Next to the love of family and a reasonable degree of health, friends are the most important thing in living.

It was in October of 1921, the golden autumn at Princeton, at a time when the country was again innocent after the first great world war; and we were sophomores, about to be initiated into the beauties of Shakespeare, the gorgeous panoply of the Renaissance, the wonderful mysteries of Platonic and Aristotelian philosophy, and the world was safe. We had no quarrel with the economic system, the Bolsheviks did not bother us, nor did President Harding in his sleepy Washington, a city which, now that normalcy had returned, had little impact on our lives. We did not think often about our government.

I had had some athletic ambitions in my freshman year and had actually made both the football and wrestling teams; but I was too light and too lazy for the varsity, and thought I would essay a literary career. It was time to try out for the daily newspaper, the *Princetonian*, and as I had known its managing editor, one Adlai Stevenson, at Choate, I thought at least I would have some prospects. In this I was wrong, and shortly turned my efforts to the literary magazine at which I made the grade.

But that first day when the candidates (heelers) assembled at the newspaper office, a slim youth spoke to me as though he would like to be a friend and said his name was Parker Lloyd-Smith. I look at the two pictures of him I own--one which seems to be in Central Park, where he stands impeccably clad in the broad-brimmed felt hat and double-breasted topcoat of that time, round-faced, with slightly receding chin, not handsome but cleareyed, alert, intelligent; the other when he was 27 (and looked 20) taken at the height of his young career, the managing editor of *Fortune*, not pompous, but happy, laughing--the world his oyster.

This was to be the man whom Henry Luce of *Time* later called one of his finest, of whom novelist Marcia Davenport wrote in glowing terms, and Margaret Bourke-White remembered as having "a headful of tight, short black curls and a profile of almost Grecian regularity." At the age of 27, Parker was the creator and first managing editor of *Fortune*, and at 29 he was dead.

I have lived more than fifty years without him, but not without the things he did for me. Brilliant, sensitive, a teacher, he was the first to make me see the color, the life, the world in the theatre, the arts, music--yes, and in nature. I believe I had never really looked at a forest, a mountain or a sky until, in the early autumn of 1923, we spent two weeks before the fall term climbing the Adirondacks where his family had a summer lodge.

The previous June, at the end of our junior year, he had asked me to room with him and I was a happy lad. Often I have thought of what it must have cost him to select an unknown Jewish boy as his roommate and closest friend. I had the decency to tell him I thought he was making a mistake; but I know now that he had thought it all out and knew what he wanted to do. For those were different days, and long ago.

There were, to be sure, a few Jews at Princeton, but they did not, as a rule, "make" the clubs, and if, as in my case, an exception were made, it would almost certainly be by one of the lesser ones. What Parker was, and the first I had really known, was a gentleman in the highest sense of the word.

Oh, I have seen his counterpart in St. Louis life many times over, in the persons of Ethan Shepley, Sam Conant, Dave Calhoun, Henry Hitchcock, Richmond Coburn, Leigh Gerdine, William McDonnell, Buster May, Charlie Thomas, Paul Reinert, Tom Eliot and so many others whose lives have not touched me as closely; but there have been, and are enough of them to give that indefinable quality, that ambiance to this city that makes it what it is, a place to live in.

*****

What then, Parker, of your friend, the companion for those years of your youth? Has he been what you would have wanted for him? Did the potentialities you thought you saw ever bear fruit? You are gone these four and a half decades and cannot answer, nor can he. He does not know whether he has done his best--or even whether to do one's best is now the way. His parents and his uncles and aunts said it was the only way and so did St. John of Choate, and the wonderful mother-in-law, Edith Aloe, he acquired when he married. Not for any of them was *dolce far niente*.

Yet the Puritan ethic and the Jewish struggle for betterment have not always been the way of the world. Many of the younger, the oncoming generation, seem to have rejected the hard path--the idea of delayed gratification. We, too, had a taste of romantic pessimism. Remember how we admired Swinburne and were fascinated by the sadness of T. S. Eliot and Matthew Arnold, those who were making

Kipling old hat and slightly ridiculous? All the same, we would not live by them, and, as year after year the poem "If" was voted the best liked by the senior classes at most universities, we too believed Kipling was the man for us.

When is a man what he is, Parker? Was Tom Jefferson at his best when he wrote his Declaration at the age of 33, or when he bought half the nation as president or, later, when in his mature upper years he created his University? When were the distilled essences of Ethan Shepley, Jim McDonnell, Ben Loeb, Edgar Queeny, Jim Hickok, Luther Smith, Jack Sverdrup? Oh, it's easy enough to determine yours because you quit the scene at 29, and therefore were the mature Parker for only a decade--the rest was silence. What of those of us who have gone on?

I know what you would say. Don't try to cast up accounts--you have been what you were, and are now what's left of where you have been and what you've done, so forget the introspection. It has never been your thing. I know too, that our kind of relationship can exist only in youth; the Damon and Pythias thing would have quickly evaporated. We were already far apart; you were traveling in very high company with the *Time* editors, and I was grubbing my way up in small industry. When you died, the romantic days, the 20's, which were the youth of the century and of you and me as well, had passed, and the serious time of the Great Depression was at hand. The romance was ending.

I have wanted for a long time to say these things to you, you who have never been wholly out of mind. It's time to stop now for the hour is late, and there's no better place to end it than right here. So I raise the glass, and quote our friends at New Haven......"We shall pass and be forgotten like the rest."

*****

301

It may be that the West is now in decline, as Spengler predicted it would be. Perhaps humanity cannot cope with its own affluence and scientific progress and, like lemmings, hurries to its own destruction. We cannot, from our small vantage point, see with any clarity where we are headed; but we do see that there is wholesale corruption accompanying all of the western constitutional governments. Indeed, more than a hundred years ago Gibbons, in his *Decline and Fall*, designated such corruption as "the unfallible symptom of constitutional liberty," as sad a commentary on our system as is to be found.

The lists of crimes honeycombing our American society grow daily and seem to pervade all levels, not just those occupied by the poor, the jobless and the underprivileged. The housewife steals from the supermarket and department store, both the employer and the employee continue to cheat the unemployment system; food stamps, child welfare and public housing are invitations to steal, and of late it appears that the sacred medical profession is not exempt.

Yet we know that, while criminal losses cost billions of dollars and thousands of lives, the culprits are a very small percentage. Most doctors are as fine as we always thought them; most shoppers, like most people, are honest; most people respect and want to obey the law--if not from true conviction, at least for fear of getting caught. And if there is malaise and unhappiness, the race problems, the crime, the increase in drug taking, all providing ample ammunition for the pessimist, it is not the end. We do seem only too ready for the man who can provide the solution, the instant answer to all our problems, the dictator. But not quite yet, and maybe not ever!

For America has its strengths.

It is now evident that the dream which Israel Zangwill disclosed to an enthusiastic nation is not to be. His concept of

America as the melting pot, a crucible in which there would be forged from the great mix of immigrants, from various nations, a strong new people, has been nearly discarded. True, there has been much intermarriage and the process will continue; but ethnic values survive, contributing strength through their diversity. Given a couple of thousand years, perhaps, the population would be leavened into an homogeneous mass, but that we cannot imagine. Except for Egypt there is no record of nations--and less of cities that long lived. And yet we do not despair.

There is no denying the personality of cities. Historians, poets, novelists, artists have doted on Florence, Venice, Paris, Prague, New York, San Francisco, New Orleans, Athens and scores more, with the same affection accorded fabled mistresses. Did not Dr. Johnson say that when a man is tired of London he is tired of life itself?

Our St. Louis is not the kind of city that inspires that rapture, the wild surmise of which Keats wrote. It does not have the ancient romantic beauty of Venice, the glorious hills and surrounding waters of San Francisco, the urbanity and humanities of London, nor the excitements of New York's hard, keen edges. But most of us would find it difficult to live constantly with such high stimulants anyhow, and the essential comfortableness of St. Louis is what comes through as the town's chief attraction. Nor do I confuse comfort with laziness; rather, the qualities of decency, respect for learning, good-nature, high good humor, respect for the other fellow together make for a good existence at this place where the rivers meet.

There is then an aura, an ambiance about the town that almost defies analysis, but is nevertheless as real as Forest Park or City Hall. Those who live here like it, and those who come here, often want to stay. When you ask them why, they speak of the slower pace, the lesser effort and strain required, perhaps, than in New York, Chicago or Los Angeles, the good education close at hand, superb medicine, vigilant newspapers, a great ethnic mix and a liberal tradition; but all these somehow do not tell the whole story. When pressed further they are likely to say, well, it's the people--they are great. I think so too.

The percentage of public-spirited citizens is perhaps no greater than in other American cities; but these persons somehow seem to be more effective, to know each other, to be willing to work in harmony. Moreover, the community is liberal in its attitudes towards its own people. Its religious mixture of Catholics, Baptists, Lutherans, Jews, Ethical Culturists, Episcopalians, and its varied background of Germans, Italians, Poles, Irish, all superimposed on the descendants of the original French and English, have eased the harshness of the race problems. It is true that diversity is often the cause of bigotry, which is not lacking here; but equally it makes for tolerance, understanding and warmth.

If the West survives, if the cities as we know them continue in vitality, then St. Louis will remain. This town, so well placed in the center of the continent on which the hopes of the western world, the envies of the dictators, the jealousies of the emerging nations are all focused, is surely a garden--a garden in which the best things of life are not free, but have flourished mightily and with the same effort will continue.

*****

In this work I have been highly critical of our local government and some of our institutions and, by implication, some of those in charge of both. I should like to think, however, that such scolding has been in the spirit of one who, out of great affection, argues for improvement. There is no bitterness--and indeed how could there be towards a city which has given so much happiness, excitement, satisfaction and laughter to, as Dr. Johnson might have said,

Its obedient servant?

St. Louis--1978